PSI SUCCESSFUL BUSIN

NAVIGATING THE MARKETPLACE

Growth Strategies for Your Business

WAYNE LOVERN & ANNA LOVERN

OASIS PRESS BOOKS & SOFTWARE

THE OASIS PRESS®

GRANTS PASS< OREGON

Published by The Oasis Press®/PSI Research

Interior design by Eliot House Productions
Cover illustration and design by Steven Burns

Please direct any comments, questions, or suggestions regarding this book to:
The Oasis Press®/PSI Research
Editorial Department
P.O. Box 3727
Central Point, Oregon 97502-0032

(541) 479-9464
(541) 476-1479 fax
info@psi-research.com e-mail

The Oasis Press® is a Registered Trademark of Publishing Services, Inc., an Oregon corporation doing business as PSI Research.

Library of Congress Cataloging-in-Publication Data
Lovern, Wayne, 1946 –
Navigating the marketplace : growth strategies for your business / Wayne Lovern & Anna Lovern.
p. cm. – – (PSI successful business library)
Includes index.
ISBN 1–55571–458-7 (pbk.)
1. Small business – – Management. I. Lovern, Anna, 1947 –
II. Title. III. Series.
HD62.7.L68 1998
658.02'2 – –dc21 98-29049
CIP

Printed and bound in the United States of America

First Edition 10 9 8 7 6 5 4 3 2 1 0

Printed on recycled paper when available.

Contents

INTRODUCTION

A Quick Overview of the Book

THIS IS TWO, VERY PRACTICAL, SMALL business books in one, and you can read either first. Book one, the competitive strategy book, offers a number of defensive business models you can adopt, copy, and modify to fit your business's needs and to solve your competitive problems. Each model contains a competitive strategy that will lessen the impact of your competitors' actions by helping you to target and highly satisfy one specific type of customer. Satisfied customers are loyal customers, and they're your best defense against aggressive competitors. Book two, the growth strategy book, contains a system of fourteen strategies that guarantees you'll find all your opportunities to increase sales and profits. Big sales figures don't automatically produce big profits; you need both sales and profit growth strategies to make your small business a success.

Strategy consultants and the country's leading university professors have been helping big corporations develop successful business strategies since 1980. Now it's your turn. This book is written for you, the owners and managers of small businesses, by two authors who founded and operated a manufacturing and retail business for 11 years. We sold our business and returned to a leading university for graduate studies. There we found a wealth of practical, strategic knowledge that would have made our lives much easier and our small business much more profitable. We are eager to share our discoveries with you.

We understand that small business people are strategic thinkers, but they don't often use three-ring binders and overhead transparencies to formalize their thinking into a slick presentation for the board of directors. Small business strategic thinking concerns fundamental problems. For instance, the small store owner battling a Wal-Mart Super Center is trying to devise a competitive strategy that will carve out a market that's protected from the big competitor's "everyday low prices." The owner of a small overhead door repair business, fighting three tough competitors, is trying to formulate a winning strategy that slams the door on the competition. Both the CEO of a small manufacturing firm and the executive director of a small not-for-profit association are trying to develop a system that will let them discover all their opportunities to grow sales and revenues. And all owners and managers of small businesses are trying to increase their profits. The competitive and growth strategies in this book will help you find solutions to these basic business problems.

Competitive Strategies: The First Half of the Book

Business owners wanting to become the next Sam Walton or wanting to avoid competing with Wal-Mart will learn how the Low-Cost Competitive Strategy is used by firms like Wal-Mart, Target, and Kmart. The Low-Cost strategy targets Prudent Shoppers with low prices for the best trade-off of products and services. This trade-off between price and the benefits that customers receive is important because all customers buy a combination of four things when they make a purchase: product, service, personnel (skills and competencies of employees in direct contact with the customer), and image. Prudent Shoppers are trade-off customers who swap seldom needed, high performance, and high prestige portions of these four factors for a lower price. They want the high performance and high prestige benefits but not enough to pay for them.

The most successful Low-Cost business is the one with the lowest price for the most desirable trade-off mix of product, service, personnel, and image. That firm captures the most sales in its market, then uses its high volume purchasing and operating strengths to amass huge cost advantages by using economy of scale, learning curves, experience curves, and several other cost-reducing concepts. This book describes how Low-Cost firms use those concepts to make good profits while charging such low prices. The success formula that triggers sales to Prudent Shoppers is standardized, commonplace, high-volume products at the lowest competitive price with the best price/benefits trade-off of product, services, personnel, and image. Shelves at Wal-Mart, Kmart, and Target stores are filled with such products, and each of these firms has its own guess about the best price/benefits trade-off mix that will make it the industry's leader.

By understanding the cost-controlling factors that big Low-Cost competitors use when building their firms, you will understand the real strengths of Low-Cost competitors. Since you never win a fight if you let a stronger opponent use his strengths, you need to know what competitive factors to avoid if you must compete with a Low-Cost giant. Or, if you dream of building your firm into a Low-Cost giant, you need to know what strengths you must develop and what competitive factors you must use.

Most owners and managers of small businesses would rather avoid cut-throat price competition. You'll learn five strategic ways to avoid competing with Low-Cost competitors and their low-priced, high-volume, standardized products and services.

1. Avoid low-price competition by using an Enhancement Competitive Strategy to target Selective Shoppers. There are five types of enhancements you'll learn to use for which this type of customer is willing to pay a higher price. You'll discover:
   - Six basic ways to enhance your products for Selective Shoppers.
   - Ways to enhance the INDICATORS customers substitute when they can't really judge a product's performance.
   - Three systems that help managers to identify the services Selective Shoppers want enhanced.
   - Three ways to enhance the skills and competencies of employees in direct contact with Selective Shoppers.
   - Three fundamental ways to enhance the image of your products, services, and business.
2. Avoid low-price competition by using a Speed Enhancement Competitive Strategy to target In-A-Hurry Shoppers with fast service. Providing products or services quickly triggers sales to some segments of Selective Shoppers.
3. Avoid low-price competition by using a Flexibility Enhancement Competitive Strategy to target I-Want-What-I-Want Shoppers. There is always a group of customers who want customized products and services.
4. Avoid low-price competition by using a Reduction Competitive Strategy to target Bargain Hunters with really cheap prices. Getting under the Low-Cost Strategy firm's low prices is done by stripping away even more portions of the product, service, personnel, and image mix. Bargain Hunters form the market for really cheap products, generic products, and severely stripped down products and services. Best of all, big firms tend to avoid this market, leaving it to small businesses.

Each competitive strategy has a few Key Success Factors (KSFs) that are responsible for triggering sales to customers, controlling costs, and limiting the effectiveness of competitors. A small business owner wanting to use any one competitive strategy as a model for his or her business must develop that strategy's Key Success Factor strengths. A competitive strategy and its KSFs combine to form a "competitive business model" that you can copy and implement to target a specific customer type, while limiting the effectiveness of competitors.

A few for-profit businesses don't have competitors and quite a few not-for-profit organizations are in that envious position. A short chapter will explore the value of competitive strategies in such situations.

Another short chapter looks at how competitive strategies are used in various industry growth phases. The computer industry is new and growing. The cabinet industry is mature with stable sales. Different industries and different products and services exist in different growth stages. You'll learn that competitive strategies aren't very useful in some growth phases and extremely valuable in others.

Growth Strategies: The Second Half of the Book

Regardless of which competitive strategy you choose to adopt, and regardless of the type of business you operate, you are always trying to find ways to increase sales and profits. The second half of the book presents 14 growth strategies that guarantee to boost your business's sales and profits. To be successful, a company must choose one competitive strategy, but that isn't the case with growth strategies. You're free to use most of the 14 growth strategies simultaneously.

In the growth strategy section, you'll learn how to find every growth opportunity for your business. The trick to finding all your business's opportunities is to examine your business using three different perspectives: a marketing sales growth perspective, a management sales growth perspective, and a management profit growth perspective. Each perspective contains its own growth strategies. After reading about each strategy, you'll be asked to stop and develop a list of ways to implement that strategy in your business. These are your opportunities to grow, and your list of growth opportunities will get longer as you complete each growth strategy. In fact, we suggest you buy a book for each of your key employees and have them develop their own list of growth opportunities. Then schedule a meeting to combine the lists and choose the best growth opportunities to pursue.

Choosing Your Best Growth Opportunities

You'll arrive at the last chapter with a list of all your potential growth opportunities. In the last chapter you'll be presented with a number of issues that you should consider before choosing which growth opportunities to pursue. After studying the issues, you may change your mind about which is the best long-term opportunity for your business. The goal of the final chapter is to help you choose the best growth options in which to invest your limited financial resources.

Two Books that Belong Together

While this seems like two books in one cover, the two books belong together. In the first book you'll learn how to carve out a market position that minimizes competitive rivalry and maximizes customer satisfaction. In the second book you'll learn how to increase sales and profits. And, most importantly, by reading both books in the order presented, you'll learn how to keep your competitive and growth strategies compatible — building a much easier business to manage.

CHAPTER 1

Competitive Strategies

GREAT SMALL BUSINESSES ARE BUILT WITH great visions, not with hard work, long hours, good intentions, and a strong desire to be your own boss. Oh, those things help, but they won't overcome either a bad business vision or trying to operate a business with no vision at all. A great vision is used to create a competitive advantage from which you build a stable, predictable, and prosperous future.

Great Visions Build Great Businesses

Before any business vision is called great, it ought to pass a few practical tests.

- A great business vision must be targeted at specific customers, aimed at creating high levels of customer satisfaction, and capable of producing a strong degree of customer loyalty.
- A great business vision must include a way to increase sales and profits continuously.
- A great vision must include a method to control business costs and limit the effectiveness of competitors.
- A great vision must make it easy for you, the manager, to make consistent decisions that continuously build the right strengths to support a growing business.
- A great vision must guide your choice of which new growth opportunities to pursue and which to avoid.

A competitive strategy from the first half of this book should be a significant part of your business vision. Each competitive strategy is an ideal model of how to boost your sales to a specific type of customer. Each competitive strategy contains a mechanism that restricts the number of competitors you have to battle. Each competitive strategy has its own, unique methods of controlling costs.

These strategies are competitive business models you can copy, and each model represents a different vision that will guide the development of your business. Your existing business may already be structured similar to one of these competitive strategy models; if so, you'll learn how to refine and improve your existing business, and how to better explain your objectives to your employees, suppliers, and financiers. After all, they have to understand your vision before they can support it. On the other hand, your existing business may not resemble any of these competitive strategy models; if not, you'll understand why customer loyalty is weak, why you're vulnerable to competitive attacks, and how to overcome your weaknesses.

Not every market is structured in such a way that a small business can achieve a perfect match with one of the competitive strategies, but every small business can move closer to its chosen competitive business model by strengthening the factors that make that strategy effective. Each strategy works by strengthening different business skills, assets, and competencies (special abilities of management and key employees). If you choose to implement one of the competitive strategies mentioned, this book will show you exactly which factors to strengthen.

Five Competitive Strategies

What's a competitive strategy? It's a number of things. It's a way to minimize the number of competitors your business has to fight for sales. It's a guiding vision for your decision-making. It's a clear choice about 1) who your target customers are and which customers you will leave to competitors, 2) which major factors actually trigger your target customers' purchases and therefore must be improved continuously, 3) which factors merely support sales and shouldn't take money away from improving your sales triggers, and 4) how to make a bigger profit.

A competitive strategy is a system of consistent beliefs and factors that will help you form the competitive boundaries for all your decision-making, whether quick or slow and deliberate, so that when confronted with a new problem, the chosen solution is the one which is best for your business. Staying within those boundaries ensures that your next decision will complement all your prior decisions and make your business stronger, not erode the effectiveness of your prior decisions or create suspicions in the minds of customers, employees, and suppliers that your objectives may be changing — again.

Each competitive strategy creates different business strengths and weaknesses. Each strategy's strengths allow certain growth opportunities to be pursued; each strategy's weaknesses cause other growth opportunities to be avoided. Therefore, your business's competitive strategy is chosen first, and then compatible growth strategies are chosen. Indeed, your choice of competitive strategy forms the basis for the development of every aspect of your business — that's why this book presents competitive strategies before growth strategies.

Your choice of a competitive strategy will lead you to hire employees with unique aptitudes, personalities, experiences, interests, education, and intelligence levels. The employees' initial uniqueness is further enhanced when your business trains them to serve its target customers.

Each competitive strategy requires its own, special equipment. The equipment to produce high volume, standardized products or services for one group of customers varies greatly from the general purpose, highly flexible equipment needed to personalize products or services for another customer group.

Each competitive strategy requires its own technology, materials, facility layout, job layouts, job designs, processes, and consumer outlet locations. A different manufacturer-wholesaler-retail store distribution chain is needed to support each competitive strategy.

Each competitive strategy requires managers of small businesses to possess and develop special abilities or competencies because each requires different types of decisions. For example, operating a business that is serving upper social class customers requires a manager who has the experience and judgment to make additional investments and to incur the additional costs needed to create a prestigious business image. By contrast, operating a business serving mass markets requires a manager who has the skills to maximize the efficiency of each business process and to minimize operating costs. Additionally, each competitive strategy requires different leadership styles, controlling tactics, communication techniques, personnel policies, wage structures, performance evaluations, and efficiency measures — all these factors over time will evolve to support your chosen competitive strategy.

In summary, managers of small businesses who choose and adhere to one competitive strategy as a cornerstone of their business vision will transform that business into a special and unique organization designed to satisfy the exact wants, needs, and desires of one particular type of customer. The corollary is profound: the satisfaction of any one type of customer can only be maximized when a manager targets those customers with the correct competitive strategy.

Managers have three competitive strategy choices: Low-Cost, Enhancement, and Reduction. These strategies exist relative to one another. To understand one strategy you must understand all the strategies. To implement one competitive vision you must know how the other competitive visions are implemented. You need to understand both how your business should compete, and how competitors are likely to react to your marketing tactics. You especially need to understand the Low-Cost strategy because the other two strategies exist relative to it; the main purpose of the other two strategies is to avoid the intense price competition from the Low-Cost strategy competitor.

The Low-Cost Competitive Strategy

A Low-Cost Competitive Strategy is most commonly used by large corporations, by firms driven by the desire to become large corporations, and occasionally by small firms who are geographically isolated from competitors. The aim of this strategy is to capture the largest sales volume in the market and to become the leader in the industry with standardized products or services. The typical characteristics of a Low-Cost strategy firm include selling the most popular version of a product or service at a low price, using highly automated equipment to hold down labor costs, and using high volume as leverage to drive costs down.

The Enhancement Competitive Strategy

An alternative to competing on the basis of price alone is to use an Enhancement Competitive Strategy to provide the market with one or more of four types of enhancements: improved products, improved services, improved personnel skills, or improved image. The typical characteristics of large and small firms using this type of strategy include higher quality or more specialized products and services, precision equipment, exclusive images, and higher prices.

Two common forms of the enhancement strategy often used by small businesses are speed enhancement and flexibility enhancement.

The Speed Enhancement Competitive Strategy

A Speed Enhancement Competitive Strategy focuses on improving only one of the four types of enhancements — *service* and only one element of service — *speed*. For example, designing a business for speed allows a small firm to guarantee each customer immediate appliance delivery or allows the small firm to change every customer's oil within 10 minutes without an appointment. The main factors supporting speed are streamlined processes, excess capacity, large inventories, and convenient locations.

The Flexibility Enhancement Competitive Strategy

A Flexibility Enhancement Competitive Strategy specializes in one-of-a-kind products or services. Each product and each service can be uniquely modified, customized, or personalized for each customer. Flexible businesses hire highly skilled employees who can adjust equipment and processes to produce tailor-made products and services for each customer. Of particular importance are the employees in direct contact with customers. These employees often need exceptionally good communication skills.

The Reduction Competitive Strategy

Another way to avoid competing with a Low-Cost strategy firm's highly popular, low priced, standardized products and services that dominate the market is to use a Reduction Competitive Strategy. While the Enhancement strategy avoids the dominant Low-Cost competitor by improving combinations of the product, service, personnel, and/or image of the business, the Reduction Competitive Strategy avoids competing with the market leader by going in the opposite direction. The firm using a Reduction strategy sells products with less performance, offers fewer services, employs personnel with fewer customer-handling skills, and/or maintains a generic image. This is a no-frills business with cheap prices. For example, Wal-Mart has everyday low prices, Dollar General uses a Reduction Competitive Strategy and has cheap prices — everyday.

Three Types of Customers

As you know, you can't please everyone, and it's ruinous to try. Customers have a wide variety of needs and a wide variety of price sensitivities, but for any product or service in any industry customers can be grouped and classified into three major types: Prudent Shoppers, Selective Shoppers, and Bargain Hunters.

Prudent Shoppers

Prudent Shoppers buy good products and good services — not the best, the best cost too much, and not the cheapest, the cheapest won't do the job. Prudent Shoppers settle for good products and good services in order to get low prices. Sure, they know high quality products provide high performance, but they reason that they seldom, if ever, really need high performance. They trade away high performance to save money.

Prudent Shoppers want some services, but each additional service increases the price, so they'll do some things for themselves and expect a lower price in return.

Prudent Shoppers will settle for adequate personnel with good attitudes instead of highly skilled, professional personnel and expect a lower price in return.

Prudent Shoppers don't want to be viewed as low-class or no-class members of society, so they shop at businesses that have some image. But they trade off excessively high prestige and status images and expect a lower price in return.

On a questionnaire, Prudent Shoppers will indicate that they would like to have improved performance, service, and personal attention. However, they aren't willing to pay for the improvements!

In almost every market, Prudent Shoppers form a huge, core group of buyers wanting a good, modestly priced product or service. Whatever product or service this customer group decides is the best trade-off will become the market's high volume, highly popular, standardized product or service.

Selective Shoppers

Selective Shoppers want one or more of four types of enhancements: improved products, improved services, more competent personnel, or enhanced image. And most importantly, these customers will pay higher prices to get what they want. However, these customers, while numerous, are not all alike. In most markets, these customers can be separated into many smaller Selective Shopper segments according to the unique wants of each group. Two very common Selective Shopper segments are of particular interest to small businesses: In-a-Hurry and I-Want-What-I-Want customer segments.

In-a-Hurry Customers are a group of Selective Shoppers who want fast service. An *American Demographics* study estimated that the U.S. society contains 43 million time-starved, busy households, and these fast-paced households form the core of In-a-Hurry consumers. To that core add the impatient shoppers, and the customers who hate shopping so much that they'll pay extra just to speed up the unpleasant but necessary experience. These consumers form a sizable group that is growing as the pace of life becomes more and more hectic, and as personal time becomes more and more valuable.

An In-a-Hurry industrial segment also exists. This segment includes businesses that want fast service. Businesses that, among other things, demand Just-In-Time deliveries, instant repair of vital equipment, and immediate communication systems.

I-Want-What-I-Want Customers are another group of Selective Shoppers that want individualized products and services, tailored to fit their exact wants and needs. They'll pay a higher price to get their products and services customized.

Bargain Hunters

Selective Shoppers, In-a-Hurry, and I-Want-What-I-Want customers buy the best, the fastest, the most personalized products and services and pay high prices; Prudent Shoppers buy good, standardized products and services and pay low prices; Bargain Hunters buy stripped-down products and services and pay *cheap* prices. Bargain Hunters sacrifice even more product performance, service, personnel skills, and image than do Prudent Shoppers. Bargain Hunters patronize no-frills businesses in low-overhead locations and expect *cheap* prices as their reward.

While fewer in number than Prudent Shoppers, Bargain Hunters form the market for generic products and services, used products, and products sold at auctions and flea markets. Bargain Hunters are motivated by a variety of factors: limited incomes, extreme price consciousness, extreme frugality, and, sometimes, simply the quest for a bargain.

Customers as Seen From the Business's Viewpoint

An individual customer may shop at Macy's for a fur coat, Kmart for toilet tissue, and Coast-to-Coast for cheap containers for the garage. In doing so, that customer is a Selective Shopper at Macy's, a Prudent Shopper at Kmart, and a Bargain Hunter at Coast-to-Coast. Each of these businesses targets one specific type of customer behavior. Macy's targets Selective Shopper behavior, Kmart targets Prudent Shopper behavior, and Coast-to-Coast targets Bargain Hunter behavior. When businesses target a customer type, they are actually targeting the portion of purchases that consumers make when exhibiting that particular behavior.

None of us as individuals can be classified as one type of customer. We tend to be Selective Shoppers when we 1) feel involved with a product or service and 2) feel that there are significant differences between each competitor's product or service. We also buy many products and services without a feeling of involvement and without feeling there are significant differences. For these products and services, we fall into the Prudent Shopper or Bargain Hunter categories.

This book looks at the issue of customer behavior strictly from the business's viewpoint. Successful businesses target one type of customer behavior;

therefore, businesses are said to target one customer type. When Macy's targets Selective Shoppers, from the store's point of view, they are targeting individuals, and those individuals become loyal to Macy's. The store satisfies a portion of their wants and needs, and the same individuals keep returning for that portion of their purchases. Since all the customers exhibit much the same purchasing behavior at Macy's, Macy's considers them a customer type.

Matching Competitive Strategies and Customer Types

Each competitive strategy is designed to serve and satisfy one targeted customer type. When your small business chooses one competitive strategy to target one customer type, it gains two valuable competitive advantages. The first advantage is a strong customer orientation that's focused directly on your chosen customers.

The second advantage of a competitive strategy is to decrease the ability of competitors in general to lure your target customers away. Most competitors target other customer types, so they are no longer "real" competitors. "Real" competitors are only those who target the same customer type and the same customer segment that your business targets. This puts distance between your business and most competitors, decreasing costly competitive rivalry. Rivalry declines because those other businesses are using other competitive strategies to develop different skills, assets, and competencies to serve other customers. Those different strengths aren't the ones needed to serve your customers, so most competitors are at a disadvantage if they try to attract your customers.

For example, when a business uses a Low-Cost Competitive Strategy that is designed to attract Prudent Shoppers, it isn't developing the strengths needed to attract Bargain Hunters. Likewise, a business using a Reduction Competitive Strategy to target Bargain Hunters isn't developing the strengths needed to attract Selective Shoppers. A Speed Enhancement Strategy designed to attract "In-a-Hurry" customers doesn't provide the business with the skills, assets, and competencies to attract and serve "I-Want-What-I-Want" customers. Competitors who use a competitive strategy other than the one you have chosen, or competitors with no competitive strategy, are not capable of satisfying your target customers.

Summing up the advantages of basing your business vision on a particular competitive strategy:

1. A competitive strategy reduces your competitive rivalry because "real" competitors are only those who target the same customer type and same customer segment that your business targets.
2. A competitive strategy maximizes target customer satisfaction and creates more customer loyalty, which makes it harder for any competitor to steal your customers.
3. Strong customer loyalty leads to stable sales and good profits.

However, each competitive strategy succeeds for different reasons. Each competitive strategy develops distinctly different skills, assets, and competencies that are used to target a unique group of customers, so each competitive strategy requires different strengths to trigger sales and create profits.

Key Success Factors

Key Success Factors (KSFs) — sometimes called the "drivers of success" or simply "drivers" — are the few very important business factors that are critical to your business's success. If the business develops superior Key Success Factors, it will be more successful than its "real" competitors. If, through incompetent management or misfortune, vital KSFs are weak, the business will lose sales to competitors, will produce poor profits, and will face a lackluster future.

There are three different types of Key Success Factors:

1. Sales triggers: Each competitive strategy has unique KSFs that trigger sales because each serves a different customer type, and each customer type has its own reason for buying. Therefore, sales to each customer type require different sales triggers.
2. Cost controllers: Each competitive strategy creates a unique business with unique skills, assets, and competencies. Any time businesses have different strengths and weaknesses, their costs will be different and their costs will have to be controlled differently. Therefore, each competitive strategy requires different KSFs to control costs.
3. Competition limiters: The last type of KSF limits competition by targeting one type of customer, developing unique strengths to serve those customers, and satisfying those customers. The result of customer targeting is that you'll only have to compete against competitors targeting both your type customers and your customer segments; you'll no longer have to battle any and all competitors. Customer targeting is used to open a direct channel of communication between you and your customers so

that information can be gathered that will guide future sales trigger improvements.

Developing Your Business Vision

Competitive strategies are the first focus of this book even though most business people are far more eager to read about growth strategies and to search for any opportunities they may be overlooking. However, your competitive strategy is the foundation of your business, and your growth strategies must be compatible with your foundation, not the other way around. You shouldn't build a house by starting with the roof, adding walls, and then building a foundation last. The building project would be a mess to manage. Similarly, you shouldn't choose opportunistic growth strategies, invest your scarce resources, and then analyze your business to determine if it has the basic strengths necessary to make your growth strategy a success. You'd be in a mess. Your competitive strengths must guide your choice of growth opportunities.

Key Success Factors are central to the success of any competitive strategy and any business. You shouldn't try to use a particular competitive strategy unless your business can generate competitively superior Key Success Factors to drive your success. KSFs must be understood before you can understand competitive strategies, so they will be presented first.

Following the discussion of Key Success Factors, the different competitive strategies are presented. Each strategy should be carefully considered before any one is chosen as part of your vision. Examples will give you an idea of how small businesses are actually using each competitive strategy. Then a more technical explanation of each is provided to teach you how to implement each strategy. The technical explanation will focus on the Key Success Factors (KSFs) that must be your business's strengths to implement a competitive strategy.

CHAPTER 2

Success Factors

THE KEY TO YOUR UNDERSTANDING competitive strategies is to understand what role various business factors play in creating a successful business. For example, personal selling skill is a *major* factor in selling automobiles and a *minor* factor in selling automobile wax. Many factors contribute to the success of your business, some are minor, some are major, and a few are critical. Some managers treat every factor, every issue, and every problem as critical, but such dedication to perfection is a waste of management time. Classifying all the parts of your business into minor, major, and critical factors will greatly improve your chances of success. Everyone in your business can spend more time and more attention on the most important factors when you've plainly identified them.

The Critical Factors for Business Success

You're probably wondering, "What do you mean by factors or business factors?" The following is a short list of business factors; you should make an exhaustive list for your business by listing every skill, asset, and competency that exists in each functional area: receiving, operations, shipping, marketing, service, purchasing, personnel, technology, finance, credit, and management. But for now, review the following short list and identify which are minor, major, or critical to the success of your business.

- Good Inventory Control
- Accurate Budgets to Control Costs
- Merchandise Turnover Rate
- Customer Credit System

- Professional Sales Force
- On-Time Shipping
- Advantageous Supplier Relationships
- Favorable Supplier Discounts
- Ability to Maintain Current, Popular Fashions
- High Employee Morale
- Scheduling Ability
- Effective Distributor Support System
- After-the-Sale Customer Service
- Ability to Recruit the Right Employees
- Ability to Raise Short or Long Term Money
- Ability to Retain Key Personnel
- Product Warranties
- Advertising
- Packaging
- Business Location
- Equipment Precision, Speed, or Flexibility

Most managers of small businesses quickly respond that a few of these are minor while many are important factors. Okay, study the important factors. For example, most business managers would pick good after-the-sale service as important, maybe even very important. After all, good after-the-sale service keeps customers satisfied and avoids getting a bad reputation, which will definitely erode future sales. But few firms need to continuously invest in improvements to after-the-sale service because this factor SUPPORTS future sales, it doesn't TRIGGER future sales. ("Support" versus "trigger" is a critical difference when implementing a competitive strategy.)

A Support Factor Example

Customers don't buy a television set because they are extremely impressed with the retailer's service-after-the-sale. The sale may be triggered by a cheap price, a low price for the best overall group of features, or because the television has the special enhancements a customer wants, but no one buys a TV because the retailer has great service-after-the-sale. On the other hand, a customer won't buy a high quality television set if they think they can't get it fixed if it breaks; the customer expects a reasonable level of service-after-the-sale. This means service-after-the-sale *supports* sales, it doesn't *trigger* sales. Bad or no service-after-the-sale will kill the sale, good service-after-the-sale supports the sale, and, a very important point, great service-after-the-sale still only supports the sale of the television — it doesn't trigger additional sales. Therefore, factors that *support* sales should be maintained at acceptable levels. Factors that *trigger* sales are critical to the future of the business and need to be improved continuously.

Knowing which of your business factors are less important and which are critical is a valuable management tool that improves the quality of your decision-making. It allows you to manage your firm's limited resources by setting appropriate spending levels for less important factors and by setting aggressive spending levels to constantly improve the critical factors. If you can fit each business factor, system, or process for your business into its proper category — minor, major, critical — you'll become a better decision maker.

Another Support Factor Example

Is customer credit a critical factor or a support factor in your business? For many expensive products, lack of credit availability will kill the sale, adequate credit will support the sale, but seldom does credit need to be improved beyond a support level. Similarly, credit approval time can kill a sale when it's so slow that customers have time to change their minds or keep shopping and discover a better deal offered by your competitor. In most cases an acceptable credit approval speed that supports the sale can be established. For most businesses, credit and credit approval time are *support* factors, and a manager should determine how much credit customers need and how quickly credit must be approved to support the sale.

For your business, the majority of the factors just listed are Support Success Factors (SSFs), and improving them beyond a reasonable level that's thoughtfully established will only increase your costs, not increase your sales and profits. Furthermore, improving SSFs beyond a support level will reduce the money available to make further improvements in your Key Success Factors.

Finding Your Key Success Factors

Identifying all the important factors in your business and sorting them into SSFs and KSFs isn't quick and it isn't easy. To discover which factors are KSFs in your market, try to determine what important skill, asset, or competency was missing that led a business similar to your own to perform poorly or shut down. Was a key product attribute weak? Was a key operating process weak? Was a key marketing skill weak? What key cost-controlling factor was missing or weak? Did the failed or weak competitor have a clear customer target or did they try to satisfy all types of customers? Did their promotions reach their customers or were they a waste of money?

Expand your study to include both failed and weak competitors. What few missing and weak critical factors can explain a competitor's poor performance? You'll find customers, suppliers, trade association personnel, bank officers, former owners, and many others very willing to discuss and speculate about the causes of business weaknesses and failures. The openness of former owners of failed businesses will surprise you. The information about KSFs and SSFs is out there, and finding it will improve your chances of success.

Next study the most successful businesses in your industry. Ask the same questions about the market leaders. What few major product strengths or organization skills, assets, and competencies made these competitors strong, profitable, and successful? Can you identify the few factors that actually trigger sales to their customers? How do the leaders in your industry control costs? Who are their target customers? How do they reach their customers with promotions? Can you identify and describe the characteristics, traits, and attitudes of their best customers?

Your Success Depends on Your Key Success Factors

As you search to identify your business's critical factors — the KSFs, that control the success of your business — you'll discover three types of KSFs. Why are there three types? Let's examine three very straightforward facts that determine the success of your business and of any business.

Fact One: *A business can only be successful if it can trigger sales.* A few, important sales triggers are the keys to your business's success. Consumer research reveals that even when a product has many benefits, customers are only thinking about a few of those benefits when they decide to pull out their wallet and purchase your product or service *(1)*. Furthermore, since each competitive strategy targets a different customer type, and each customer type has unique needs, wants, desires, and consumer behaviors, then each competitive strategy must have different sales triggers.

Sales triggers exist in every market for every product, for every service, and for every business. For example, in the gourmet frozen food market, quality of taste is a sales trigger. For Southwest Airlines, who competes in the discount air passenger market, price is a sales trigger. In upscale beer markets, image is a sales trigger.

On the other hand, product price is an important supporting factor in the gourmet frozen food segment; a low price will actually hurt sales. Seating comfort is an important supporting factor in the discount air passenger market; uncomfortable seating can hurt sales by driving customers to competitors. An attractive label is an important supporting factor in the upscale beer market; an unattractive label can kill sales by damaging the product's image.

Support factors are important, but doubling the performance of a supporting factor will not double customer satisfaction and will not double sales. By contrast, increasing the customer benefits provided by the Key Success Factor does increase customer satisfaction and will trigger additional sales. For example, lowering a gourmet food's price will decrease sales because it erodes the food's superior image. Most customers believe *you get what you pay for,* so lowering the price causes them to expect an inferior product.

Likewise, Southwest Airline's customers need adequate seat comfort, but additional improvements beyond the adequate level in seat comfort will not increase sales. However, if Southwest could further cut its costs, it could further cut its price, and sales would certainly increase.

Every product and every business will have one or more sales triggers. If your business can improve its sales triggers RELATIVE to your competitor's sales triggers, you'll have the best sales volume, you'll have growing sales.

Improvements to sales triggers are also RELATIVE improvements — an important point. Your business or your product can only have superior sales triggers relative to your competitor's sales triggers. Since all competing businesses are trying to improve their sales triggers, your success depends on maintaining long-term sales trigger superiority relative to those of your "real" competitors. Maintaining better KSFs than your competitors is an ongoing improvement battle.

Fact Two: *A business can only be successful if it generates profits.* The skills, assets, and competencies that control your business's costs are also keys to your business success because no business can make a profit or stay solvent if costs run amok.

Factors such as supplier discounts, purchasing expertise, processing efficiencies, Just-in-Time inventory procedures, strict budgets, and other cost-controlling techniques can maximize your firm's profits without having a negative effect on its sales triggers. Every successful firm has a few critical factors they use to control costs. These are Key Success Factors.

Returning to our gourmet frozen food segment example, one key cost-controlling factor in that industry is having a parent company in the food business. Therefore, Le Menu can control costs because it is owned by Campbell Soup who has tremendous purchasing, processing, and distribution strengths. This alliance allows the smaller Le Menu business access to the larger Campbell Soup Company's cost-controlling knowledge, efficiency expertise, and purchasing clout. Thus, ownership by the big parent company has been found to be a major cost-controlling KSF that explains all of the smaller cost-controlling techniques used by Le Menu. In your search for KSFs, you'll often identify smaller cost-controlling elements before you realize how the smaller elements fit together to form a major cost-controlling system that becomes the firm's KSF.

For Southwest Airlines, a major cost-controlling KSF is its "No-Frills" system. The "No-Frills" system has many smaller cost-controlling elements, like stripping away less needed product and service features, like limiting the variety of planes it flies to only two types, which significantly lowers training and repair costs, and like operating with an organizational culture that motivates each employee to reduce costs by being highly productive. All are elements of a bigger system, the "no-frills" system. When you analyze another business's cost-controlling techniques, you are likely to see the smaller elements before understanding how they fit together to form a cost-controlling system, a KSF.

In the beer industry, manufacturers control costs by operating plants near capacity. The "Peak Capacity" KSF controls costs by minimizing the plant, equipment, and marketing overhead costs per beer. This, in part, explains how the largest company in the beer industry, Anheuser Busch, generates the highest level of profits. They are able to operate their plants at near peak efficiency.

Every business, profit or non-profit, must have one or more KSFs that control costs. Having the best sales trigger in your industry will generate the highest sales volume, but without a key method of controlling costs, high sales can lead to the poor house.

Equally important, KSFs that control costs must be continuously improved so that profits can be continuously increased.

Fact Three: *A business can only be successful if it can limit the number of competitors it has to battle.* Any system that limits the effectiveness of your competitors or the ability of competitors to affect your business is a key to the success of your business.

Consider the pharmaceutical industry where there are hundreds of competitors, a scary prospect for any business. Any one firm, no matter how large, would go bankrupt if it had to fight hundreds of competitors for sales. However, all those pharmaceutical firms thrive because of target marketing where only a few firms make products for any one physical ailment. In most product areas of the pharmaceutical industry, only two or three firms are in actual competition, making similar medicines targeted to exactly the same ailment; therefore, because of customer targeting, most firms have only a few competitors for each medicine that can be called "real" competitors.

In the beer industry, Heineken targets upscale beer customers with high prices and high prestige while Old Milwaukee targets price-sensitive customers with low prices. By using customer targeting, the two firms avoid being "real" competitors.

A small business can limit competitors the same way — through customer targeting. Targeting customers means specializing in one customer type and in a few carefully selected customer segments.

Businesses have long limited competition with customer specialization. For example, Le Menu chose to specialize in gourmet foods and to avoid competitors targeting other customers in the main-stream frozen food market. When Southwest Airlines entered the intrastate market, it chose to specialize by targeting price-sensitive customers who were being ignored by the full service airlines. The new microbrewery businesses have avoided competition with Anheuser Busch, Miller, and Coors by making their own specialty beers and targeting local customers who want a unique taste, a connoisseur image, an adventure in beer drinking, and, in some cases, local entertainment.

Competitive Strategies and Key Success Factors

To understand a competitive strategy, you must understand its Key Success Factors. All businesses, regardless of which competitive strategy they use, have three types of KSFs:

- Sales Triggers
- Cost Controllers
- Competition Limiters

Each competitive strategy triggers sales to its target customer type by using different sales triggers. Different sales triggers are developed with different business skills, assets, and competencies. Not surprisingly, businesses using different competitive strategies need different cost controllers because they face dissimilar cost problems.

Each competitive strategy has its own Key Success Factors, which will be clearly marked with a 🔑 symbol, that create its effectiveness, and those KSFs will be closely examined in the coming chapters. To understand a competitive strategy, you must understand its KSFs. To implement a competitive strategy, you must develop its KSF strengths and use them in your market.

As you read the next few chapters you should reflect about how each competitive strategy is used and could be used in your market. And, if you decide to adopt one of the competitive strategies as your *competitive business model,* you must develop a creative plan to use that strategy in your market or industry. You'll learn the basic concepts from this book, but you must devise your own way to implement the competitive strategy concepts in your unique situation.

CHAPTER 3

Low-Cost Competitive Strategy

Understanding Small Business's Most Dangerous Competitor

A Low-Cost Competitive Strategy is used by a business to generate the lowest per unit costs for the market's most common product or service. The strategy uses the firm's low-cost advantage to charge the lowest market price in order to capture the largest market share and make a big profit. The Low-Cost strategy firm uses its purchasing power to drive down suppliers' prices, advertisers' prices, transportation charges, and any other volume-related expense. When the firm achieves the market's highest sales volume, it can then use the industry's most efficient production systems, most efficient business systems, and most efficient business processes to achieve exceptionally low per-product or per service costs.

Low-Cost strategy success depends on an ever-growing sales volume. The Low-Cost strategy is growth driven; it feeds on fast growth; it succeeds through rapid growth. This strategy builds big corporations, and, once built, keeps them big. So, as a manager of a small business, why should you care about a big business strategy? Why should you care if big corporations like McDonalds, Wal-Mart, Bic, Home Depot, and Toys R Us use a Low-Cost Competitive Strategy? Why should you spend your time to understand this strategy? Three reasons. First, you might be interested in creating a big business like Wal-Mart. Sam Walton steered his rural Arkansas discount department store to an industry leader in just 30 years by shrewdly using the Low-Cost Competitive Strategy. If you yearn for rapid expansion of your small business, this strategy may be the roadmap to your dreams.

Second, under the right circumstances this strategy can be used effectively by a small business in an isolated, local market. If the competition in your market is confined geographically, you can use this strategy to carve out a profitable local position without pressure to expand outside your region. However, you will have to expand inside your community or region to maintain your local cost advantage.

Third, you need to understand this strategy to protect yourself. Most small businesses are looking for alternative strategies to help them avoid low-price competition from big, aggressive companies. You can't avoid cut-throat, Low-Cost competitors unless you understand their Key Success Factors, and unless you understand how to avoid competing against their strengths. Just as the formulation of any military strategy begins by understanding the enemy's strengths, the formulation of your competitive strategy begins by understanding the Low-Cost competitor's strengths.

Also, you can't ignore Low-Cost competitors by simply choosing to use an alternative competitive strategy because all the alternative competitive strategies are formed RELATIVE to the Low-Cost strategy. Therefore, your understanding and implementation of alternative competitive strategies depends on your understanding of the Low-Cost Competitive Strategy. Moreover, even if you don't offer the same product or service as the Low-Cost competition, customers are making comparisons, so you'll need to understand the comparisons.

Finally, every Low-Cost strategy action demands a reaction, even when you use an alternative competitive strategy. When the Low-Cost firm changes its standardized product to include new features and new benefits, your firm will be affected, and your firm has to respond. When the Low-Cost strategy firm acts, it does so in order to expand sales by widening the appeal of its products and services. By understanding the Low-Cost Competitive Strategy and particularly by understanding this strategy's customers, you will understand what actions to anticipate from businesses using this strategy.

Prudent Shoppers: The Largest Customer Group

Established markets consist of a wide variety of products and services being sold to a variety of customer types. For example, consider the broad range of products sold in the lawn mower market: cheap mowers, expensive mowers, push mowers, self-propelled mowers, riding mowers, mowers with bagging systems, mulching mowers, prestige mowers, used mowers, smooth-cutting mowers, commercial mowers, mowers for golf courses, and mowers for tennis courts.

Instead of thinking about the variety of products sold to customers, turn this around; think of the variety of customer groups or segments wanting to buy each type of mower. It's an easy concept to grasp that the customers who purchase one type of mower represent a separate group wanting the unique benefits offered by that particular mower. Since the Low-Cost strategy targets

Prudent Shoppers, the logical question is, what benefits do Prudent Shoppers want? Prudent Shoppers are price-driven buyers. They trade away the product attributes that provide peak performance in favor of a lower price because they know they will seldom need peak product performance. Prudent Shoppers trade away a lot of luxury, status, and prestige attributes to get a lower price — sure, they want higher status but not enough to pay for it. Prudent Shoppers are compromise shoppers driven toward the best balance of good features, good performance, good status, and a modest price. Prudent Shoppers settle for the best bang for the buck.

Prudent Shoppers form the largest customer group with huge buying demand, and they are intensely sought after by large businesses. The company who best satisfies Prudent Shoppers is the one with the optimum product/price version or service/price version that delivers top value. That product or service emerges as the industry standard.

If you want to see Prudent Shoppers and what they buy, go to your local discount department store and look around. In stores like Target, Wal-Mart, and Kmart, who target Prudent Shoppers, you'll find the lawnmower industry's low-cost winner, the Murray which sells for around $100.

The inexpensive Murray Lawn Mower is typical of all standardized products that Prudent Shoppers buy in any industry. The Murray mower has a good engine that is adequate for the average homeowner; higher priced competitors offer more expensive, powerful engines to handle tough jobs. The Murray mower has a thin steel frame with little plastic wheels and small plastic axle sleeves; higher priced competitors offer strong frames with special grass-flow features and metal wheel hubs with steel ball bearings for great performance. Every feature of the Murray is "good." Well, every feature except one — price — and that's where the Murray is superior — it has the best price. The Murray mower is a highly affordable new mower, a great trade-off between features and price — the best lawn mower value. Change the Murray mower's oil once a year, sharpen and balance its blade occasionally, don't hit big rocks, and it will last 10 years. That makes it cheaper per year than a used mower — that's real value. No wonder the Murray mower is the choice of so many Prudent Shoppers.

Prudent Shoppers in most markets are members of the two largest social classes, the middle class and the working class, which make up 72 percent of the U.S. population. These two social classes have limited financial resources and make many cautious purchases. Because of their huge numbers, Prudent Shoppers profoundly affect every market and every type of product and service. Not only do they form the core or center of each market, the company who wins the largest share of their business is able to wield exceptional influence over its own costs.

Massive Purchasing Power of the Low-Cost Strategy

Powerful, large competitors have ruined many small businesses with their unbelievably low prices. How are they able to charge such low prices for their products and services? Let's examine how purchasing power grows as a manufacturer achieves success with a low-priced product.

The combination of low price and a good product naturally attracts a horde of Prudent Shoppers who understandably need to stretch their bucks. As sales climb for the winning standardized product, the firm that produces it takes advantage of its growing market strength through a number of cost reduction steps that can't be matched by any competitor. First, with the largest sales, Low-Cost strategy manufacturers, distributors, and retailers can justify installing the industry's most economical and efficient operating systems. Manufacturers can afford to install highly automated, mechanized manufacturing equipment and processes to drive down per product overhead and labor costs. Distributors can afford to install high volume material-handling systems and efficient delivery systems to achieve the lowest per product freight costs. Retailers can afford to keep their markups low and make their profits by selling large volumes. Thus, at every step in the process — from manufacturing through distribution to retailing — every member plays a part in keeping costs low to keep prices low in order that all of them can make high profits producing, distributing, and selling big volumes.

Second, the suppliers to the winning Low-Cost strategy manufacturer compete for big orders of raw materials and components by offering large price discounts. With big volumes, a supplier can greatly reduce costs by automating, making long production runs, and reducing overhead and labor costs. As suppliers lower their prices, the Low-Cost manufacturer again lowers his price, which stimulates additional sales volume for the leading low-price product.

Third, the winning Low-Cost manufacturer becomes the most powerful industry buyer of raw materials and components, and this purchasing muscle is next used to force suppliers into quality concessions. Suppliers are pressured to improve their quality beyond normal levels or face the loss of future orders. As suppliers raise the quality of the components that go into the standardized product, the performance, reliability, and durability of the standardized product is improved without increasing its cost. Improved product performance without a price increase fuels still more sales growth by attracting some quality-conscious customers to the low-price product.

With every increase in sales volume, the manufacturer's purchasing clout grows larger and is again used to further push down the supplier's price and is again used to demand additional quality concessions from suppliers. As a result, costs continue to decline, quality continues to increase, price continues to decline, and the standardized product's value continues to increase.

Fourth, just as rising quality attracts some customers who might have purchased higher quality products, declining prices pull some bargain hunting customers away from buying used products, adding more sales growth.

The Danger of Challenging the Low-Cost Leader

Low-Cost industry leaders are usually national and international corporations because they must seek every opportunity for growth to increase their purchasing muscle faster than that of their rivals. Many small businesses have tried unsuccessfully to compete with these Low-Cost leaders by selling modestly priced televisions, appliances, jeans, beverages, tools, furniture, food, and a host of other products. Whenever the prices that can be charged by each firm in an industry are determined predominately by the costs that result from each firm's purchasing power, small businesses should avoid competing with price alone.

Because the Low-Cost strategy is very volume-sensitive, before challenging the Low-Cost leader a small business needs a strategic vision that enables it to capture the largest competitive sales volume and the biggest market share in order to maintain the lowest costs. Don't think you can set your sales goals high and achieve reasonable success if you capture the second-best market share — second place with this strategy could bankrupt your business.

When two businesses both use a Low-Cost Competitive Strategy to target the same customers, the second-place competitor has to match the price of the leader without having the same low costs of the leader — a formula for bad profits and poor cash flow that won't allow the second-place competitor to finance further expansion that's necessary to catch the leader. Usually the second-best competitor's prices are a little higher, and Prudent Shoppers, being price sensitive, punish the second-best competitor.

Large national and international corporations not only currently dominate today's product and service areas with their Low-Cost Competitive Strategies, these giant corporations are in a position to dominate in tomorrow's markets because of their enormous past earnings. For example, Philip Morris, the cigarette giant who makes Marlboro, had a war chest of $21 billion in cash, yes that's billion not million, to use in buying or diversifying into new businesses. With this amount of money, Philip Morris could easily take a non-patented concept away from your small business by duplicating your product or service and expanding quickly to capture the cost advantages produced by high volumes. Overnight, they could charge a price below your costs and still make a good profit.

In most cases, these big, Low-Cost corporations have billion dollar manufacturing and distribution investments in commodity chemical, food, clothing, furniture, housewares, electronics, and automobile plants. Before your small business can compete head-to-head with one of these established giants, you have to find a way to beat their price, without relying on high volumes, and still make a profit — unlikely without a technological breakthrough, a good patent, or an exceptional business vision.

Great Low-Cost Small Business Visions

Now that you're thoroughly discouraged and have given up any hope of using a Low-Cost strategy, you should know that it can be successfully used by small businesses. Sears and Montgomery Ward were huge when Sam Walton spotted their weakness.

Walton's vision was to become the low-price leader in small, rural towns. Because of his experience, Walton realized these communities were isolated from national markets, so in rural communities he only had to beat the prices of mom-and-pop stores — local retailers. As Wal-Mart grew, Walton could qualify for ever-increasing price discounts from suppliers. Plus, with increasing sales, he could continuously increase Wal-Mart's efficiencies to drive down the costs of merchandising, promoting, warehousing, and distributing.

The vision worked. Wal-Mart drove costs down by combining its growth in small towns before entering small city markets. Then Wal-Mart combined its growth in small cities before entering the large city markets. When Wal-Mart finally entered the Dallas, Chicago, Atlanta, and Phoenix markets, it was a powerful company with major cost advantages to use in those cities. Wal-Mart could never have survived if it had started in the big cities, and Sam Walton knew this. Wal-Mart could never have survived if a firm like Sears or Montgomery Ward had realized early enough what Sam Walton's vision was and duplicated it; in Wal-Mart's formative years, lots of retailers had the sales volume muscle to undercut Wal-Mart's prices in rural communities and send Sam Walton back to his old job managing a Ben Franklin's store. But competitors reacted too late, and the rest is history.

This example demonstrates how a competitive strategy becomes an important part of a business vision, but not the only part. Sam Walton's vision combined a Low-Cost Competitive Strategy with a Concentrated Growth Strategy, one of fourteen growth strategies presented in the second section of this book.

Using a Low-Cost Competitive Strategy in Local Markets

Sam Walton demonstrated that because many markets are competitively isolated, a Low-Cost Competitive Strategy can be used successfully in local communities. Except for a few lost sales to catalog companies, many small businesses are locally isolated and, thank goodness, not easily combined into a national business like Wal-Mart. For example, local homebuilders in most communities don't compete with national homebuilders; neither do local cabinetmakers, barbers, repair shops, retail boat sellers, and plumbing businesses. Local service businesses are normally isolated. The more services and less products your business sells, the greater the likelihood that you can use a Low-Cost strategy in your local market and go after the large local volumes. Service businesses implement a Low-Cost strategy by limiting the services offered to those few that are most valued by customers and streamlining those few to become highly productive. Increased service productivity leads to lower costs and lower prices.

Now that you have a practical understanding of how a Low-Cost Competitive Strategy builds a big business, let's look more closely at the key factors used to implement this strategy.

Key Success Factors for the Low-Cost Competitive Strategy

This strategy is used to target Prudent Shoppers with low prices. Obviously a product's cost must be lower than a product's price if the business is going to make a profit. What factors make this type of business successful? What special skills, assets, and competencies does a business using a Low-Cost Competitive Strategy need to develop?

The remainder of this chapter focuses on the KSFs that trigger sales, control costs, and limit competitors — the technical side of this strategy. To be successful with this strategy, you must build these strengths, and you must develop a vision for how you will achieve and maintain relative KSF superiority among competitors in your market.

On the other hand, to avoid competing against this strategy, you must understand its KSF strengths and abstain from competing with these factors.

Key Success Factors that Trigger Sales

A Low-Cost Competitive Strategy targets Prudent Shoppers who stretch their incomes by purchasing low-priced, good products. Therefore, this strategy has a single KSF to trigger sales.

Low Price: Low Price is the KSF that triggers the sale, and good products and services are support factors that must be maintained at levels acceptable to Prudent Shoppers. At the support level, nothing is either outstandingly good or egregiously bad about the low-cost product; it's a trade-off product or a trade-off service that swaps unnecessary product performance, service, personnel assistance, and image for a lower price. Again, the best bang for the buck, a good price/benefits value.

However, this trade-off must not be confused with what Prudent Shoppers want. Whether interviewed or given a questionnaire, they will indicate that they would like higher performance or better services, but this doesn't mean they will pay a higher price for them. They won't.

Other factors can be significant enough to be rated as Low-Cost sales triggers in a few industries. For example, in the fast food industry, competing Low-Cost hamburger chains offer slightly different products, services, and store designs to create some differentiation between firms. By differentiating, these firms create a second, weaker KSF that triggers sales — product taste — and a third, weaker KSF that triggers sales — image. Together, these two weaker KSFs allow McDonalds' Low-Cost competitors to build enough customer loyalty to deflect some head-to-head price competition.

Such differentiation is more difficult in other industries. For example, Wal-Mart, Kmart, and Target all compete with a Low-Cost Competitive Strategy and very similar products. So far, Wal-Mart has the best lowest prices, so the other firms have struggled in their attempts to differentiate their stores with far weaker sales triggers and to attract a viable share of Prudent Shoppers.

Key Success Factors that Control Costs

A low price for a good product or service wins the sales battle, but big sales certainly don't guarantee big profits. The formula for big profits is to support a low price with even lower costs, and lower costs for this strategy are achieved with a total of six cost controlling KSFs.

Economy of Scale — A Cost Controlling KSF: Earlier, the purchasing muscle of the low-cost business was explained, but the purchasing muscle is just one aspect of what's called economy of scale.

Economy of scale is the powerful cost-controlling engine used by this strategy to generate low costs, support low prices, and produce big profits. When several firms compete, each using a Low-Cost Competitive Strategy, the business with the best economy of scale will have the lowest costs. Economy of scale rewards the market leader (the business with the biggest market share) and punishes everyone else. With this strategy, achieving some economy of scale isn't good enough, being second best can have cruel consequences.

The word "economy" in economy of scale means "to lower costs." For example, if you improved your economy in advertising, your advertising cost per sales dollar would go down. If you improved your economy in operations, your production cost per product or per service would go down. The word "scale" means "to get larger." So, economy of scale means that even though total costs will increase as your business gets larger, as it operates at a larger scale, the per product or per service costs can decrease.

For example, suppose the total cost to produce 100,000 furniture casters is $150,000 or $1.50 per caster. The business grows and produces 200,000 casters, total costs climb to $200,000, but the cost per caster declines to $1.00. In this case, total cost increases, but per product cost decreases — that's economy of scale, and that's this strategy's major cost-controlling engine, driving costs down.

Economy of scale affects advertising costs. For example, a small firm with $300,000 in annual sales might spend $18,000 in advertising, or six cents per sales dollar. When annual sales growth reaches $500,000, the firm might spend $25,000 in advertising; advertising cost drops to five cents per sales dollar. Therefore, sales go up 67 percent; total advertising cost goes up 39 percent, but advertising cost per sales dollar declines by 17 percent. That's economy of scale in action; that's the most important KSF pushing all costs ever lower with a Low-Cost Competitive Strategy.

Economy of scale benefits push the Low-Cost strategy firm to pursue every opportunity to grow, so it can build up more and more economy of scale cost advantages. Many of the cost-reducing effects of economy of scale happen naturally. The firm grows larger; suppliers lower their prices. But managers of Low-Cost firms also aggressively use their purchasing muscle to force down the per unit costs of advertising, transportation, labor, training, warehousing, production equipment, services, and technology. When managers spot a new opportunity, they aggressively use their large size to negotiate, bargain, and force their unit costs lower than their competitors.

Much of Wal-Mart's climb from a small business to a giant corporation was due to the cost savings from economy of scale cost reductions in their warehouse and distribution area. As Wal-Mart grew, it was able to build its own warehouses to gain two early cost advantages. First, building central warehouses and delivering to each of their stores in their own trucks allowed them to operate with less inventory, and the cash they didn't have to put into inventory was used to finance more new stores. Second, suppliers gave Wal-Mart additional price discounts because they saved money delivering to a central warehouse instead of delivering to each store.

Today, Wal-Mart has grown large enough to use cross-docking warehouse techniques. After a Wal-Mart truck delivers to a Wal-Mart store, it goes to a supplier's plant and saves freight costs by hauling a truckload of merchandise back to the Wal-Mart cross-docking warehouse. Here, most new supplies are immediately broken into small lots and placed on out-going trucks for tomorrow's store deliveries — much of Wal-Mart's merchandise isn't stored, it keeps moving. Cross-docking economy of scale is credited with lowering Wal-Mart's operating costs by an additional 5 percent, which drives their warehousing and distribution cost to 1.3 percent of sale. By comparison, Sears distribution cost is 5 percent of sales and Kmart's is 3.5 percent *(1)*. Based just on warehouse and distribution costs, in order to make the same profit, a lawn mower that Wal-Mart could sell for around $100 would have to be priced about $3.00 higher at a competitor's store.

Yet, even with these natural economy of scale advantages, Wal-Mart has a reputation as a fierce negotiator who continuously pushes suppliers' prices down. Top management knows that some economy of scale advantages occur naturally with growth, and others occur only with pressure or only by re-designing the business as it grows.

Economy of scale advantages usually accrue to big businesses, but alert small business owners can also benefit from them. Richard Moody created a very profitable small business by using economy of scale.

Moody understood that the most expensive phone call was an operator assisted, long distance, business conference call made during the regular workweek, 8 A.M. to 5 P.M., Monday through Friday. Moody spotted a chance to enter the conference call business using a Low-Cost Competitive Strategy, and Aloha Conferencing was born.

The premise for Moody's strategy was that the cheapest calls are those made before 8 A.M., and conference calls are cheaper if a company operator handles the connections instead of the long-distance telephone operator.

Aloha Conferencing was established to provide conference calling from Honolulu, Hawaii, because Honolulu's time is five hours behind New York's — when it's 10:00 A.M. in New York, it's 5 A.M. in Honolulu — where the call originates. Moody realized that if Aloha placed morning conference calls for New York businesses, the costs would be so cheap that Aloha could make a good profit and still give corporate customers a significant cost reduction.

Aloha's call volume quickly increased. As the volume of calls increased, Aloha's economy of scale advantages kicked in, and the telephone company began lowering Aloha's phone rates. Aloha eventually received the long distance carrier's cheapest rate — their total phone bill went up, but their cost per telephone call went down drastically.

The economy of scale success was so great that it allowed Aloha to become debt free within three years. Their sales topped $3.5 million by the mid 1990s *(2)*.

Learning Curves — A Cost Controlling KSF: Learning curves also push costs down for the Low-Cost strategy firm. Learning curves describe what happens to labor costs per product or per service as employees do their jobs over and over. As a manager, you've observed that workers get faster the more times they perform a task. Learning curves are mathematical proofs of that observed fact: the more often an employee performs a manual task, the less time it *should* take the employee to do the task, so labor costs per product or per service *should* continuously go down.

Furthermore, learning curves reward high sales volumes, so the Low-Cost strategy business can generate more learning curve cost reductions than other types of businesses — another big competitive cost advantage. Additionally, the Low-Cost industry leader is able to combine economy of scale effects and learning curve effects to hammer down costs.

In practical terms, learning curves establish the right of a manager to expect, and even demand, that employees get faster and more efficient at repetitive jobs. Learning curves don't always automatically produce faster employees and cheaper labor costs. Learning curves only guarantee managers the chance to improve efficiencies and the opportunity to drive costs down; managers have to take advantage of the opportunity to reduce costs. Managers who understand the learning curve effect must plan to use their employees' improved abilities, and must reorganize the work system to use employees' improved abilities — managers make it happen.

Successful Low-Cost strategy managers are aggressive cost fighters who set higher performance standards and work quotas for more experienced workers. They reward a worker's improved efficiency. They motivate the entire organization to believe that each worker's output should continuously increase with experience in order to keep the business healthy.

During World War II the government used learning rates to predict future building times for a new ship. Suppose past data (see Figure 3.1) showed the Gulf Coast Shipyard to have a 90 percent learning curve and the shipyard took 2,000,000 man-hours to build the first of a new style ship. The second ship could be predicted to take 1,800,000 man-hours (90 percent x

FIGURE 3.1

The Discovery of Learning Curves

Learning curves were mathematically proven during World War II when the U.S. Government's industrial engineers attempted to estimate the time it would require to build a new style ship or airplane by examining the time it took to build previous war ships and airplanes. Historic records revealed that every time the production volume of one type ship or plane doubled — not increased but doubled — the time it took to build the next ship or plane went down by a predictable amount. The time reduction was so predictable that the learning pattern was easily plotted on graph paper. Those graphs of total labor versus the number of ships built were called learning curves. For example, the government's numbers might look like these:

- 1st ship — 1,371,742 total man-hours
- 2nd ship — 1,234,567 total man-hours
- 4th ship — 1,111,111 total man-hours
- 8th ship — 1,000,000 total man-hours
- 16th ship — 900,000 total man-hours

Each building time shown above is 90 percent of the previous building time, so each time the shipyard doubled the number of ships it built, the total time to build a ship went down by 10 percent. Stated another way, the time to build the 16th ship was 90 percent of the time to build the 8th ship. Therefore, this shipyard had a 90 percent learning curve.

2,000,000), the fourth 1,620,000 man-hours (90 percent x 1,800,000), the eighth 1,458,000 man-hours, the sixteenth 1,312,200 man-hours, and so forth. Each time the number of ships built was doubled, the man-hours required could be predicted to go down to 90 percent of the previous total — that's the effect of learning curves.

If a shipyard stopped building a type of ship for a while, then started up again, they would lose some of their learning curve advantage because of forgetting — a forgetting curve also exists but hasn't been plotted and named by industrial engineers.

Of course, wartime employees were dedicated to helping win a popular war and were motivated by patriotism to apply any extra time gained from learning to building the next ship. Today's employees, in some circumstances, may be less likely to voluntarily apply extra time gained from learning to the next task, so Low-Cost strategy managers need to stimulate workers by creating a business climate that encourages and motivates workers to strive for higher levels of productivity, or if necessary, requires them to become more productive.

Learning rates vary greatly from one business to the next. A business may have a 95, 80, 70, or any other percentage learning curve rate. This means that employees at a plant assembling motorcycles and employees at a flower shop creating floral arrangements may have different learning curve rates, but employees at each facility are capable of faster assembly speeds as they learn from their prior work. Furthermore, managers in both businesses should use learning curves as their justification to set higher work standards as workers and crews gain more experience.

While learning curve effects can be used in any business and with any competitive strategy to lower costs, learning curve effects are a particularly important KSF for firms using a Low-Cost Competitive Strategy. Their high sales volumes provide them more opportunities for learning curve cost reductions.

Experience Curves — A Cost Controlling KSF: Experience curves are similar to learning curves, but experience curves apply to work that's more mental and less manual, such as the tasks done by managers, purchasing agents, sales people, editors, computer programmers, etc. In general, it is useful to think of learning curves applying more to blue collar workers, and experience curves applying to white collar workers. However, the mix of mental and manual work content can vary for workers with any color of collar.

Experience curve effects aren't mathematically proven and aren't shown on charts and graphs, but evidence of their existence is convincing. For example, consider a purchasing agent's experience over time as new "product A" emerges from the product development stage and goes into regular production. Initially, the purchasing agent is asked to find a supplier for a new component that is used in "product A." The agent spends a great deal of time finding a new supplier, qualifying the supplier, establishing credit with the new supplier, and entering the first order. The second order is much quicker because of the experience gained from the initial purchase; hence, white-collar labor costs go down. As the purchasing task is repeated, the new supplier's phone number goes into the phone memory pad, and the new task picks up additional speed.

Eventually "product A" is commercialized, and the ordering task for the new component for "product A" gets highly automated. By the 500th order, a blanket purchase order for the year is issued with a schedule of deliveries. By now, the time to enter a 100,000 unit order is far less than the initial order for 10 units.

The declining labor cost of purchasing a new component is due to the experience curve. The more often any white-collar task is repeated, the less time it should take to do the task, and the less it should cost — that's the effect of the experience curve. Of course, as the tasks take less and less time, the white collar worker could goof off, tell jokes, spend too much time visiting with supplier's salespeople, take long lunches, and do personal chores on company time — sound familiar? However, Low-Cost strategy firms, being aggressive cost controllers, make sure the time saved is productively used, not wasted.

However, white-collar workers are harder to monitor and control than blue-collar workers. Low-Cost firms capture the major benefits of the experience curve only when professional employees are highly motivated and when their jobs are enlarged as they gain experience. Enlarging and changing job content is called restructuring, and, unfortunately, restructuring may mean downsizing the organization, combining jobs, and forcing the remaining white collar workers to use their experience to become more productive.

This explains why Wal-Mart recently eliminated some jobs at its headquarters in Bentonville, Arkansas, even as it announced record profits and sales. Wal-Mart was managing its learning and experience curve effects; white collar workers had gained experience, had become more productive, thus Wal-Mart made adjustments that forced employees to use their improved abilities to increase their personal productivity. Wal-Mart clearly intends to remain the industry's low-price leader for a long time, and they are not going to squander their learning and experience curve opportunities.

Economy of scale, learning curve effects, and experience curve effects are powerful KSFs that Low-Cost firms use to control costs. Some of the following factors are frequently important to various Low-Cost strategy businesses and can be important enough to be considered KSFs for some businesses.

Low Overhead — A Cost Controlling KSF: The first purpose of low overhead is to keep costs down. Low-Cost manufacturers, wholesalers, and distributors choose locations that minimize the combined cost of land, buildings, labor, in-bound freight, and out-bound freight. Reducing the cost of one of these factors can cause the cost of one or more of the other factors to soar; therefore, a total overhead KSF can be created by shrewdly finding the optimum balance of all location-affected costs.

Low-Cost retailers cannot follow the same cost minimization formula. A retail location provides important customer benefits such as ease of access and status. Prudent Shoppers trade-off *some* of these benefits for a lower price, but they don't trade-off all of these benefits. Prudent Shoppers still want reasonable access to the retail facility. They still want some status and prestige; they don't want to feel ashamed to be caught shopping at the low-cost retail business. Therefore, a Low-Cost strategy store usually avoids the high overhead expense of the community mall in favor of a more economical location close to the mall. However, the retail store using a Low-Cost strategy avoids the inferior location next to an abandoned building with a collapsed roof even if it is extraordinarily cheap. The best image location isn't needed, but the worst image location must be avoided.

The second purpose is symbolic because keeping overhead low is a highly visible demonstration of management's commitment to controlling costs.

Maintaining low overhead is a major management leadership tool that conditions employees to believe that management truly values cost cutting. If the headquarters, plant offices, or the retail store owner's office is allowed to become a fancy, showy, or ostentatious symbol of the business's success, employees will decide that stringent low-cost controls are no longer essential. Management perks can signal a "do as I say, not as I do" attitude that is resented and resisted by employees. Visual displays of luxurious offices, luxury cars, and company planes erode both the employees' willingness to support current cost-controlling tactics and erode their willingness to continuously strive to improve the firm's cost-controlling ability.

Constrained Technology — A Cost Controlling KSF: Investing in new technologies is a budget buster, so Low-Cost strategy firms in high-tech and other markets have developed ways to control the cost of technology.

First, Low-Cost firms invest in process technologies much more heavily than in product technologies. Process is the sequence of steps used to do work, so process technological improvements are those that make the operation more efficient to drive down costs. Since Low-Cost firms seek to make and provide Prudent Shoppers with good, but not great products, being first to offer expensive state-of-the-art improvements is not necessary.

Second, technological improvements are not confined to product and service changes. Low-Cost firms continuously search throughout their organizations for opportunities to streamline the marketing process, the inventory replacement process, the credit approval process, the customer complaint resolution process, the employee training process, etc. Costs are often reduced by reinventing these supporting processes to make them more productive.

Third, Low-Cost firms are copycats. They excel at quickly copying the expensive, new products and services invented by other firms. The result is easily seen on the Low-Cost retailer's shelves where you'll find low-priced versions of high-priced products, private store brands, and products using last year's technology to keep prices low.

Culture — A Cost Controlling KSF: Culture is the term used to describe the general beliefs and attitudes that are widely held by the majority of your employees. Establishing the appropriate culture is important because only when employees believe in your business vision will they help you achieve it.

In a supportive Low-Cost culture, employees believe offering customers good products and services at the lowest price possible is the right way to do business. Because employees believe this, they will voluntarily help to keep costs low by keeping their personal productivity high.

In a supportive cultural environment, instead of being pushed by management, employees are internally motivated to find every possible economy of scale savings. They enthusiastically re-invest the time saved because of their learning curves and experience curves to help push costs down. This creates a powerful KSF to control costs because employees are the only ones who intimately know their actual work processes and who best know how to make those processes more cost efficient. Properly motivated employees can identify ways of cutting costs and improving efficiency that management would never discover. Also, in supportive cultures, when key management people are away at a conference or on vacation, the employees continue to make good decisions and take actions that are consistent with the Low-Cost strategy because they share the belief that it's the right way to behave.

A supportive Low-Cost culture allows a manager to operate with a wider span of control and supervise a greater number of employees because employees with good work attitudes need less direct supervision.

This collective employee conscience that supports the firm's competitive strategy is created by managers in a number of ways:

- Managers hire people whose personal values and beliefs are similar to the organization's.
- Managers model appropriate behavior and appropriate decision-making.
- Managers create supportive cultures by including employees in the planning of new cost-reduction programs.
- Top managers tell stories that support a Low-Cost culture. Stories about great cost-reducing ideas of current and former employees, about times when the company shrewdly beat a competitor's price, and about providing good customer value at low prices. Studies have shown that top management storytelling is a powerful and subtle tool that can shape

employee attitudes and beliefs without preaching, teaching, pontificating, or talking down to employees (3).

- Managers reward employee cost-cutting actions, supportive attitudes, and decisions that are consistent with a Low-Cost strategy. They discourage waste and punish employee actions that do not support the competitive strategy.
- Managers use effective Low-Cost symbols such as spartan offices and frugal ceremonies that are fun, but not lavish. Managers wear moderately priced clothing, drive moderately priced vehicles, and avoid showy perks.

The Key Success Factor that Limits Competition

Competition is significantly limited by customer targeting, so customer targeting is a KSF. For example, two women's dress shops happily exist side by side in the community mall when one targets petite women and the other targets big women. A third store opens to target pregnant women without upsetting the first two in the least. These stores are not competing for the same customer dollars. A sale by one store is not a sale lost by the other stores. All are in the women's dress industry, but they aren't "real" competitors.

Customer Targeting: These three women's clothing stores limit the effectiveness of their competitors by targeting different types of customers.

Unfortunately, defining and describing your business's target customers may require some effort, but the objective of customer targeting is simple: isolate a group of customers to serve and leave the rest of the customers for other firms to fight over.

A business using a Low-Cost Competitive Strategy targets Prudent Shoppers and leaves Selective Shoppers, and Bargain Hunters for its competitors. The Low-Cost firm's "real" competitors are only those also targeting Prudent Shoppers.

Prudent Shoppers are a complex group to describe. They are customers with modest incomes who seek out low-priced products, and they are customers with high incomes who are Prudent Shoppers for products for which they feel no involvement. There are some high-income customers who don't feel that they have high incomes, and their consumer behavior is more in line with low-income customers. Other consumers with low incomes will stretch to buy low-priced products, instead of cheap products, to hide their true financial circumstances. For all these reasons it's difficult to form an accurate, descriptive profile of Prudent Shoppers.

Some firms establish an artificial profile of Prudent Shoppers. Wal-Mart, for example, divides all customers into three groups: upscale families with over $50,000 in annual income, middle income families, and downscale families with under $25,000 in annual income. Wal-Mart then targets downscale families, and if they can keep their prices low enough to win the loyalty of downscale customers, they will attract a great portion of the middle and upper income groups who are price sensitive for various reasons.

Continuously Improving Your Ability to Limit Competitors

Here's how customer targeting, a KSF, is continuously improved. First, the Low-Cost business constantly strives to identify the characteristics that identify and describe its target customers, its best customers. Descriptions can include any characteristics commonly found among target customers that seem important, such as a certain age, occupation, education level, ethnic group, income level, religion, lifestyle, personality trait, attitude, opinion, interest, media habits, or any combination of these. Descriptions may include the Prudent Shoppers' attitudes about themselves, their view of how they want others to see them, or the ideal self image they are striving to achieve.

Second, as the Low-Cost firm's initial Prudent Shopper profile is built, it becomes extremely valuable in guiding efforts to find additional customers who match the profile. Customer profiles help the firm to make contact with new, prospective customers with advertising, promotions, and personal selling efforts. Every time improvements are made in the accuracy of the target customer profile, the firm's ability to communicate to its target customers is further improved.

Third, as the firm's knowledge of target customers grows, the ability to get good feedback from target customers grows. With better feedback, the firm can continuously adjust its products, services, personal skills, and image to further improve Prudent Shoppers' satisfaction. Increased customer satisfaction further limits competition by making it more costly for competitors to steal your customers.

Customer targeting is a KSF whose strength can be measured by the amount of customer knowledge that a firm possesses. That knowledge must continuously be improved for three reasons. First, no firm will ever have as much customer information as it needs. Second, customer profiles change over time, thus a firm needs to periodically adjust its target customer description to maintain its customer focus. Third, customer wants and needs change over time and the business must continuously improve its ability to monitor those changes.

The Limitations of a Low-Cost Competitive Strategy

Using this strategy, a business faces some unusual problems. First, normally only one business in a market can prosper using a Low-Cost Competitive Strategy. The business with the lowest long-term pricing wins, and low long-term pricing must be supported with the lowest long-term costs. For example, in the discount department store industry, Wal-Mart is highly successful while Kmart has been flirting with bankruptcy for years. Wal-Mart and Kmart have many similar product lines, but Wal-Mart has higher sales and therefore a larger economy of scale advantage, a larger learning curve advantage, and a larger experience curve advantage. Due to its superior cost-controlling ability, Wal-Mart has lower costs and lower prices than its competitors.

Second, a small business must exercise great caution when attempting to establish itself in a big market. What typically happens is that the small business grows large enough to attract a big competitor's attention. The competitor then builds a huge, highly efficient, automated plant or retail network and pushes the small competitor out of the market. Large competitors can afford to set their prices below the small business's cost in order to build sales rapidly while they wait for the economy of scale, learning curve, and experience curve cost-reduction advantages to kick in, producing big future profits as their costs predictably drop. This is how big businesses drive small businesses out of fast growing new markets. If you're lucky and discover a big new market, perhaps they will buy you out instead of driving you out. Yet, remember Sam Walton. The fear of big competitors shouldn't stop you, but it should make you slow down and formulate a highly effective growth strategy.

Third, some businesses achieve low costs through technological breakthroughs; they invent a cheap way to make something. They will be the low-cost leader until a competitor invents an even more cost-efficient technology. The limitation of any Low-Cost technology is that it can become obsolete. For example, in today's small battery market, the current Low-Cost leader uses a cheap, nickel-cadmium technology. The next generation of even lower cost batteries may be a new style lead acid battery being pursued by Portable Energy Products, Inc.

CHAPTER 4

Enhancement Competitive Strategy

A Small-Business-Friendly Strategy

THE ENHANCEMENT COMPETITIVE STRATEGY is a business plan that provides improved products, services, personnel and/or image to a more demanding type of customer. "Improved" means that something is added to the industry's low-priced standard product or service. This strategy allows your business to compete on the basis of improved products and services instead of strictly on the basis of low prices.

Just as every customer isn't satisfied with the lawn mower industry's inexpensive Murray sold at the local discount department store, there are many customers who seek enhanced, more expensive, more specialized products and services that better fit their special needs in every market and every industry.

Firms using a Low-Cost strategy can't serve enhancement customers effectively. Implementing the Low-Cost strategy requires these firms to develop efficiency-oriented skills, highly automated equipment and systems, and cost-minimizing competencies. Their aim is to make and sell a high volume of low-priced, adequately performing products and services.

On the other hand, the Enhancement strategy requires special skills, automated equipment designed for more precision, and cost-containment competencies. Firms using an Enhancement strategy offer high-performance products, full-service systems, more professional employees, and strive to maintain a more exclusive image — offering specially enhanced products and services for higher prices for special customers. Any business trying to compete with both low-priced, trade-off products and services and high-priced, high performance products and services will do neither well and will become vulnerable to a competitor who concentrates on just one competitive strategy.

While the Low-Cost strategy is often used by large firms to target the huge number of Prudent Shoppers, the Enhancement Competitive Strategy is often used by small businesses to target smaller customer segments. Because many of the Enhancement segments are small, they don't attract the attention of big competitors and big corporations. In fact, the big guys are happy to leave the small segments to small businesses; they have much larger appetites. This is great for a small business because it doesn't have to compete on the basis of price, and it doesn't have to compete with big corporations. Also, the small firm doesn't have to depend on large sales volumes to be profitable because it can make its profits by charging higher prices.

The target customers for the Enhancement strategy are dubbed "Selective Shoppers" because they want something better than the standard products and services purchased by Prudent Shoppers.

In this chapter, Selective Shoppers are examined in depth in order to help you develop techniques to identify and target their wants and needs. As you will see, some segments have practical needs and some have hidden needs, but both types of needs can be served.

Regardless of which Selective Shopper segment you choose to serve, only a few product, service, personnel, or image factors will trigger sales to your customers. Enhancement sales triggers are studied in depth to help you understand the type of Key Success Factors that will make your business more successful. The sales trigger section should be used as a guide when designing new products and new services or as a roadmap for reinvigorating your existing business.

Only a few Key Success Factors control costs, and the cost controllers for this strategy are difficult to use. Costs are naturally higher when using an Enhancement strategy to make costly improvements to products and services. As employees become conditioned to passing the extra improvement costs on to customers in the form of higher prices, a pass-it-along attitude develops which must be controlled or profits will evaporate. Costs can be controlled by using one or more of the KSFs presented in this chapter.

Finally, the Enhancement strategy can easily limit the effectiveness of most competitors with *customer targeting*. The targeting KSF that limits competitors is closely examined because it also determines the quality of feedback a business gets from its customers, which is used to help a manager decide which product and service attributes to further improve.

Selective Shoppers: Willing to Pay a Higher Price

Everyone's a customer. We all purchase various products and services, and we buy a lot of routine stuff without much thought except to check the price. At the same time, we feel more involvement with some products and services, and in these cases we want something better, something improved. These are the times we reject the ordinary products and services offered to Prudent Shoppers; we become picky, more demanding, more selective. Price is less important than getting the exact enhancements we want. We become Selective Shoppers for these particular purchases. Every consumer becomes a Selective Shopper for the purchases they consider special, purchases for which they feel a higher level of involvement.

Selective Shoppers form a large customer type made up of all the consumers rejecting the Low-Cost strategy offerings, each for their own reason. They're looking for something better, but Selective Shoppers aren't one big homogeneous group who all want the same thing. The term "Selective Shopper" is really a big umbrella under which many smaller segments of customers are found, and each segment is a group of consumers wanting its own personalized mix of product, service, personnel, and image improvements. Your business cannot succeed by targeting Selective Shoppers in general; your business will succeed by targeting one or more of the Selective Shopper customer segments in your market.

For example, in the lawn mower industry lots of small retailers, using an Enhancement strategy, target Selective Shoppers in order to avoid having to compete against the Low-Cost strategy's winning mower, the inexpensive Murray. However, these enhancement businesses aren't trying to make or sell the one improved mower wanted by all Selective Shoppers. These small firms fully appreciate that Selective Shoppers aren't one homogeneous group who all want one set of improvements. Selective Shoppers in the lawn mower industry are clearly divided into separate segments, and each buys a different and more expensive product because each segment wants or needs its own special improvements. One segment wants a self-propelled mower, another wants a riding lawn mower, another wants a mulching mower, another wants the high status and prestige of owning a Snapper Lawn Mower, another wants a mower that will give a perfectly smooth cut on rough terrain. Lots of different consumer segments exist in the lawn mower industry and each has its own wants and needs.

Commercial or industrial segments of Selective Shoppers also exist in the mower industry. One segment of commercial Selective Shoppers wants a highly maneuverable mower to cut grass in and around heavily landscaped buildings such as colleges, corporate headquarters, and government buildings. Another needs a mower to cut very rough terrain such as uneven fields or ditches. Another commercial segment needs to cut unusually high grass. Another needs three different mowers to cut the rough, fairways, and greens at golf courses. Each of these segments could be further divided by the size of their operation, and the resultant need for larger or smaller mowers. Clearly, lots of different industrial segments also exist in the mower industry.

The term "Prudent Shopper" refers to the prudent behavior of individuals seeking a good, low-price product or service. Prudent Shoppers become a largely homogeneous group through the process of making trade-offs that result in them purchasing the same, standardized product or service. The term "Selective Shopper," on the other hand, refers to the selective behavior of enhancement customers. Selective Shoppers are heterogeneous buyers because they can be separated into different segments of customers who want different product and service enhancements. Each segment is willing to pay a higher price, but aside from this common trait, each segment can be unique.

All Selective Shoppers Are Not the Same

Therefore, to use an Enhancement strategy you must divide the Selective Shoppers in your market into separate segments according to the different products and services each wants, then identify what few improvements will trigger sales to each segment. Next, look at your business and identify its current strengths and weaknesses as well as the strengths that can realistically be developed or purchased; after which you can determine which segments your business is best suited to serve. Finally, target the segment or segments where your business has the best competitive advantage. These are the steps to success with an Enhancement strategy, except for one problem. Identifying the improvements a particular segment wants is sometimes easy, sometimes difficult, sometimes impossible. The most difficult task in designing your business to satisfy your target customers is figuring out exactly what it is that they want.

Since Selective Shoppers are paying higher prices to get certain improvements, you would expect them to be highly motivated and able to explain precisely what they want. Not always. When Selective Shopper segments have practical and functional improvement needs, you can, with their help, determine exactly what improvements to make. However, when the desires of Selective Shoppers are less practical, less directly functional, or more emotional and psychological in nature, you'll have to study their purchase behaviors and purchase patterns and then make informed guesses about what improvements to make.

Big businesses often use sophisticated market research to collect information from which to make analytical decisions about the hidden motivations of their customers. But this is still only a form of guesswork. After collecting lots of expensive insights with consumer research, big firms usually test market their products, services, and promotional concepts before committing to full commercialization. If the big firm's market research was accurate, they wouldn't need test markets. The truth is that managers in both big and small businesses are making informed guesses.

Serving the Practical Needs of Selective Shoppers

The practical wants and needs of Selective Shopper segments are the easiest to identify and understand. For example, older consumers who tire quickly, lazy consumers, disabled consumers, consumers with larger areas to mow, and consumers who find riding a lawnmower fun all combine to form a segment of Selective Shoppers with a practical need for a riding mower, which is a much-enhanced version of the inexpensive Murray. This segment of customers willingly pays a much higher price for a riding mower. Just as the practical need for an enhanced mower is easy to identify and understand, many segments in other markets also have practical enhancement needs that are easy to identify.

For example, customers who regularly run or walk for exercise will understandably need shoes that are better fitting, lighter, and more shock absorbing than regular sneakers. Professional stock market traders have a real need for faster computer software. Professional loggers need a more reliable chain saw that's less likely to break down deep in the woods.

It's easy to identify the practical needs of Selective Shopper segments when those needs are understandable. And if you need help clarifying practical needs, customers will work with you to develop the optimum product enhancements to maximize their satisfaction. These customers will fill out questionnaires, answer questions, and test your prototypes.

Enhanced service needs can be just as practical. Consumers lacking mechanical aptitude form a segment that needs to purchase mowers that are completely assembled. Busy people form a customer segment that needs a pizza delivery service. Dual income couples form a segment that needs your retail store to stay open in the evenings. Inexperienced do-it-yourselfers need demonstration clinics to give them the confidence to make purchases. If you don't fully understand the practical service needs of Selective Shoppers, ask them. They'll work with you to develop the perfectly enhanced service.

Serving the Hidden Needs of Selective Shoppers

On the other hand, the wants and needs of some Selective Shopper segments are less practical, less straightforward, and essentially hidden. Hidden needs present a problem for the manager of a small business because you can't afford the expense of motivational research to identify and describe your customers' real needs. In these situations, a manager has to instead study the *purchase behaviors* of target customers in an attempt to discover *consistent purchase patterns.* Obscure and hidden buyer motives can be served anytime a manager can accurately predict customers' behaviors.

For example, managers of The Fort in Colorado, a gourmet restaurant with an outstanding reputation that specializes in buffalo cuisine, were experiencing low sales of buffalo tongue hors d'oeuvre which sold for $1.75. They needed to better understand why customers were reluctant to purchase this product. They needed to know more about the needs and wants of their hors d'oeuvre customers in general. Unfortunately, the cheapest market research The Fort could buy would involve a small focus group study and would cost at least $10,000. That's a lot of money just to generate a few theories about what motivates a customer to eat a buffalo's tongue.

Fortunately, management had a wealth of knowledge about the purchase behavior and patterns of their customers. From past experience, management knew that their customers had shown a pattern of attraction to higher priced hors d'oeuvres. Acting on this observation, The Fort raised its price to $6.75 and, in small print under the listing on the menu, made the product more exclusive by limiting customers to two helpings. Sales immediately jumped. They now sell out of buffalo tongue every night *(1)*.

The managers of The Fort do not completely understand the hidden, psychological needs of their segment of Selective Shoppers, but they do understand the purchase behavior of those customers, and so they can make enhancements that target the *purchasing patterns* of their customers. You can do the same with your customers. If you can't clearly identify the enhancement needs of your Selective Shoppers, then study their purchase behaviors, and experiment with some enhancements that target those behaviors. With some cautious experimentation, you'll soon discover that predictable purchase patterns can be served. Your success will also provide some insight into your customers' needs. For example, managers at The Fort can now speculate that buffalo tongue customers seem to be buying an adventure in eating, fun, excitement — and price and exclusivity are important signals that heighten their customers' expectations.

As managers of The Fort demonstrate, unclear needs or motives of customers can be served. In fact, many owners of small businesses have built successful firms catering to the buried, subconscious yearnings of their customers by identifying and understanding their customers' purchase behaviors, not their actual needs.

Hidden needs are common among enhancement customers, and a manager of a small business must accept their existence and their impact on sales. Noted psychologists from Sigmund Freud and Carl Jung through to modern day experts acknowledge the existence of these unconscious, hidden needs and wants that drive consumer choices. Today's consumer behavior researchers agree that consumer purchases are often motivated by emotions, feelings, and moods of which the consumers are unaware. Consumers have hidden feelings that have never been expressed in words, and these feelings are stored in consumers' memories and then used to shape what they think, say, and buy. Researchers have discovered many of the emotional influences that affect consumers' behavior.

For example, researchers have found that each person is really three people, three inner selves. There's the real inner-self with likes, dislikes, good habits, bad habits, warts, and pimples. The real-self may be a regular guy who buys beer and pizza simply because he likes them. There's the others-self, the way the customer wants to be seen by others. The others-self may want to buy products and services to hide the bad habits, deficiencies, warts, and pimples. So, the others-self guy may buy stonewashed jeans and L. L. Bean hiking boots because his others-self is trying to portray an outdoorsy image. There's the ideal-self, the person the customer wants to be, perhaps beautiful, macho, self-confident, intelligent, or in control of his or her destiny. The same guy may attend night classes at the local community college because his ideal-self is to be an educated person. Since most customers don't realize they have inner selves, the needs of each self are somewhat hidden. But some customers clearly buy products and services because they want to be seen using them. And some such customers are clearly pursuing various self-improvement programs to achieve some personal ideal. These are purchase patterns and behaviors that can be served.

Researchers have shown that hidden needs are sometimes connected to fantasies, and lots of enhanced products and services fulfill fantasy needs. Studies suggest that people who have a wide gulf between their real-self and ideal-self are most proned to have fantasy needs *(2)*. If a woman perceives her real-self as plain while her ideal-self is to be beautiful, she'll buy large amounts of cosmetics and stylish clothes to help her become her ideal-self. Men often buy sports cars and four-wheel drive vehicles to satisfy their fantasy macho needs. Businesses often target the fantasy behavior patterns of their customers; business advertisements routinely offer solutions to fantasy needs. For example, the advertisement for a very successful cologne shows an attractive nude man carrying an attractive nude woman over his shoulder through a wooded park to suggest the cologne's ability to solve the man's fantasy needs. But don't waste your time asking your customers to tell you about their hidden fantasy needs. They'll think you're bonkers.

Researchers have described consumers' self-image fulfillment behavior. One common self-image fulfillment example is when customers achieve financial success and move up to a higher social class, they suddenly have a not-so-hidden pattern of showing others they have "arrived." They buy the best houses, cars, clothes, furniture, club memberships, and lawn services — they would wear a billboard that says, "I now have big bucks" if it were socially acceptable. Their needs are not practical, but their purchase behavior and patterns are easy to identify and serve. They will spend lavishly at your Enhanced Strategy business to fulfill their higher social class image.

Closely related to the self-image fulfillment behavior is the "symbolic self-completion" behavior. Many hidden needs are driven by this behavior which describes how customers are motivated to purchase products that complete their identity. Customers who believe they are sexy, manly, smart, religious, a master craftsman, and so forth, buy products and services that help them become that type person. In other words, people make themselves into the type of person they want to be with their purchases — you are what you buy. Similarly, customers who want to belong to a fraternity, sorority, country club, church group, bowling league, or professional group will make purchases that symbolically show they belong to those groups. A business appeals to those customers by demonstrating that its products and services will help them become a member of their chosen group. While most customers will not readily discuss their symbolic needs, it shouldn't keep you from identifying and serving these types of behavior patterns.

Consumers also buy products that match and display their personalities, but only extremely expensive psychological tests can measure the hidden personality traits of your customers. Small businesses often enhance the ambiance of their business to increase its appeal to a particular personality type. For example, sporting goods stores, mountain bike shops, neighborhood taverns, and shops that specialize in lingerie frequently adjust the atmosphere of their business to make it more appealing to a specific personality type. Building the correct ambiance is how you target a particular personality type whether it's bookworms, party animals, or sports fans.

A small business uses an Enhancement Competitive Strategy to target a Selective Shopper segment with improvements designed to satisfy that segment. Yet, for many reasons, the exact needs and wants of those target customers will remain hidden. This is a common phenomenon among Selective Shoppers, and a manager of a small business must accept it and learn how to deal with it. When buyers' needs and wants are hidden, study their purchasing patterns, shopping behaviors, and habits. If your target segment demonstrates consistent patterns, behaviors, and habits, you can successfully serve those patterns without fully understanding your customers' actual needs or motives.

Key Success Factors for the Enhancement Strategy

The road to business success with this strategy begins by making enhancements to satisfy either the practical or the hidden needs of your chosen Selective Shopper segments. A few enhancements will be important enough to become the Key Success Factors (KSFs) that trigger sales to your customers. You must decide which factors are the keys to your success and must continuously be improved, and which factors support sales and should be maintained at a support level. Separating your business factors into a few KSFs and many SSFs is your job; you know more about your customers, business, market, industry, and competitors than anyone else. But the remainder of this chapter will help you to 1) examine the factors that are frequently KSFs for various enhancement firms, and to 2) help you identify your firm's KSFs.

If you correctly identify the KSFs that trigger sales to your target customers and if you strengthen those KSFs to build a competitive advantage, your business will generate lots of sales. The next step is to install the right KSFs to control costs, so your business can generate a good profit. Finally, the likelihood of your success increases if your competition can be limited. Competition is limited by choosing the right Selective Shoppers to target. This three-part formula for success depends on your ability to achieve superiority in the three business areas pointed out in Chapter 2:

- Sales Triggers
- Cost Controllers
- Competition Limiters

You'll recall that sales trigger and cost controller KSFs for the Low-Cost Competitive Strategy were directly related — keeping costs low allowed the business to charge low prices. Low prices increased sales, thus increasing economy of scale and other cost advantages which helped to push costs even lower, which allowed the business to charge even lower prices, which increased sales ... you remember the downward cost/price spiral. This easy-to-manage cost/price relationship does not exist for the Enhancement Competitive Strategy because the sales trigger and costs controller KSFs oppose each other. In other words, providing enhancements to satisfy your target customers pushes costs up, while making a profit requires holding costs down. This enhancement/costs tug-of-war requires extensive management planning, organization, leadership, and control. Management has to know which factors are KSFs and which factors are not, and management has to control the costs of each.

There are a few enhancement business pitfalls you should avoid. Don't set out to make your business unique; set out to satisfy a unique segment of customers. Making the wrong enhancements or making improvements not desired by your customers leads to failure. For example, one small business enhanced the common mousetrap, so it would trap the mouse in a plastic sleeve instead of smashing it with a spring-loaded wire. While an interesting enhancement that made the firm's product unique, the new product created a big problem for customers — what to do with the live mouse in the trap, short of grinding it up in the garbage disposal. The enhancement seemed like a neat idea, so the business developed it, but it didn't satisfy the needs of any target customers. Avoid the unique product pitfall by keeping your sights on your reason for enhancing a product or service — to provide the improvements that will satisfy your customers. Successful enhancements are those desired by a clearly identified target segment. Whenever possible, use the feedback from your target customers to guide your choice of which enhancements to make.

Another enhancement pitfall concerns the concept of "quality." Some confusion exists between "quality" and "enhancement." Making an enhancement isn't the same thing as improving quality; an enhanced product isn't necessarily a quality product. Also, quality doesn't sell, so don't improve something because "quality sells." Don't make improvements to increase quality and expect to automatically increase sales. Instead, start thinking of quality as "conformance with my target customers' expectations." Any product meeting the performance level desired by target customers is a quality product because the target customers get exactly what they want — they are highly satisfied. Therefore, a very cheap product can be a "quality" product if it meets customers' expectations. The Enhancement Competitive Strategy isn't about making or selling quality products and services, the Enhancement strategy is about making the improvements that Selective Shoppers want.

Five Key Success Factors that Trigger Sales

Above all else, success depends on sales, but enhancement sales don't hinge on price. Price is a key factor that triggers sales to Bargain Hunters and Prudent

Shoppers, but not Selective Shoppers. Selective Shoppers are willing to pay a higher price to get the enhancements they desire. Thus, the Enhancement Competitive Strategy depends less on price and more on making the exact improvements that customers want and need. The enhancements that trigger sales to Selective Shoppers will mostly be product, services, personnel, and image enhancements, although most enhancement businesses will not improve all four factors.

Most products and services have multiple attributes that create multiple benefits, but each benefit doesn't need to be improved. Studies have shown that even for very complex products with many features that are valued by customers, only a few enhancements actually trigger the sale *(3)*. Therefore, you must isolate the few improvements that are critical to your customers.

Let's look at an enhancement example from one part of the home furnishings industry which demonstrates that only a few factors trigger sales and should be classified as KSFs. This example will also show that the Enhancement strategy can be used to target customers in any social class. Rent-to-own furniture and appliance businesses enhance only a few marketing factors, and all of them are services. They don't depend on price to make the sale. In fact, their prices are quite high.

Rent-to-own retailers have three KSFs that trigger sales. First, their customers have credit problems and need *easy credit*. Second, their customers have low incomes and need *low weekly payments*. Third, like most Americans, their customers want instant gratification with *instant product availability*. Therefore, the three KSFs that trigger sales to rent-to-own customers, in the order of importance, are:

- Easy Credit
- Low Weekly Payments
- Instant Product Availability

Enhancing each of these KSFs will increase sales but costs will also increase. For example, easing credit restrictions for customers with poor credit histories will increase sales but will also cause credit losses to escalate. Likewise, providing low weekly payments will increase sales but will also increase the cost of carrying inventory. Each new sale is followed by small amounts of cash received weekly, while each item sold must be replaced immediately. Therefore, as sales increase, the business will put a great deal of money into inventory and slowly recover its cash flow — a costly operation.

Easy credit and weekly payments also increase collection expenses, as rent-to-own businesses have to send employees to many households every week to collect overdue payments.

Providing instant product availability requires maintaining additional crews and trucks to provide immediate deliveries, which raises costs.

All of these extra costs are passed on to rent-to-own customers through higher prices, but the customers don't object to the higher prices, which proves that price does not trigger the sale. If low price were a KSF, customers wouldn't purchase any of the products sold at rent-to-own businesses; instead, customers would use the free layaway program at places like Wal-Mart. But "price" does not trigger the sale and is not a KSF; price is only an SSF (Support Success Factor) that must be maintained at a reasonable competitive level to support sales. This doesn't mean that rent-to-own managers shouldn't push suppliers for price discounts, only that those discounts should be used to enhance the firm's KSFs, not to lower prices.

Knowing their KSFs, rent-to-own managers also know that the following marketing and sales factors are SSFs for their business:

- Product Performance
- Product Features
- Product Reliability
- Product Durability
- Product Quality
- Price
- Product Serviceability
- Sales Force Skills
- Prestige
- Location
- Convenience
- Merchandising Skills
- Image
- Breadth of Product Line
- Trendy Styling
- After-the-Sale Repair Service
- Brand Loyalty
- Customer Loyalty
- Advertising
- State-of-the-Art Technology
- Distributor Support System
- Order-Handling Skills
- Early Trend-Spotting Ability
- Warranties and Guaranties

Because these are SSFs, managers should establish support levels for each and develop a budget which allows each SSF to be maintained at the proper level. Money saved by holding these factors at the support level allows the firm to further ease credit requirements and to further decrease weekly payments by extending the payment period — improving these KSFs will further increase sales.

What are the proper support levels for a rent-to-own business's SSFs? Each factor will have to be analyzed separately. For example, what is the correct support level for a rent-to-own store location? First of all, location is a SSF and not a KSF because great locations don't trigger sales to rent-to-own customers. Customers need easy access to a pleasant store located reasonably close to where they live. If the location is too far away from where customers live or too inconvenient, it will kill sales. On the other hand, customers don't need the convenience of an expensive mall location. Therefore, the proper location is close to where most customers live with easy access, pleasant surroundings, and a modest rent. Money saved by choosing a modestly priced location can be spent to further improve the firm's sales triggers.

What's the proper support level for sales force training? Sales people don't have to be product experts or skilled at customer negotiations. Sales people need to be outgoing and friendly, be trained on-the-job, and be willing to do collections — all three skills can be achieved with a minimal training budget. Likewise, advertising is a SSF. It doesn't trigger sales; it's only used to create store awareness and an image of easy credit, low weekly payments, and quick deliveries. Therefore, advertising should be budgeted at a support level that depends on the level of awareness that exists among target customers about the business. The more widely known the business becomes, the smaller its advertising budget needs to be.

For any business, whether selling primarily to low-income customers like rent-to-own firms, or selling to middle- or high-income customers, knowing KSFs from SSFs improves a manager's decision-making ability. A manager can spend more time, money, and mental effort improving the KSFs to trigger additional sales because he or she has not wasted time, money, and effort over-strengthening factors that don't trigger sales. When a problem arises, the manager will invest the right effort and resources to find the proper solution. A great amount of effort will be spent identifying the best solution to a KSF problem; a reasonable amount of effort will be spent identifying a good solution to a SSF problem.

The rent-to-own KSFs are unique to that type of business, but all Enhancement businesses have KSFs that trigger sales, and most firms' KSFs differ greatly. Since all purchases involve a mix of product, service, personnel, and image, each of those four factors could be enhanced. But, as you will see, customers aren't always able to judge a product's performance, so their purchase decisions may also hinge on indicators of product performance. Therefore, there are five categories of possible KSFs that trigger sales for this strategy:

- Product Enhancement
- Indicators of Product Enhancement
- Service Enhancement
- Personnel Enhancement
- Image Enhancement

Each of these five categories of enhancements will be thoroughly explored which will help you to find the KSFs that trigger sales to your customers. But there are other reasons for you to study these five categories. If you're trying to develop a new product or service for your existing business, the enhancement categories can be used like a list of potential product or service improvement options for your consideration. If you're considering establishing a new business, these categories can be used as a list of enhancement options that could be used to design the right enhancements to maximize the satisfaction of your target customers. We'll begin by exploring the first of the five categories of enhancement sales triggers — product enhancement.

Product Enhancement — A Sales Trigger KSF

Of the five enhancement categories, product enhancement most often triggers sales to Selective Shoppers. Of course, not every part of the product should be enhanced. Most products consist of many parts, called product attributes, and usually only a few attributes need be improved for your customer segment. For example, a bicycle has wheels, spokes, a seat, handlebars, a frame, weight, a particular gear ratio, etc. Each is an attribute, each provides a separate benefit for customers, and each can be enhanced. The bicycle wheels can be enhanced for either racing customers, street riding customers, or off-road riding customers. The same is true of the seat, the frame, and the gear ratio — each can be enhanced in different ways for different segments of customers. Different customer segments want different attributes enhanced, so different enhancements will trigger sales to different Selective Shopper segments.

The few product benefits that are most important to customers are the improvements which will trigger sales to those customers; these benefits are the KSFs. The other product attributes are SSFs that must be maintained at a reasonable competitive level to support the sale, and the required support level will differ for various customer segments. However, support factors need not be improved continuously while KSFs must be improved continuously for the business to maintain its competitive edge.

Product enhancements have created many interesting small business success stories:

- California Pizza Kitchens grew from one startup location to 12 stores by making "designer pizzas" for a small customer segment of gourmet pizza lovers. They serve socially up-scale customers with discriminating tastes. Using expensive ingredients, a slower cooking process, and more cooking skills, they produce taste-enhanced pizza that sells for prices that are considerably higher than Domino's, Pizza Hut, and Pizza Inn *(4)*.

- Kayla Beverly Hills in Los Angeles makes cosmetics that are specially enhanced for Asian-Americans. The University of Missouri boasts that 169 nationalities are represented on their campus, that leaves lots of room for other small businesses to target other minorities with specially enhanced cosmetics *(5)*.
- African Eye makes designer clothes enhanced for African-Americans whose sense of taste and style are formed by their own cultural experiences *(6)*.
- Pyramid Books targets African-Americans with special book selections *(7)*.
- Gulf Atlantic Life Insurance Company serves the special needs of Southern California's Spanish-speaking residents *(8)*.
- The Moose Preserve Bar & Grill in Bloomfield Hills, Michigan, targets local tastes with venison chili garnished with sour cream — Wendy's, look out *(9)*.
- Boochee's dominates the gourmet hamburger market in Columbia, Missouri.

These are a small sample of business successes achieved through product enhancements. A larger sample reveals an interesting pattern of six types of product enhancements. The six types of product improvements that trigger sales to various segments of Selective Shoppers are:

- Performance
- Features
- Reliability
- Consistency
- Durability
- Serviceability

Product Performance is a product's most important benefit. Selective Shoppers most frequently want a product's performance enhanced, so improved performance is often a KSF that triggers sales. Most products have more than one type of performance, and it isn't necessary to enhance them all. Enhance only the performance attributes your targeted customers want improved and are willing to pay a higher price to get.

For instance, if you were a toothpaste manufacturer, you would have several improvement choices. Toothpaste has many performance attributes and many corresponding types of performance benefits (see Figure 4.1).

FIGURE 4.1: Toothpaste Attributes and Performance Benefits

ATTRIBUTES	PERFORMANCE BENEFITS
a mild mouth soap	a gentle cleaner that helps prevent cavities
a gel	a product that will cling to the brush
a mint flavoring	a pleasant taste and pleasant smelling breath
a fluoride additive	a strong cavity fighter
a tartar removal additive	protection from gum disease
a whitener additive	more attractive teeth
approval by an association of dental experts	assurance that the product really works
acceptance	social compliance

A list of product attributes and performance benefits for toothpaste could easily be expanded to 20 or 30, but the ones listed will demonstrate an important concept.

Which of the listed toothpaste benefits should be enhanced for Selective Shoppers? The answer, as with all products and services, depends on which customer segment you want to target. If you want to target smokers, you'd enhance the toothpaste's ability to whiten teeth and remove ugly stains. If you want to target young singles, you'd enhance the toothpaste's breath freshening ability. If you want to target parents of young teenagers, you'd enhance both the toothpaste's decay fighting ability along with the independent proof of its decay fighting ability (an endorsement by an association of dental experts). Like most products, different benefits are enhanced to trigger sales to different groups of Selective Shoppers, so there is no simple answer about what to enhance — it depends on which customer segment of Selective Shoppers you are trying to target.

The number of ways to enhance performance is even more enormous than the number of products that exist. Here is a small sample of some of the common ways performance is enhanced for a few products:

- Speed is enhanced in sports cars.
- Power is enhanced in trucks.
- Safety is enhanced in baby toys.
- Quietness is enhanced in refrigerators.
- Strength is enhanced in rope.
- Stability is enhanced in swing sets.
- Environmental Safety is enhanced in pesticides.
- Gentleness is enhanced in stomach medicines.
- Operating cost is enhanced in home air conditioners.
- Shelf life is enhanced in precooked foods.
- Precision is enhanced in airplane instruments.

Since there is an enormous variety of products and an even larger number of product attributes and benefits, a complete list of the all performance attributes that could be enhanced for all products is impossible. Imagine the multiple performance benefits of pharmaceuticals, snack foods, clothes, nudist camps, boats, airplanes, computers, garden tools, cameras, toys, underwear, and adhesives. Since a list of all product performance measures is impractical, you'll have to develop your list for your products, and you'll have to decide which to enhance to trigger sales to your enhancement customers. But, here's a procedure called "Situation Analysis" that will help you locate those few product performance factors that should be enhanced — these will be your KSFs.

First, list each situation in which your product is used. For example, a food product may be consumed in these *use situations*: breakfast, lunch, dinner, snack time, parties, backpacking, picnics, sports events, formal entertaining, or informal entertaining. Your task is to determine which performance benefits are most important to your customers in each use situation. If you discover that customers' needs vary by situation, then different product enhancements and indeed different products are needed for each situation. Remember, Low-Cost strategy firms supply general-use products; Enhancement strategy firms provide special products. Products are special when they're made for a specific *use situation* instead of for general use.

Business managers don't always know about every use situation, so ask your customers about when and where and why they use the product. You may discover a new opportunity, as recently happened to Black & Decker, the tool manufacturer. Black & Decker's simple observation technique led them to discover another use situation for their power tools. Previously the company had identified only two use situations: do-it-yourselfer use and professional use. After sending employees to many customers' homes to observe them actually using power tools, Black & Decker discovered that do-it-yourselfers should be divided into casual do-it-yourselfers and serious do-it-yourselfers — a use situation they hadn't previous known about.

Serious do-it-yourselfers use their tools more frequently and they tackle larger and more complex projects. They need more powerful and precise tools than the average handyman. These customers are willing to pay a higher price, but aren't willing to pay a professional tool price. As a result of use situation analysis, the company now makes tools designed for a new situation: serious do-it-yourself use. By studying your customers, you may discover a new *use situation* your competitors don't know about.

The second step is to prepare an exhaustive list of all the benefits needed by customers for each use situation. For this, you'll need to involve your customers by asking them to identify which product benefits are most important to them in each situation. After you've developed your list, go back to the customers and have them pick the three most important benefits for each use situation.

Use situation analysis has three benefits. First, it will confirm which KSFs trigger sales in different situations. Second, it will help you better target your product improvement efforts to give your business a competitive advantage in each situation. Third, it will help you identify new growth opportunities by identifying use situations where no current product satisfies a segment of customers.

Product Features are secondary, less important benefits of a product that can be enhanced to trigger sales in highly competitive markets. For example, a professional contractor's prime reason for buying a power tool is because the tool can perform the tough tasks required — the tool's power and precision have been improved to do the hard jobs. But, given a competitive choice between several tools that all meet the necessary performance specifications, the contractor's ultimate purchase choice will be the tool that has the best features, such as being lightweight or being comfortable to use. In any use situation where several competitive products or businesses have the same product performances, *features* will become secondary KSFs that trigger sales.

Similarly, the performances desired by VCR customers are quality of image and sound reproduction, but if the picture and sound quality of several competing models are equal, features, like ease of on-screen programming, styling, or a remote control device with additional functions will trigger sales. Also, price enters the picture as a feature for Selective Shoppers when competing products have equivalent performances. If consumers think all the competing products are about equal, price becomes a secondary feature, and the lowest price will trigger the sale.

Product Reliability as a product benefit refers to the length of time between breakdowns of your product. Increased reliability means that your product breaks less often, which is a critical benefit for some Selective Shoppers. For example, professional mechanics depend on highly reliable tools in order to make a living, airplane operators depend on reliable avionics to avoid losing their way, business travelers depend on reliable laptop computer batteries so they can continue working, and busy women executives depend on reliable cosmetics that don't have to be reapplied during inconvenient moments. Enhanced product reliability is critical if the product's failure has grave consequences, like loss of income, a threat to the customer's safety, a major inconvenience, a major embarrassment, etc.

Product Consistency as a benefit refers to the variations that Selective Shoppers can detect when they repeatedly buy and use the same firm's product. When customers purchase and use a product frequently, they become particularly sensitive to changes in performance of different batches of the product. This suggests that consistency should be enhanced when you target high-use customer segments who are experienced or experts in their field. For instance, gourmet chefs (cooking experts) must produce high quality meals every time they cook, so they purchase the most consistent ingredients. Likewise, experienced gardeners pay extra for dependable seeds, better root stimulants, and high quality fertilizers. Enhanced consistency is important to such segments, since it can reduce problems, mistakes, and failures. In addition, improved consistency can provide a valuable emotional benefit by decreasing the customer's fear of failure; some customers will purchase the same product that the experts use in hope of avoiding problems. Finally, industrial customers seek enhanced consistency because it saves them money by reducing production problems.

Product Durability as a product benefit describes the amount of abuse your product can withstand before it breaks — how easily it breaks. You should enhance durability to trigger sales to Selective Shoppers who use your product in physically demanding situations. For example, professional loggers need chain saws with enhanced durability that can survive rough treatment in remote spots without breaking down. Hunters need highly dependable winches to pull their vehicles out of mud when they get stuck deep in the woods. Most people want at least one highly durable flashlight for emergencies. General aviation schools need training planes with durable landing gear. Enhanced product durability is important any time the product is regularly used in an abusive situation.

Product Serviceability as a product benefit refers to the combined time and trouble required to fix a broken product and is usually determined by the way the product is designed. A product's serviceability can be enhanced to trigger sales. When continuous product performance with a minimum of interruptions is highly valued by Selective Shoppers, serviceability should be enhanced to minimize the product's downtime for repair. For example, many of today's business offices can't function without their copiers, printers, computers, and other machines. These businesses will pay extra to get highly serviceable equipment, so if the equipment does break, it can be returned to service quickly.

Many industrial customers need enhanced serviceability. For example, furniture factories, cabinet shops, and housing contractors can't work if their nailing guns break. Most breakdowns are caused by jammed nails, which often cause the guns to be set-aside until the repairman's next visit. Senco Products, Inc. redesigned its nailing guns to allow customers to easily and quickly remove jammed nails and put their guns back in use. Customers benefited from increased production; Senco benefited from increased nail sales and decreased repair work. For Senco, enhanced serviceability triggered additional sales and cut costs.

One of the main complaints of the users of battery-operated drills was the length of time required to recharge a dead battery and get the drill back in use. One manufacturer improved the serviceability of its drills merely by packaging the drill with two rechargeable batteries and one recharger. One battery was always charging while the other was being used.

In summary, products, as you have just seen, have six types of attributes that can be enhanced to trigger sales to different segments of Selective Shoppers. As a manager of a small business, you already possess a tremendous amount of unorganized knowledge about your customers. You've often observed customers' actions and reactions to product changes, past promotions, changes in price, various store locations, and different merchandising tactics. You've listened to customer requests and complaints. Now it's time to organize your knowledge and fill in the unknowns. Ask your customers what product benefits are important to them. Ask customers what attributes they are comparing among competitive products — even customers with hidden needs make product comparisons.

The more you know about which product benefits to enhance for your target customers, the more successful you'll become. *Use situation* analysis is very helpful. As you have seen, it involves three steps:

1. Identify every situation in which the product is consumed or used.
2. Identify the needs and wants of customers for each use situation.
3. Have customers prioritize their needs and wants for each use situation.

Armed with better customer information, you can develop a short list of suspected sales triggers. Then talk to customers about your list, and listen carefully to their replies. Try to combine the comments of various customers; believe it or not, semantics researchers get paid big bucks to combine customer comments and reduce them to a short statement of needs and wants. The job of customer analysis is the manager's most important responsibility and the most fun. You can identify the KSFs that trigger sales to your customers.

Indicators of Product Performance — A Sales Trigger KSF

While it's true that Selective Shoppers most often want improved product performance, it's a mistake for you to believe that building a better mousetrap will trigger a lot of sales. The truth is that customers often don't know a better mousetrap when they see it, and customers sometimes, even after all your efforts, don't perceive your product as enhanced. *Most customers can't really judge a product's performance*, and that's understandable. After all, customers can't perform controlled laboratory tests on competitive products to prove objectively which product is superior. Most customers have neither a technical degree nor the scientific knowledge required to read the product's engineering specification sheets, which aren't given to them anyway. Customers often don't have the sort of in-depth product experience that's required to make well-informed product choices, but they still make purchases, so what information do they use?

When customers can't judge the very benefits that are supposed to trigger the sale, an interesting phenomenon takes place. They substitute an *indicator of performance* they can judge for the actual performance feature they can't judge. When substitution occurs, the indicator of performance becomes the sales trigger. Therefore, you may have to enhance your product's performance and enhance your product's *indicator of performance* to trigger the sale, which makes the indicator of performance a KSF that triggers the sale. And, making matters worse, customers are unaware that they are substituting indicators. It's an unintentional error.

Indicators work clandestinely. For example, suppose you are a manufacturer of laundry detergents, and you introduce an enhanced product that is scientifically proven in your laboratory to be a strong but gentle cleaner. In other words, this laundry product is proven to be a highly efficient cleaner that doesn't harm delicate fabrics — it's strong and gentle, it works, and you can prove it works.

You market the detergent, but sales turn out to be lower than expected. Market research discovers that customers don't believe the product is both a strong cleaner and gentle on delicate fabrics. Suppose they believe it's gentle but not strong. Therefore, a gap exists between the actual product performance and the perceived product performance. To solve the problem, the company dyes a few granules green and mixes them with the white detergent. Then they launch a new advertising campaign claiming a new, improved laundry detergent, even though it is chemically the same product.

The new product is successful. Sales soar. Market research now reports that customers believe the claims of gentle for delicate fabrics but a strong cleaner. All this because the green-colored granule is an indicator of performance, a signal of performance. Actual research has shown that either adding a color granule or making the detergent granules coarser causes customers to believe a dry detergent is a stronger cleaner.

The existence of indicators that signal performance has important ramifications for small businesses. Customers often use indicators to judge the product's performance or the entire business's performance. The firm's success may hinge on discovering the performance indicators used by customers and enhancing them. Your goal is to create a match between the actual product performance and the product performance perceived by customers.

Still not convinced about the role of indicators in altering customer perceptions? Okay, here's another example. One university study demonstrated another color-related collision between perception and reality. The university fed students several batches of vanilla pudding, but each vanilla pudding batch was colored a different shade of brown. The students were not told the flavor. After eating the puddings, students identified all the puddings as chocolate and reported that the darkest batch of vanilla pudding had the richest chocolate flavor *(10)*. These students were using color as an indicator of flavor, and their expectations were so strong that their taste buds were fooled. Customers are often fooled in similar ways by indicators of performance.

You're probably thinking, I've eaten dorm food and had to guess what is was by the color. Then consider con artists. Con artists use indicators to trigger false customer perceptions to make their "score." Con artists carefully study the signals their "marks" rely upon when making a decision, and manipulate the signals to make their sale. If indicators of performance didn't exist, con artists couldn't exist.

Some commonly used indicators of performance are well known, and probably used by you when you shop:

- A good guarantee signals a good product.
- A good business reputation signals good products.
- A good brand name signals a good product.
- The professional demeanor of the store's salesperson signals quality products.

- The attractive exterior of a retail building signals good products.
- The general appearance of the surrounding commercial area signals product quality.
- A solid door-closure sound indicates good automobile workmanship.
- Speaker size indicates stereo speaker quality.
- Good suds signal a dishwashing liquid's ability to clean.
- A lemon scent indicates high cleaning power in household cleaners.
- Fresh, attractive produce in the grocery store signals high quality products throughout the store.
- High price signals high quality.

Price is a frequent indicator of performance for your enhanced product or enhanced service. Selective Shoppers want improvements, but they aren't always capable of judging an enhanced product. Thus, they often assume that a higher price signals that costly enhancements have been made to a product or service. Therefore, price can become a KSF that triggers the sale when it is an indicator of performance that customers often substitute for the actual performance they can't judge — remember the $1.75 buffalo tongue hors d'oeuvre that wouldn't sell until managers increased the price to signal a gourmet delight. Besides, most consumers are conditioned to believe that higher prices mean higher quality. As an old maxim goes, "You get what you pay for."

One customer explained his thought process for choosing a contractor to remove a dead tree at the side of his house. After getting estimates from five businesses, he hired the firm with the highest price. He explained that only an expert could charge those rates, and that only an expert could be trusted to keep the tree from falling through his house. No, he didn't check the expert's references! He let price signal quality. He used an indicator of performance because he wasn't capable of judging each contractor's real ability to perform.

The scary thing about signals or indicators is that customers aren't aware they are judging an indicator of performance instead of actual performance. The customer unconsciously accepts the relationship between things like the size of stereo speakers and the quality of sound. No thought process has to occur — just a feeling about the relationship between speaker size and sound performance that guides a purchase decision. So, if you asked the customer what factors signal high quality, they might not name speaker size. Your customers probably don't know which indicators of performance they are using.

Suspected indicators can be tested. Suppose we place a number of differently sized stereo speakers in a test room. We ask various customers seated on the other side of the room to judge the sound quality. Sometimes we tell the customers that the large speakers are playing when the small speakers are actually playing. If most customers judge the sound as best when told that the large speakers are working, even when they aren't, speaker size is being used as an indicator of performance.

Analyzing behavior patterns will help you discover the indicators used by customers. If one salesperson is more successful than others, try to isolate the reason for the unusual success. What is the difference between highly successful and moderately successful salespeople? Is it honesty, competency, responsiveness, self-confidence, or non-verbal communication techniques such as gestures, body language, or appearance? When customers can't judge a product's performance, they often judge the personal traits of the salesperson serving them. Without realizing it, the customer substitutes the salesperson's 1) ability to communicate, 2) willingness to respond openly to every question, and 3) appearance of honesty for the product's performance. In fact, one reason many firms hire college graduates for sales positions is that while earning a college degree the students polish their indicators of performance. When the college graduate goes to work, their polished personal appearance, speech patterns, and confidence become significant indicators of performance used by their employer's customers.

When searching for indicators, ask customers what convinced them to buy the product then listen to exactly what they say. Research has shown that the few things a customer mentions without being prompted by you are the factors most important in the customer's decision-making. If the first thing your customer says is, "Well, Joan was very persuasive, she really knows the product," note that the salesperson's personal traits were mentioned before product benefits were mentioned — the customer appears focused on indicators rather than on product performance.

When searching for indicators, watch customers' behavior closely. Watching is a valid research method that trained professionals call "observation research." Through observation you may discover that the sales of a modestly priced product are higher when it's placed beside a very well known and expensive product. If you observe this relationship, the expensive item may be an indicator. It's not uncommon for a relatively modest priced item to sell well when placed next to a high priced item — proximity signals similarity — then for sales to drop dramatically when the high priced item is removed. Now that you understand the use of indicators, instead of removing the modestly priced item when its sales drop, you may first put the higher priced item back next to the modestly priced item just to check the effect on sales.

Since your customers usually can't help you, you have to search for the indicators of performance your customers use by studying their patterns of behavior. But remember, very few indicators will be important enough to trigger sales. Very few indicators need to be improved continuously. More often, a few indicators will be SSFs for which you must establish the correct support level.

Service Enhancement —A Sales Trigger KSF

All of the enhancement categories help small firms avoid competing on the basis of price alone; however, as you will see, service improvements often are the most helpful. But what's a service? A service is an intangible customer benefit; you can't touch it or pick it up — you experience it. A service is ephemeral — the teacher instructs, the waitress serves, the theater entertains. A service disappears as it is performed. Yet a service is real and valued by Selective Shoppers. Since a service is real, it can be stripped down or enhanced. And enhanced services do trigger sales.

Enhanced service is largely responsible for Domino's Pizza becoming a giant corporation. Other fast food franchises had already proven that customers wanted convenience, which is a service, but Domino's further enhanced convenience by adding a quick home delivery service. The new service was a hit; Domino's grew to a giant corporation and competitors were forced to add their own home delivery service to compete with Domino's.

Enhanced service wasn't the only factor that helped the company succeed. Domino's had more than just a good idea; they had some very supportive remote trends creating a favorable environment for sales growth. First, a demographic trend helped as the number of dual income families kept increasing. This created lots of working families who didn't have enough time to prepare food at home, but whose combined incomes let them easily afford to have prepared food delivered to their home.

Second, a societal attitude trend helped fuel Domino's growth. The number of consumers who responded to questionnaires saying they were time-starved, or short on time, kept increasing. These customers said they didn't have time to cook and clean dishes.

Both trends combined to make Domino's new home delivery service so popular that it has become a standardized service with mass appeal, and the service is now offered by many businesses.

To use this strategy as Domino's did, you need to identify all the services that could be enhanced by your business. You need to examine your customers' service needs from many different angles to identify every possible service that could potentially be enhanced or added. This section offers you three approaches to help you find all the services you could add or could improve to trigger sales to your segment of Selective Shoppers.

But, what if you only sell products? Sure, services are the mainstays of the service industry, yet services and products are inseparable. For instance, a consulting firm provides information services for its clients and products — like written reports. Likewise, a quick oil and lube business provides a maintenance service for its customers and products — like oil and filters and grease. On the other hand, a small boat dealership sells boats, which are products, and provides services — a service warranty plus repair services. The local furniture store sells products and provides services — home delivery and credit. Providing services is part of every business.

Managers face the same problems asking customers about their service needs as they do when asking them about their product needs. Customers articulate some needs, forget to mention basic needs they assume are well understood, and can't imagine exotic, new needs. The burden falls on your shoulders to discover all the potential service improvement options, to present customers with those options, and to ask them which they are willing to purchase.

Three search methods or viewpoints will help you find all the potential services your business might enhance for various Selective Shopper segments. The three service viewpoints are:

- Performance
- Shifting
- Explicit and Implicit Benefits of Services

By examining your customers and your industry with all three different perspectives, you will identify every possible service that could be added or enhanced. Then you can add or enhance the services your target customers want. Searching with all three viewpoints will produce overlap, which means many of the same service enhancement options will be discovered with each viewpoint. If you develop a list of possible service enhancements using one method, it will look very similar to a list you develop using another method. Similar, but not identical. New service enhancement options will be discovered using each viewpoint; therefore, it's important to examine your business and your customers' wants using each viewpoint to develop an exhaustive list of service options.

Performance — Finding Service Enhancements

The performance viewpoint is used to develop two categories of services: primary and secondary. Primary services are the main services your target customers expect. Primary services are the basic services already performed by your business that are easily identified, frequently enhanced, and often the KSFs that trigger sales. Secondary services are more subtle. When asked why they frequent your business, customers may mention the atmosphere or ambiance. That atmosphere or ambiance is created by a host of small services, each invisible, but together they create an ambiance that may trigger sales and become a service KSF. Identifying all the possible secondary services you might add or enhance can require some extra effort on your part.

Primary Services can become KSFs. Primary services provide the main service benefits wanted by customers; these are the benefits that support or even trigger current sales. Primary services (there can be several in a business) are easy to identify because they are the ones that customers most often ask for, the ones you already perform and advertise. Because they're easy to identify, they're easy to enhance when targeting Selective Shoppers. For example, customers call an office equipment repair service to get repairs — a primary service. A repair service can be enhanced by using better diagnostic equipment, highly trained personnel, and better quality replacement parts. Customers willing to pay a higher price would get an improved repair job, better machine performance, and experience fewer subsequent breakdowns — all worth a higher price for many Selective Shopper segments, but not for Prudent Shoppers.

Because primary services are of major importance to customers, they are frequently enhanced. Entertainment is the primary service of the movie theater industry which has been enhanced by adding new theaters, bigger screens, Dolby Speaker systems, and by showing films that are created especially for big screen enjoyment. Education is the primary service of community colleges which is often enhanced to be more convenient and flexible for local citizens by adding evening and weekend courses. Some appliance stores have enhanced their service warranty by automatically covering breakdowns for five years instead of trying to sell extended warranties.

Make a list of the primary services your business provides. For example, transportation, speed, and convenience are the primary services of small trucking firms and commuter airlines. Entertainment and variety of entertainment are the major services of a local cable firm. Easy credit, low weekly payments, and speedy delivery are the primary services of a rent-to-own firm. Accommodation and creature comforts are the primary services of a bed-and-breakfast inn. Recreation is the primary service of a marina. Based on your knowledge of your industry, make a list of every possible service you could enhance to provide more benefits for Selective Shoppers. Present your list of enhancement ideas to some of your customers for their reactions. You may be surprised by the encouragement you receive.

One frequently enhanced service is speed; speed has been enhanced repeatedly for busy and impatient customers. Speed enhancement has given customers fast food, overnight replacement parts, drive-through windows, catalog ordering, home shopping networks, Internet shopping, ordering by fax,

800 numbers, home delivery, ATM machines, boarding passes issued with your airline tickets, automatic car washes, email, voicemail, 10-minute oil changes, one hour photo processing, express lanes, overnight package delivery, and supersonic airline service.

Convenience is another service that's often enhanced. Enhanced convenience has given customers frozen foods, prepared foods, and easy-to-prepare food mixes. Enhanced convenience has given customers easy access locations, telephone ordering systems, and convenience stores. Enhanced convenience has led to a complete reversal of some previous business practices. For example, a few retail stores are enhancing convenience by placing the most sought-after products near the store entrance to minimize the customers' purchasing efforts, reversing the old practice of making customers walk to the back of the store past unwanted merchandise to get frequently sought items.

Secondary Services often become KSFs. Secondary services are minor services that can trigger Selective Shopper sales in highly competitive situations. Secondary services are important to an Enhancement Strategy because these are the services that firms using a Low-Cost strategy cut out to keep their costs low. For example, Low-Cost firms don't provide an abundance of sales people to assist customers, don't carry the customer's purchases to their vehicles, don't make deliveries, don't provide a pick-up service for broken merchandise, and don't provide a host of other services which would increase their cost of doing business. Performing the secondary services that Low-Cost firms avoid can often trigger sales to any Selective Shopper segments who want to be pampered and are quite willing to pay for pampering. Make a list of all the small services your business could provide if it wanted to pamper and coddle customers or offer a special experience to customers.

Enhancement firms offer additional services, which are also secondary services. For example, Low-Cost firms will change the customers' oil and filter, but enhancement firms can offer additional services such as straining the oil as it comes out of the vehicle to search for metal particles and analyzing the chemical composition of the old oil to provide customers with valuable information about the condition of their engines. Selective Shoppers often want additional services.

The difference between primary and secondary services is subtle. For example, if a customer calls a firm to get technical assistance, the primary service performed by the business is to return the customer's call and provide accurate technical advice. Secondary services would include 1) a fast call-back, 2) easy-to-follow instructions, and 3) a follow-up call to see if the customer's problem was solved. Prudent Shoppers are unwilling to pay extra for more costly secondary services, but such secondary services are often the added benefits wanted by Selective Shoppers.

Secondary services can be used to alter customers' moods and attitudes. Added or enhanced services can make your customers feel the work done by your business is more thorough and complete, more professional. Or, services can be added to increase your customers' fun, to put them in a lighthearted mood, or to increase their sense of happiness. If you can describe the moods and attitudes you'd like your customers to have, you can often design and add secondary services to create those attitudes. For example, a hotel wanting its convention customers to have fun and be happy can add golf, fishing, and sailplane excursions — these secondary services are fun and put guests in a good mood. Better hotels want customers to feel pampered, so they enhance customer satisfaction by building a computer database of the likes and dislikes of each customer. When the customer makes the next reservation, the hotel can consult the computer file and supply the customer's creature comforts by setting the room temperature where the customer left it when he or she last visited, by stocking the room's refrigerator with the customer's favorite beverages, and by having the customer's favorite newspaper delivered to the room in the morning — all secondary services designed to make Selective Shoppers feel pampered.

Many secondary services are complementary services added to enhance the physical comfort of customers, such as adding comfortable seats for waiting spouses and designing the store layout to minimize walking for elderly, pregnant, and overweight customers.

In summary, primary services fulfill the basic needs of customers. Secondary services are those small, added services that make your business special for Selective Shoppers. You'll discover more opportunities to add and enhance secondary services than to enhance primary services.

Shifting — Another Tool to Find Service KSFs

A second search method to identify important services that you might choose to enhance for Selective Shoppers is to use the concept of shifting — identifying opportunities to shift work and shift risks from customers to your business. For example, the small lawn care firms that have sprung up in suburbia provide a work-shifting service; busy homeowners shift their lawn work to the local lawn care firm. With the number of dual-income families and the number of people with "out-of-time" attitudes growing, the opportunities for small businesses to provide many other types of work-shifting services are bound to increase dramatically.

Work-Shifting Services are KSFs that pamper selective shoppers. Most services shift actual work from the customer to the business, and Enhancement firms typically shift more work than do Low-Cost firms. For example, work is shifted from the customer to your business when you provide deliveries, installations, training sessions, alterations, easy product return systems, and catalog ordering. To find your work-shifting opportunities, make a list of all possible customer work that could potentially be shifted to your business. Your list might include an in-home repair service, an in-home replacement service for products broken while under warranty, and a product disposal service at the end of the product's life.

This is a creative search exercise, so don't limit your thinking to the types of services typically offered only in your industry. Borrow new service ideas from businesses outside your industry. Pretend you're developing a menu of services to offer your customers, a big comprehensive menu like you find in restaurants that try to serve every type of food.

Work-shifting also involves enhancing existing services to improve current customer benefits. For example, one small oil and lube business in Springfield, Illinois, enhanced its existing service speed so it could offer a guaranteed 10-minute service for those Selective Shoppers who really want to minimize their inconvenience.

Work shifting can be used to trigger the sales to a chosen customer segment. For example, some customers may need enhanced work-shifting because they don't know how to perform some type of task. In the computer industry, customers have been segmented into two types: experienced and novices. Accordingly, computer retailers have split into two types of firms: one type targets experienced customers with less service and cheaper prices, a second type offers enhanced support services and higher prices to trigger sales to novice customers who need the extra help.

Identifying work-shifting opportunities can be done three ways. First, listen to the requests and questions from your customers. They often begin work-shifting requests with "Do You ...," "Would you ...," or "Can you ...," etc. These customers are asking you to do some type of work they don't want to do or can't do. These requests can lead to the discovery of new opportunities to target customers with a new work-shifting service.

Second, analyze your services and your competitor's services. Jot down each service performed for customers by any competitor in your industry. If it involves work-shifting, analyze it to see if it can be improved.

Third, prepare a customer work process map for customers who use your products and services. Work process maps identify each work task the customer performs in order to use your product or service. The maps include searching for information about products and services, searching for information about stores that carry the product, shopping, comparing, purchasing, transporting the product home, installation steps, using the product, perhaps repairs and adjustments, and disposal. You can ask a few customers to make personal work process maps, or pay a few to make them. Then analyze the process maps for opportunities to shift work from your customers to your business. Some small firms have given customers tape recorders, so they can make verbal process maps.

Risk-Shifting Services are KSFs that protect Selective Shoppers. Selective Shoppers face a variety of financial and emotional risks that could be shifted to your business. For example, customers would like to shift the risk of losing money to your business if the product fails. Customers risk losing their money if they misjudge a product's performance and need to replace it, so they would like to shift this risk to your business. They risk disappointment if they take the product home and it doesn't match their carpet, wallpaper, dress, or suit. They risk embarrassment if friends disapprove of their purchase. They risk that an accident might damage the product. They risk that they might get sick and be unable to make the payments. Shifting these and other risks from the customer to your business might trigger sales to your segment of Selective Shoppers. Some customers are eager to pay extra to shift financial or emotional risks to your business.

1. Financial Risk-Shifting Services. Financial risk-shifting has become quite common. Insurance companies sell a variety of risk-shifting services from insuring homes, health, and incomes to insuring a good-looking pair of legs or an athlete's career. Retail businesses have added a variety of risk-shifting services such as satisfaction-guaranteed-or-your-money-back policies, no-questions-asked return policies, and various types of extended and improved warranty programs. Many risk-shifting services are designed to encourage the customer to purchase quickly without shopping around because the financial risk of making a mistake is shifted to the business. If the customer makes a mistake, the retailer will refund the customer's money, and no questions asked.

Enhanced financial risk-shifting services are waiting to be invented. Perhaps your customers would be willing to pay extra if they could get a full refund should the product need a repair during its first year of use. Perhaps you could offer to provide the next product upgrade for free or guarantee a certain trade-in price if Selective Shoppers decide to purchase next year's model. Shifting the financial risks from the customer to your business can trigger sales. Make a list of all the financial risks that you'd be willing to offer in exchange for a higher price. Discuss your list with your target customers.

2. ***Emotional Risk-Shifting Services.*** Emotional risk-shifting requires that your business be willing to forgo an immediate sale to protect Selective Shoppers from any mental trauma in order to build a long-term customer relationship. For example, upper class Selective Shoppers are often socially sensitive to the judgment of their peers. They want help avoiding products that might be questionable for a person of their caliber and status. Status-seeking customers want to be served by a salesperson with the confidence to say, "Don't buy that product; it's not right for you." Telling customers not to buy lowers immediate sales, but protects the customers from possible embarrassment and builds long-term customer loyalties that will increase long-term sales.

Interior decorators, for example, provide a combination of work-shifting for busy customers and emotional risk-shifting for customers who don't feel competent to decorate their own homes or offices. Similarly, other firms specialize in gift buying, landscaping, or party planning for customers who are afraid to tackle the projects themselves as well as for customers who are too busy.

When you search for all the possible enhancements your firm could make, consider your customers' emotional needs. Emotional risk-shifting services can trigger sales.

Explicit and Implicit Benefits of Services

Another method to identify every service enhancement opportunity available to your business is to divide all service benefits into two categories: explicit and implicit. While these categories overlap both the performance and shifting viewpoints, they can yield additional opportunities for service enhancements.

Explicit Service Benefits. Explicit benefits are those service benefits that are easy to see, easy to measure, and easy to enhance. For example, a "fast" service is explicit because you can put a stopwatch on it, you can measure it, you can enhance it, and you can easily prove that you've enhanced it — by simply measuring it again. Your services are comprehensive or not comprehensive, consistent or not consistent, readily available or not readily available. When searching for all the services you can enhance, make a list of all the ones you can easily measure. If you can easily measure some aspect of a service, you can probably easily enhance it.

Implicit Service Benefits. Implicit benefits are those service benefits that are elusive, less tangible, harder to identify, more psychological in nature, and tend to be valued differently by each customer. For example, convenience is an implicit service because it's hard to measure. A store can be convenient to customers living or working close by and inconvenient for customers located farther away. Sometimes a store is convenient only for customers traveling in one direction. Sometimes implicit benefits need to be enhanced to attract more customers.

Implicit benefits are valued differently by each customer. For example, security is an implicit service, which is why some customers feel safe in the neighborhood surrounding your business while others feel less safe. Privacy is an implicit service, which is why some customers feel their transactions are private while others don't. Implicit services often have psychological benefits which are harder to measure because they are perceived differently by each customer. To find your opportunities to enhance implicit services, first describe the state-of-mind you want customers to achieve when dealing with your business. Then search for service improvements that will create that state-of-mind.

Your search for implicit services should include identifying the less tangible services you could improve — like convenience, atmosphere, waiting line activities to mask delays, and other services that customers often don't think about but that heighten their enjoyment.

Personnel Improvement — A Sales Trigger KSF

Enhancing the skills and competencies of employees in direct contact with Selective Shoppers will often allow you to charge higher prices. Personnel enhancements are frequently used to trigger sales to Selective Shoppers. In this case, *personnel refers only to employees who are in direct contact with your customers.*

Contact employees control the quality of the customers' experience with a business and can make a business appear professional or unprofessional. Contact employees can make the customers' experience enjoyable or detestable. A business using a Low-Cost competitive strategy provides low-skilled employees to keep prices low for Prudent Shoppers, and a business using an Enhancement Competitive Strategy provides high-skilled and motivated employees to better serve Selective Shoppers — of course, at a higher price.

Personnel enhancements often trigger sales. For example, Barbara Rackes succeeded in the women's clothing business by enhancing her contact employees' personal skills to target a segment of busy middle- and upper-class women. Barbara knew that most women's clothing stores had separate departments for different types of apparel and accessories, and those stores staffed each department with competent employees who thoroughly knew that department's merchandise, but only that department's merchandise. Barbara knew this didn't satisfy busy women; she knew personnel enhancements were valued by her target customers when she entered the clothing business.

In her clothing store, Barbara carefully screens applicants and hires helpful salespeople; then, she cross-trains her sales people to know all her store's merchandise — not just one department's merchandise. When the busy, In-a-Hurry woman buys an item in any area of Barbara's stores, the knowledgeable sales counselor can quickly design a complete, matching ensemble. For example, if a customer picks out a suit, the sales counselor can rapidly traverse the store and offer the customer a choice of appropriate blouses, pins, scarves, and other accessories. The customer gets a complete outfit; the store gets a larger sale and a larger profit *(11)*.

Personnel enhancements increase costs and push up prices. So, like Barbara Rackes, you must be sure the Selective Shopper segment you're targeting is willing to pay extra for the extra value created by personnel improvements.

Selective Shoppers often want personnel with enhanced skills waiting on them, selling to them, and performing services for them. The personnel improvements that your customers want usually fall into three categories: enhanced attitudes, enhanced people-handling skills, and enhanced judgment.

Attitudes. Employee attitudes should be enhanced differently for different business situations. Your employees' attitudes can be enhanced to be more:

- Professional
- Communicative
- Friendly
- Cheerful
- Kind
- Moral
- Superior
- Soothing
- Joyful
- Happy
- Confident
- Attentive
- Involved
- Playful
- Entertaining
- Lighthearted

Firms often enhance employees' attitudes to attract Selective Shoppers who want an enhanced experience. For example, a small, prestigious nursing home might attract customers with employees who are professional, attentive, and friendly; an upscale bar might attract customers with employees who are cheerful, entertaining, and lighthearted; a general aviation flight training center specializing in business pilot training might attract customers with employees who are professional, communicative, and nurturing. Likewise, different employee attitudes are appropriate in a day care center for gifted children, an advertising agency specializing in status products, and a religious bookstore. The right enhanced attitude can often trigger sales to Selective Shoppers. In fact, many small businesses are successful because of the enhanced personnel traits of the owners, who create such an enjoyable and special experience for customers that they are able to overcome their higher prices.

Once you identify the attitudes you want to enhance, you teach employees to project those attitudes using two methods: 1) by making sure that managers and senior employees model the correct attitudes and 2) by giving clear instructions. Giving clear instructions isn't as easy as it sounds. For example, telling employees to be more friendly is unclear. "Friendly" is a subjective term. It means different things to different people. Each employee will make a personal decision as to what actions to take to become "more friendly." And, it's unlikely that you will agree with each employee's personal decision. By contrast, a clear instruction on how to be more friendly might include telling employees to look straight at any customer who comes within 15 feet of the employee, smile, and, with a pleasant voice, offer assistance.

Good instructions are *specific* and *measurable*. Specific instructions tell employees exactly what attitude component is to be improved and exactly what actions to take. The 15-foot policy is an example of a *specific* action a friendly employee should perform, and the 15-foot policy is *measurable*. With a specific and measurable policy, both the employee and the employer can agree on what's "friendly." You should never tell employees to project a certain attitude without giving specific and measurable examples of how they are to display that attitude. Try always to include objective ways to measure the employee's attitude.

List the enhanced attitudes that your Selective Shoppers might want from your contact employees. Then, determine which of these are worth higher prices to your target customers by discussing them with customers.

Customer-Handling Skills. The customer-handling skills of employees can be enhanced to more effectively handle large groups, small intimate groups, conflicts, problems, complaints, etc. For example, the normal reaction in most restaurants when the server is given an overcharged credit card is to return and inform the customer that the card's credit limit has been reached and ask for another method of payment. In a restaurant that has improved its employee's customer-handling skills, the server might approach the customer, who may be entertaining guests, and calmly inform the customer that he or she has a phone call. Then the matter can be delicately handled in private. Such enhanced customer-handling skills are greatly valued by Selective Shoppers and will trigger sales.

You should keep an up-to-date list of each type of customer problem, complaint, and conflict that has occurred or can occur in your business. Then train employees to handle each type of situation that is important to your target customers.

Employee Judgment. Enhancing employee judgment means training employees to give customers better advice. For example, a clothing store can enhance a salesperson's judgment about which accessories to recommend with each type suit. A craft store can enhance a salesperson's judgment about which projects to recommend for each level of customer competency and about how to judge each customer's level of competency. Make a list of enhanced employee judgments that might be important to your target customers.

A new employee's attitude, people-handling skill, and judgment are easier to improve if the employee already possesses some of the needed personal attributes. Enhancing traits the new employee already has is far easier than creating new traits that are foreign to the employee. The hiring process can be designed to identify potential employees who actually possess the needed traits.

A recommended hiring process that will teach you how to find employees with the right traits is *Swan's How To Pick The Right People Program* by William Swan (Wiley and Sons). Swan's interview system has three simple parts. The first part tells you how to identify employees who CAN DO the job because they have the right training, experience, skills, and education. The second part tells you how to identify employees who WILL DO the job because they have the right behavior traits — the right attitudes. The third part tells you how to identify employees who FIT into your type business.

Swan observes that most employment interviews focus exclusively on the first part — hiring people with the right qualifications. Therefore, managers like yourself usually don't discover until after the new employee is on the job that they don't have the right attitudes to support your business strategy, and worse yet, aren't capable of developing the right attitudes.

As for training, most managers of small businesses say they don't have a training program, but every business has a training program. Small business training is predominately on-the-job training where the employee observes and copies your behavior and the behavior of your more experienced employees. In this environment, employees will not develop better behavior traits, judgments, and attitudes than the ones you and your experienced employees display. You must consistently display the behaviors you want to instill in your employees — it's called leadership.

If you hire the right employees, set a proper and consistent example, and provide some personnel skills training, you can build a personnel enhancement KSF that will trigger sales to some Selective Shopper segments.

Image Improvement — A Sales Trigger KSF

Image enhancements can significantly lower your customers' resistance to higher prices. Image is particularly important to Selective Shoppers who buy designer clothes, expensive cars, fancy homes, exclusive country club memberships, and first class accommodation. The prestige and status connected with such products or services are important to some Selective Shopper segments; in fact, much of what they're buying is often image. Customers buy expensive products and services in part because they are trying to subtly display their success. When a customer buys a Porsche from Isringhausen Imports in Springfield, Illinois, the purchase becomes a conspicuous display of the customer's personal image, success, and social class. The Porsche, sitting in the circle drive in front of the owner's expensive home in the exclusive part of the city, lets the customer brag about individual achievements without uttering a word. Surely the owner of such a fine vehicle is a special human being, an uncommon human being. Such image-enhancing displays are the socially acceptable manner of bragging. Enhanced image is a vital factor when targeting upper-class, Selective Shopper segments.

However, the image of almost anything can be enhanced. Take ordinary fruit juice. Frozen, concentrated, and canned juice are common, but fresh-squeezed fruit is special. Though no more nutritious than the others, fresh-squeezed beverages have prestige and status because they are prepared by a server, a paid servant. They are unlike canned juices that are prepared by nameless, faceless factory workers and have no image at all. Capitalizing on the appeal of image, Odwalla Inc. formed a small business in 1980 to sell fresh-squeezed juices. Image-conscious customers have lined up to be served. This small business grew to $13 million in annual sales by the mid 1990s *(12)*.

Image improvements can be an important part of your firm's Enhancement strategy. The best jewelry store, best bridal shop, and best furniture emporium in your community sell more than great merchandise, they sell an enhanced business image and that enhanced image is transferred to their customers.

Image is usually enhanced simultaneously with product, service, or personnel enhancements for two reasons. First, sales to many customer segments are triggered by the combination of these enhancements. Second, image is frequently an indicator of performance. Customers may not be able to actually judge the product's performance, so they substitute the image of the firm and assume that the image is earned. For either reason, image can become a powerful sales trigger for some Selective Shoppers.

Image enhancements are achieved with three tools: differentiation, exclusivity, and price.

Differentiation. You achieve differentiation by targeting a different segment of Selective Shoppers than your competitors. You also achieve differentiation by offering different products and services and personnel skills than those offered by your competitors. Therefore, image is enhanced simply by being the unique source of improved products and services for your customers — being different is differentiation.

Advertising techniques are instrumental in differentiating your business and its products and services — in the minds of your customers — by stressing and elaborating an enhanced image. Advertisements should be designed to portray the special and exclusive qualities of your products, services, and business. Advertisements for new products typically include older, accepted, high-image products in an effort to transfer their image to the new products. Image transference is also passed from your business spokesperson to your products and services. That is why image-enhanced firms are careful to hire spokespersons with exemplary images.

Exclusivity. Exclusivity enhances image through scarcity. Improved products, services, and personnel become exclusive if you limit them to only a few special customers. By limiting the number of students who can gain access to an expensive Ivy League University, by limiting the number of members of a prestigious club, and by limiting the number of deluxe suites at the football dome, these products and services become coveted and special. Your products and services cannot be exclusive if you allow them to become commonplace.

Price. High price creates an aura of prestige, status, and exclusivity. High price validates image enhancement by making it impossible for the experiences of your customers to become commonplace. For example, a Rolls Royce Silver Shadow is image-enhanced by its extremely high price; its price guarantees it will never be driven by an ordinary person — unless he's the chauffeur.

The use of price to create exclusivity and image was explained by a Houston resident of an expensive, but otherwise average, apartment complex. When asked why she was willing to pay such a high price, the woman replied that the very high rent bought her the prestige of living among the upper social class and avoiding common people. The apartment complex was full due to an enhanced image achieved solely by charging high prices.

Make a list of the ways you can use differentiation, exclusivity, and high prices to enhance your business image. When image is important to your Selective Shopper segment, it can become a KSF that triggers sales.

Combining all Five KSFs

It's common for some small businesses using an enhancement strategy to improve all enhancement factors. For example, the popular Crescent Cottage

Bed and Breakfast Inn in Eureka Springs, Arkansas, improves all of them. The Crescent enhances its product and image by decorating its rooms with Victorian antiques. The inn further enhances its product by serving a gourmet breakfast. It enhances its personnel and service by training employees to anticipate and take care of each customer's every need. As a result, the Crescent Inn has a waiting list despite high prices and big corporate competitors. The Crescent targets customers wanting a special weekend adventure with lots of enhancements.

In conclusion, a business using an enhancement competitive strategy has five categories of sales triggers:

- Product Enhancement
- Indicators of Product Enhancement
- Service Enhancement
- Personnel Enhancement
- Image Enhancement

Each of the five categories contains many elements or factors that can be improved individually to trigger sales to your segment of Selective Shoppers. The few enhancements that are the most important to your target customers will be KSFs for your business. Your objective or goal is, year after year, to strengthen your KSFs to maintain a long-term competitive sales advantage. However, a sales trigger advantage will only guarantee great sales, not great profits. Other KSFs produce profits.

Key Success Factors that Control Costs

Enhancement organizations aren't inclined to control costs. All five categories of enhancements will cause your expenses to rise, so expect higher costs with this strategy. This puts great pressure on a manager to keep costs constrained. Management must provide cost leadership by installing and judiciously maintaining one or more Key Success Factors to control costs. Unless you, the manager, do your job, escalating costs, a natural consequence of this strategy, will gobble up all your profits.

Your Enhancement Business Won't Be Cost Conscious

When you use an Enhancement strategy, the KSFs that trigger sales are expected to push up costs because you hire more highly skilled labor, extensively train employees, provide more services, buy better equipment, choose better locations, invest in image, and continuously make new investments to maintain your competitive sales advantage. You pass along your higher enhancement costs to your customers through higher prices. In doing so, everyone in your organization becomes conditioned to expect that every extra cost can be passed along automatically. That pass-it-along attitude, unless controlled, results in costs getting out of control, or prices rising to levels that are unacceptable to your Selective Shopper segments.

Selective Shoppers, excluding those seeking an exclusive image, are willing to pay only a reasonably higher price for the enhancements they want. Thus, for most enhancement firms, there's an upper limit to the price the business can charge, but no upper limit to the height to which costs can climb. If prices get too high, customers will quit buying, and "real" competitors will begin to target your customers with reasonable prices for similar enhancements. Managers using an Enhancement Competitive Strategy must install a cost-controlling system to make a great profit.

Cost-Controlling Key Success Factors

Since making enhancements and controlling costs are inconsistent goals, employees need a manager's clear and strong guidance to achieve both goals. Good enhancement managers install a cost-controlling system to balance the twin objectives of making the right improvements and making a profit. Take for example Larry Dinny's small, four-employee company, Den-Con of Oklahoma City, Oklahoma, that manufactures enhanced oil-drilling equipment. Den-Con's more expensive products are sought after because of their enhanced performance, but Den-Con still faces a limit to the price it can charge. If Den-Con is to make a profit, Dinny must control costs. That's why Dinny installed a Total Quality Management (TQM) program. TQM stresses doing things right the first time, reducing scrap, and eliminating re-work to control costs. Using TQM, Dinny's employees develop an understanding that turning out a good part takes the same amount of time, the same amount of raw materials, and the same amount of labor as turning out a defective part — in fact, turning out a good part is cheaper because a bad part has to be fixed or disposed of, which costs extra. Dinny knows that turning out only good parts leads to on-time customer deliveries, lower costs, lower prices, and good profits *(13)*.

Den-Con demonstrates that in an enhancement environment the KSFs that control costs and generate profits are created, installed, and enforced by the operating manager. It's management's job to provide good cost leadership, and it's management's job to control the dangerous "pass-it-along" attitude that can become part of this strategy.

Managers of small businesses can choose from a wide variety of cost-controlling systems that are each best for minimizing costs in different industries and in different situations. Some common programs that are often KSFs include:

- Rigid Budgets
- Project Go/No-Go Evaluation Points
- Management by Objectives — targeted improvements
- Just-in-Time Philosophy
- Process Re-Invention
- Total Quality Management

For example, rigid budgets and Go/No-Go Evaluation points can be combined to control the cost of an improvement program or a special enhancement project. When you begin an improvement project to enhance some critical aspect of your product, service, personnel, or image, start by developing a rigid budget to limit the spending freedom of the employees involved. Tell employees they cannot spend more money than is budgeted in a certain time period. When the project is authorized, automatically pick a few future dates for full project reviews of all costs to date, progress to date, and likelihood of the complete success of the project. For example, if you begin a nine-month project on January 1, the first planned review might be scheduled for April 1, and the second on June 1. On those dates all involved employees should know that, following a complete review, a decision will be made to either continue or terminate the project. These Go/No-Go evaluation dates let project employees know, before the project begins, that they are being held responsible for both making timely progress and controlling costs. The same system should be used if you're operating a one-person business. Go ahead and set Go/No-Go review dates and budgets for yourself — don't let your costs get out of control.

These six key cost-controlling systems and programs are well known and widely used. The first four are briefly explained in Appendix B at the end of the book, and the last two are explained in some depth in Chapter 14. For more details on each topic, books on each can be found in the "Books in Print: Subject" reference guides at your public library. But be warned, a manager of a small business must choose, implement, and control at least one of these cost controlling systems in order to make a profit with an Enhancement strategy.

The Key Success Factor that Limits Competition

An Enhancement strategy gives a small business two ways to limit the number of "real" competitors with which it has to contend. First, the Enhancement strategy targets Selective Shoppers, so the business distances itself from Low-Cost competitors targeting Prudent Shoppers and no-frills competitors targeting Bargain Hunters. Second, Selective Shoppers can be further divided into segments of customers, and by targeting different segments of Selective Shoppers, the business distances itself from other businesses using an Enhancement strategy. Therefore, "real" competitors are limited in two ways with this strategy.

For example, in order to avoid competing with mass-produced cabinets, one small cabinet shop targets Selective Shoppers wanting custom-built Oak cabinets while another cabinet shop targets Selective Shoppers wanting exotic Cherry and Walnut cabinets. Each cabinet shop uses an Enhancement strategy, but each targets a different Selective Shopper segment with a different set of enhancements. Each business develops unique skills, assets, and competencies, and each business earns the loyalty of a different group of customers.

Customer Targeting

Customer targeting reduces competition and allows many small Enhancement businesses using an Enhancement strategy to coexist peacefully. For example, three gourmet restaurants in a community escape direct competition when they specialize in different ethnic foods: Chinese, Italian, and American. Two bike shops in a community limit their competition when one specializes in Mountain bikes and the other in up-scale street bikes. In the boat-building industry, many small manufacturers avoid head-to-head competition when each specializes in a boat designed for a different end use.

Targeting can also be viewed as a way to pick your competitors. For example, by targeting customers wanting taste-enhanced ice cream made from all natural ingredients, Ben & Jerry's Homemade Ice Cream, Inc., chose to compete with Breyers and Steve's Ice Cream and chose not to compete with Dairy Queen.

Hone your targeting skills by trying to determine the size of the market for each possible improvement you thought of for each of the five categories of enhancements. Estimate how many customers would purchase due to the type of product, service, personnel, and/or image improvement you're willing to make. Be sure to consider combinations of improvements. As you study your market, you're sure to identify lots of different sized groups of customers — segments — that you could choose to target.

In general, the best segments to target should meet a few basic requirements. You should be able to actually measure the number of customers in the segment to be sure the segment is worth pursuing. The segment should be the right size and, hopefully, growing. There should be some way to reach the customers in the segment with advertising and promotions so that customers will know you have what they want. Your business should be capable of building a competitive advantage with the segments because you have the right strengths or can add the right strengths. For additional information on segmenting, see Appendix A.

Continuously Improving your Ability to Limit Competitors

As you have learned, customer targeting is vital to the success of an Enhancement strategy because it guarantees that the firm's improvements will be purchased by some group of customers in the marketplace. At the same time, aiming at a special group of Selective Shoppers limits your direct competition by avoiding competitors who target other customers — a to-each-his-own concept. For both reasons, customer targeting is a KSF that should be improved continuously through four steps.

Step one, begin to clarify who your target customers are by defining your business in terms of the overall product and service benefits your business offers customers.

Step two, develop, over time, the ability to identify and to describe the characteristics of your target customers.

Step three, using the knowledge gained in step two, improve your communications with your target customers. Develop advertisements and promotions that 1) reach more targeted customers, 2) are more easily comprehended by targeted customers, and 3) make a more lasting impression on targeted customers. This means that as you study your target customers and gain knowledge about them and their habits, you should be able 1) to have each promotional message received by more target customers, 2) to use customers' language and symbols to improve their ability to comprehend your promotional and personal selling messages, and 3) to improve your messages' impact on your target customers.

Step four, begin to ask your target customers for feedback which you will use to make the next enhancement changes, further increasing their satisfaction with your business, products, services, personnel, and image.

Step two is a lot of trouble. How do you identify and describe the characteristics of your target customers? You can begin by studying your best customers to discover what they have in common in terms of geodemographics, demographics, and psychographics.

Geodemographics is a fancy term that describes where most of your best customers live. Do your best or target customers come from the most expensive parts of town, rural areas, low-income housing areas, certain subdivisions, inner city, outer city, West Coast tourist, etc.? This knowledge may help you to improve your ability to reach target customers with future promotional campaigns because you are smarter about where to target your promotions.

Demographics is a term that describes the traits that your best customers have in common in terms of their media habits, age, income, occupation, family size, education, religion, ethnic group, nationality, and so forth. Your best customers might be high school graduates working in blue-collar jobs at local factories, or they might be upper income, born-again Christians. Knowledge of target customers' personal characteristics helps you to create more effective promotional messages, and knowledge of their media habits helps you to target your promotional campaigns to better reach them.

Psychographics is a term that describes the lifestyles, attitudes, interests, hobbies, or opinions that your best customers have in common. Perhaps your best customers are outdoor types, movie buffs, conservative republicans, or library patrons. This knowledge can help you choose the best tone and content for your promotional message to increase its impact and impression on your target customers.

So, how do you get all these wonderful, but intimate, details about your customers' lives? There are many ways to collect information about your customers. You can use observation, written and telephone surveys, questions on warranty cards, and contests. Contests are fun for customers. As part of your contest, print up a short questionnaire in two colors. Have a detachable portion for the customer's name, address, and phone number. Give one color of your questionnaire to target or best customers, give the other color questionnaire to all others. Use the detachable portion for a random drawing and award prizes — have fun!

Then sort the questionnaire responses by color and analyze the information for each group of customers. Search for any meaningful differences between information from the questionnaires filled out by target and best customers and information from the rest of the customers. You'll immediately get two things from your study: increased ability to describe and understand your best customers, and more questions you want to ask next time. Maybe next time you can have customers jot down the radio stations they listen to and the time of day they listen, and you'll give away some radios as prizes. You'll develop lots of creative ideas when you get started.

Devise your own contest or information collection system, but always try to separate your best or target customers' answers from the other customers' answers. Build a profile of your best customers that describes their important characteristics, lifestyles, attitudes, opinions, and personalities.

An interesting way to discover your customers' lifestyles, attitudes, opinions, and personalities is to run a magazine contest. Use the same color-coded system, and ask customers to write down the three magazines they like best. As a prize, pay for a few customers' subscriptions. If you discover common magazine choices among your target and best customers, read those magazines carefully to identify what lifestyles, personality, and attitudes those magazines target. Read the advertisements in those magazines, and study their tone, language, symbols, and general content. Also, call the magazines and ask for a *psychographic profile of their subscribers*, so you can consider placing ads in the magazine. Even if you don't place ads, you may benefit from reading their subscribers' profiles.

Along with building up a descriptive profile of your target customers, techniques like these let you build up a collection of the names and addresses of your best customers. In addition to the obvious promotional advantages of such a direct mail list, the list is a gold mine for improving your ability to make further enhancements and improve your customers' satisfaction. These are the ideal Selective Shoppers to give you the feedback you need to guide your next enhancement efforts. Use mail or telephone questionnaires to find out what customers like and dislike. Combine this information with personal interviews.

Let your target customers steer your next enhancement decisions which will improve customer satisfaction and further diminish the appeal of "real" competitors. To use customer feedback, you need to be aware that customers have three types of needs: *basic, articulated,* and *exotic*. When you ask customers what specific performance, service, and personnel attributes or benefits are most important, be aware that customers routinely forget to mention their *basic* needs, which they assume you already know. They mention (*articulate*) a few, currently important needs, but they seldom mention *exotic* enhancements they would love your firm to develop *(14)*.

Understanding the limitations of basic, articulated, and exotic feedback can help you avoid mistakes. For example, suppose you want to make an enhanced toothpaste. You ask customers what product attributes they want in a toothpaste, and the articulated replies will probably include fresh breath, white teeth, and a clean mouth. Surprisingly, they'll forget to mention their *basic* desire for cavity prevention. They'll assume you already know that cavity prevention is the most important benefit of a toothpaste.

Also, customers won't mention *exotic* needs. For example, no customer will say they want a toothpaste that can repair small cavities. Yet a cavity-repairing toothpaste would satisfy a need and obviously have tremendous sales. Cavity repair would be a great sales trigger. But customers won't ask for such a benefit because customers aren't normally that creative. They don't give exotic feedback, unless you help them.

You can overcome the exotic feedback limitation by giving customers a list of your exotic benefit ideas and asking them which benefits they want and which benefits they will pay extra to get. So, the good news is that you can test your exotic enhancement ideas to see if customers really want them, just don't expect your target customers to think up exotic ideas for you.

Another limitation is that customers sometimes give inaccurate feedback to your enhancement questions in a few predictable situations. Some customers will give politically correct answers instead of truthful replies. So, customers can be expected to give misleading answers when asked if they want more healthy food choices in the grocery store or on the restaurant's menu — it's politically correct to answer "yes," so you should expect too many "yes" answers. Shy customers will avoid questions that are too personal and will predictably give evasive answers. Some customers even try to be extra helpful and give you the answers they think you want to hear. Be careful not to signal your preferred answers. Using a small dose of common sense, you'll be able to get great customer feedback to guide the implementation of your Enhancement Competitive Strategy.

In conclusion, the Enhancement Competitive Strategy is frequently used by small businesses to target one or more Selective Shopper segments with improved products, improved services, an improved shopping experience provided by the business's contact personnel, and/or an improved image. By catering to the needs of a particular segment of Selective Shoppers, your firm can prosper without having to compete solely on the basis of price. Be sure to use a cost-controlling system to generate good profits, and use customer targeting to build customer loyalty which will limit the number of "real" competitors you'll have to fight.

CHAPTER 5

Speed Enhancement Competitive Strategy

Another Small-Business-Friendly Strategy

SPEED ENHANCEMENT IS A SPECIAL form of the Enhancement Competitive Strategy. It targets Selective Shoppers who want faster service. The Speed Enhancement strategy has the same KSFs that control costs and limit competition as the previously presented Enhancement Competitive Strategy, but this strategy uses speed to trigger sales. Speed Enhancement deserves special attention because it is a form of enhancement frequently used by owners and managers of small businesses.

Many customer segments need fast service, and many small businesses excel at providing it. In comparison to the other competitive strategies, this one is easier for you to implement. While the typical business using an Enhancement Competitive Strategy is wrestling with a complex mix of product, indicators, service, personnel, and image improvements, a business using a Speed Enhancement Competitive Strategy focuses on one factor: service. Fewer enhancements mean fewer management obstacles and fewer complications for your business. The Speed Enhancement business doesn't have to conduct product research, attract and retain the best and the brightest employees, or maintain an exclusive image. Speed Enhancement businesses do simple things — very quickly.

Speed refers to the time it takes to perform a service for a customer, the time it takes to respond to a customer inquiry, the time it takes to complete a customer project, or the time it takes to serve a customer. Speed Enhancement may involve products, but the products aren't fast, the service is fast. In other words, the term fast food doesn't refer to speeding food, it refers to a food served quickly.

However, speed should always be evaluated and measured from a customer's perspective. Service may not seem fast to a customer who found it time consuming to get to your business then to get across the lanes of traffic and into your parking lot. Speedy service only triggers sales when the customer thinks the service is speedy, and the customer will judge the entire service process, not just the one part of it you enhanced.

Speed: A Common Small Business Advantage

Busy people need speed, and trends show that an increasing number of people are leading busy lives. The number of two-wage-earner households who have little time for domestic chores is increasing. The number of single head of households, who carry the entire burden of work and care for their children, is increasing. The number of consumers who respond to surveys by saying they hate shopping, are time-starved, or are impatient shoppers is increasing. The number of people holding down more than one job is increasing. The number of high-income customers who can afford to pay higher prices for speed is increasing. The result of all these trends is an ever-growing number of In-a-Hurry customers, and an ever-growing number of Speed Enhancement opportunities for small businesses.

Small businesses are fond of Speed Enhancement. For example, one office supply firm spotted a recurring need for rush orders of printed labels from its commercial customers. The firm prints labels like those often found on a catsup bottle in the grocery store, a shoe box in the department store, and a box of envelopes.

This small firm had been charging higher prices for rush orders of labels, but despite the higher prices, sales continued to grow. It studied the demand for a speedy label service and found that customers needed emergency orders for several reasons. Businesses would sometimes miscount their inventory of product labels and run out, creating an emergency, and their regular label suppliers weren't set up to respond quickly to emergencies. Business customers who normally keep good inventories of labels would occasionally experience prolonged periods of high demand that depleted their normal label inventory. Some industrial firms would receive unexpected rush orders for their products, creating a shortage of labels. And of course, the regular label suppliers would sometimes experience production problems that caused shipping delays.

When a product manufacturer, food processor, or shoebox company runs out of labels, they can't ship their products. At the same time, they can't afford to keep their customers waiting. The result is a desperate need for an emergency shipment of labels.

The small office supply firm identified and described an ongoing stream of emergencies which they were convinced created a sizable customer segment that could be targeted. Responding to the opportunity, the firm designed its label equipment to minimize setup times, so they could print one rush order and quickly set up to print the next customer's rush order. Reducing job setup time was the key that let them print labels quickly. In fact, fast setups allowed the firm to offer a 24-hour, small-volume label service. In the next 14 years, using a Speed Enhancement Competitive Strategy, the firm grew to a $27 million a year firm, making it the nation's largest short-run manufacturer of printed labels *(1)*.

Focus Packaging Inc. is a Kansas City packaging company employing 33 people that serves just one customer — quickly. They are the sole packaging supplier to the Colgate-Palmolive Company's nearby soap plant. The Colgate plant gets what they want, when they want it, because Focus Packaging is dedicated to providing complete, instant customer service. The speedy service reduces Colgate's packaging inventory to near zero which boosts Colgate's profit. In fact, Colgate likes the speedy inventory arrangement so well, they asked Focus Packaging to build a second small plant in Louisville, Kentucky, that would be dedicated to their toothpaste plant *(2)*.

Repair businesses can also be speedballs. Repair speed is enhanced by stocking large inventories of parts and components and by employing extra repair crews. Of course, this drives costs up and prices up; quick isn't cheap. Vortex Industries discovered that customers with broken warehouse doors would gladly pay an additional $200 for a one-day repair service rather than wait three weeks for a cheaper competitor who had to order parts and then schedule the repairs *(3)*.

When a paper manufacturing machine costing $7,000 an hour to operate breaks a gear at the Scott Paper Company in Mobile, Alabama, they can't wait for the company that made the equipment to ship a replacement gear. Scott depends on a small local machine shop that specializes in gear making to fabricate a replacement part immediately. The machine shop's employees are on 24-hour-a-day call to handle Scott's problems, and service speed has made the small machine shop very successful.

Sales to small retailers are frequently triggered by speedy deliveries. Several small furniture retailers explained they have limited warehouse space and limited money for either additional space or additional inventory. Not surprisingly, these retailers are willing to pay extra to speedy suppliers who make frequent, small deliveries. The higher prices are offset by avoiding the warehouse, material handling, and insurance expenses these retailers would incur in order to stock more inventory. Furthermore, small inventories reduced the retailers' product obsolescence and pilferage losses. The biggest advantage of using speedy suppliers is to increase sales and profits by avoiding stockouts.

The popular Just-in-Time business practice is a Speed Enhancement system. According to the Small Business Administration, the growing use of Just-in-Time inventory controls by industrial businesses has provided sales growth for many small manufacturers. Big corporations use Just-in-Time to reduce and even totally eliminate inventories of raw materials and components. Instead, these firms rely on frequent, fast, small deliveries from suppliers who make deliveries as they're needed. The deliveries are timed to arrive just in time to keep production running, and small manufacturers located close to large corporations are benefiting because they are able to manage the short time schedules.

In summary, small businesses frequently excel at doing things fast. The ability to do things fast increases if a business specializes in doing just a few things. All of these examples show small businesses who are focused on doing a few things quickly. By comparison, big businesses with their committees and consensus building management styles are dependable suppliers but not often fast suppliers. Speedy service is often a small business specialty.

Key Success Factors for Speed Enhancement

Again, Speed Enhancement is a type of Enhancement Competitive Strategy, and, like all forms of the Enhancement Competitive Strategy, Speed Enhancement succeeds when the business develops three types of KSFs:

- Sales Triggers
- Cost Controllers
- Competition Limiters

Key Success Factors that Trigger Sales

Speed. The *Speed* of a service is the most important KSF that triggers sales and is the one factor that must be improved continuously. Speed is enhanced by simplifying the service process through the following steps:

- Reduce the number of services the business performs to as few as possible. Employees get faster through repetition, and restricting the number of services performed means they will perform the same ones more often, becoming more skilled. The favorable effects of the learning and experience curves are gained only through repetition.

- Limit customizing services. Customizing adds additional planning, setup time and other non-repetitive work tasks, causing workers to slow down.
- Simplify manual jobs. Assembling products or performing services requires many individual tasks. Jobs such as assembling computers, assembling cars, preparing food, and repairing cars can be speeded up if each employee's job consists of only a few simple tasks that are repeated frequently. Each worker learns to do the manual tasks quickly then pass the work to the next worker. Repetition increases speed.
- Reduce the number of employees necessary to perform a mental job. White-collar jobs are also made up of many tasks. Because these jobs are more mental and less manual, job speed is increased when one person does as many tasks as possible without handing the work off to another person. For example, in a loan approval system or an insurance claim adjustment system, each time the work is handed off to the next worker, time is lost while the next worker familiarizes themselves with what the last worker did and what problems remain to be solved. The next worker has to waste time preparing to do their work. Speed when performing white-collar jobs is often achieved by minimizing the number of workers that contribute to each job.
- Cross-train employees if demand frequently varies. When market demand frequently fluctuates, forcing the workforce to go through expansion and contraction cycles, employees should be cross-trained by rotating them from job to job to make work-force adjustments easier. This way when the workforce is shrunk, no key skills are lost. When the workforce is expanded, experienced workers can more easily train new workers because every worker is a trainer in a cross-training environment.
- Design each employee's work area for efficiency. For example, a common high-efficiency job layout is the simple U-shaped work area, which allows the worker to perform several tasks with a minimum of physical movement.

All these improvements speed up service for In-a-Hurry customers. In-a-Hurry customer segments frequently place more emphasis on service speed than the products accompanying the service; often only standardized products are needed to support sales. This means that some In-a-Hurry customers are pleased with the performance of the Low-Cost strategy firm's products, but they want the service speed enhanced.

Services become fast only if the service process is designed to be fast. When speedy service is the KSF that determines which competitor gets the sales, speed must be improved continuously to maintain a competitive advantage over speedy competitors. Speed is always relative. So, in order to trigger sales, you need a significant advantage in speed compared to that of your competitors. Therefore, your business must constantly measure not only its own speed, but its competitors' speeds as well.

Furthermore, customer perception is the key to the success of a Speed Enhancement Strategy — speed is always in the *eye of the customer*. A service isn't fast unless customers think it's fast. For instance, some businesses think they have speedy deliveries just because they keep their delivery schedules. While an applaudable record, real delivery speed is measured from the customer's point of view. Do customers get deliveries when they want them? Do customers have complete control over the delivery times? For a delivery to be speedy, customers must get their deliveries when and where they want them.

Also, customers' speed perceptions can sometimes be fooled. For example, a hotel that received many complaints from customers having to wait for its elevators installed full-length mirrors next to every elevator door. Complaints dropped immediately because customers were distracted as they straightened their clothes and checked their appearance. It seems that having something to do while waiting makes the waiting time seem shorter. Similarly, a small restaurant in the Midwest has many amusing, perpetual-motion toys arranged along the waiting line to distract waiting customers, which shortens the perceived waiting time. These examples suggest that some service delays can occasionally be masked by distorting the customers' perception of time.

High Inventory Levels are a KSF because high inventories are necessary for the service to be speedy. For example, a fast oil change business wouldn't be very fast if it ran out of oil. Likewise, a speedy overnight parts delivery service wouldn't be speedy if it ran out of parts. Or, a Speed Enhanced small manufacturer wouldn't be speedy if it waited until after the customer's order was received to produce products, instead of maintaining lots of finished goods inventory in their warehouse, ready for an instant shipment. To trigger sales with speed, businesses have to carry large inventories of products that are connected to the service.

A Speed strategy requires large inventories of finished goods which in turn requires large storage areas or warehouses and fast stock retrieval systems to provide speedy services. When products are part of your speedy service, your costs will be pushed up by the cost of maintaining large inventories and the costs of storing and handling those inventories.

Under-Utilized Capacity is a KSF that triggers sales because it guarantees services will continue to be speedy. However, the reason for setting up a business to operate at less than full capacity differs for service versus manufacturing businesses.

Unlike products, services can't be placed into inventory. For example, oil and lube businesses can't perform oil changes in advance; workers must perform them after customers arrive. Barbers can't store haircuts, funeral homes can't store funeral services, and the theater can't store customer entertainment — none of these services can be inventoried ahead of time, they must be performed after the customer arrives. While a speedy manufacturing firm simply fills the customer's order out of inventory immediately upon receiving the order, a speedy service firm has to perform the service immediately after the customer arrives.

To maintain a speedy service, the service firm has to be able to handle normal customer traffic fast, it has to be able to handle heavy customer traffic fast, and it has to be able to handle peak customer traffic fast. If the firm isn't prepared for peak demands, waiting lines will grow, and customers will occasionally experience unusually long waiting times, creating dissatisfaction and eroding the firm's main KSF that triggers sales — fast service. Therefore, service speed can only be maintained if the business has more operating capacity than is normally needed.

For example, suppose a quick lube and oil business wants to promise a 25-minute oil change service without asking customers to make appointments. If three service bays and three service crews are needed just to keep up with the flow of customers on normal weekends, a fourth service bay will be necessary to handle peak demand. At a three-bay capacity, customers will have to show up in steady, uniform streams for the firm to keep its commitment to service speed. Unfortunately, customers never show up in a steady stream. They show up in small bunches, big bunches, peaks, and valleys. With three bays, the firm will often get behind, fail to live up to its 25-minute service claim, struggle to catch up, and run behind for long periods of time. Four bays and four crews will be necessary to catch up during periods of high demand; yet, some of the four crews will be idle during times of normal demand which will raise costs.

Speed Enhancement in a service business always involves building excess capacity. Of course, during slower than peak periods the service business can reduce its number of part-time employees to lower costs, but it can't reduce the size of the building, the amount of equipment, or the monthly payments on both.

Manufacturing businesses using a Speed strategy face similar fluctuations in demand. They build big warehouses, maintain lots of finished goods inventory, and expect to fill customer orders immediately from those inventories.

However, every manufacturing firm experiences occasional periods of sustained high demand which depletes their inventory. During those periods, the manufacturer must be able to increase its production speed to replenish its inventory while shipping goods to customers. This is possible only if the manufacturer normally operates below full capacity and has extra production capacity to use during difficult times.

Also, manufacturers operating at less than full capacity still pay the same salaries, equipment payments, building payments, and insurance premiums as they would operating at full capacity. Therefore, per product costs increase for speedy manufacturers.

Location is often a KSF. Location becomes a KSF when it significantly increases the speed of service. From a customer's perspective, the time it takes to acquire a speedy service from a business is a combination of the time *to reach the store* plus the time *to be served* after reaching the store. Location determines the time it takes the customer to reach the business. Only easy-to-reach and easy-to-access businesses are convenient, so only convenient businesses can be speedy. From a customer's perspective, even a nearby business isn't convenient if they encounter traffic bottlenecks every time they try to visit the store. Being stuck in traffic, being unable to find a break in oncoming traffic to access the store, and being unable to get back into traffic when leaving the store makes the location inconvenient because they all lengthen the service time for the customer.

Bad locations can sometimes be overcome with technology. Reaching the business is convenient when target customers can relay their orders by phone, fax, or computer. With today's technology, reaching a business may have nothing to do with actually traveling to the business.

Site convenience is sometimes enhanced by installing one-way traffic patterns around the business to speed up parking and minimize traffic conflicts. The inside of the business can also be designed to improve convenience. Contrary to the common practice of putting frequently desired items at the back of a store to force customers to make contact with unwanted products before getting what they came after, Speed Enhancement firms maximize the convenience of their target customers by placing the most frequently purchased items close to the entrance — it's faster.

KSFs that Control Costs and Limit Competition

Speed Enhancement is a type of Enhancement Competitive Strategy; thus the KSFs that control costs and limit competition are the same. Please refer to Chapter 4 for a discussion of these topics.

Speed Enhancement Limitations

Speed Enhancement pushes up both costs and prices; therefore, the business must be sure that enough target customers exist to support this strategy. If only one customer in one hundred is willing to pay the extra price for speed in your industry, then only larger communities will have the necessary volume of customers to support a business using Speed Enhancement. Many Speed strategies cannot be used in small towns because there aren't enough target customers willing to pay the higher prices.

No business can risk building large inventories of products that have unstable, unpredictable sales. Therefore, this strategy can only be used with products having predictable life cycles. Many commonplace products have predictable and stable sales like motor oil, fertilizers, dry cleaning fluids, photo developing chemicals, soft drinks, coffee, carpet, furniture, food stuffs, and basic clothing items. Other products either become obsolete or go out of style too rapidly for this strategy, like computers, fax machines, beepers, and fad products such as Pet Rocks and hula hoops — how would you like to own a huge inventory of Pet Rocks?

Success based on speed can sometimes be short lived. Success can weaken the business's most important sales trigger anytime demand for the firm's fast service grows more rapidly than the firm's capacity to supply that service. Unfortunately, the first effect of rapid growth is a rapid increase in profits as the firm begins to operate at full capacity, which often lulls management into blissful complacency. Then comes the second effect — a slow-down in service speed as demand becomes higher than the business's capacity. Lines of customers begin to form. This excess demand creates widespread customer dissatisfaction, causing sales to decline and profits to plummet. Success must be managed by either expanding capacity to keep up with expanding demand or by raising prices to dampen demand.

CHAPTER 6

Flexibility Enhancement Competitive Strategy

A Very Small-Business-Friendly Strategy

FLEXIBILITY ENHANCEMENT IS ANOTHER popular form of the Enhancement Competitive Strategy that deserves your special attention. This strategy places the maximum competitive distance between a small, flexible business and the brutal low-price competition of big competitors using a Low-Cost strategy.

Flexibility refers to the ability of the business to alter a service or a product to fit the wants and needs of individual customers — not groups of customers, not a customer segment, but one customer at a time. A flexible business is the complete opposite of the Low-Cost business because it doesn't make any routine products or provide any standard services. Unlike the Low-Cost firm that employs efficiency-minded managers to supervise lots of low-skilled employees who operate automated equipment, the flexible manager of a small business must be creative and must supervise high-skilled workers who operate adjustable equipment to tailor-make each high priced product or service for each customer.

I-Want-What-I-Want Customers

Sometimes consumers want personalized services, and many different types of small businesses supply them with customized services:

- Chartered Air Services
- Clothing Alterations
- Custom Computer Software
- Investigative Work

- Convention Planning
- Personal Fitness

Sometimes consumers want personalized products, and many different types of small businesses supply them with customized products:

- Custom Cabinets
- Automotive Customizing
- Home and Business Remodeling
- Art Work
- Custom Furniture
- Custom Jewelry

Most consumers have some individual wants, and businesses using a Flexibility strategy serve those wants. Home remodeling contractors tailor their expertise and materials to transform individual ideas into reality. Custom cabinetmakers tailor their products to each customer's space, style, and house plans. Home decorators and landscapers specialize in catering to each individual's taste.

Customers wanting individualized products make up the "I-Want-What-I-Want" customer type. These customers have many differences, and they form a loose customer type whose common trait is that they don't have much in common. However, these individualists are willing to pay higher prices to get products and services tailored to fit their exact wants and needs.

Flexibility: A Common Small Business Competitive Edge

One size fits all? Forget that nonsense, say I-Want-What-I-Want customers, and they go searching for small businesses who'll give them exactly what they want. Lots of small businesses use this strategy to serve them.

Tired of off-the-rack swimwear that's too tight in one spot and too loose in another? Here's a solution. Software Sportswear of Greenwich, Connecticut, uses Flexibility Enhancement and can make a swimsuit tailored to your body. First, Software Sportswear uses a video camera and a computer to photograph, measure, and record an individual's image and dimensions. Second, the computer displays various types of fabrics and styles of swimsuits for the customer's consideration. Third, each suit the customer likes is shown on the customer's body on the TV screen — the customers see themselves as others will see them at poolside. When the final choice is made, the computer creates a pattern exactly proportioned to fit the I-Want-What-I-Want customer's body.

Software Sportswear's prices are much higher than off-the-rack swimwear, as much as 50 percent higher than a department store's swimwear.

Instead of complaining, customers rave about the customized fit and pay the higher price *(1)*.

Each disabled person's needs differ greatly, so Sunrise Medical makes wheelchairs to fit each individual customer. Sunrise's chairs come in one-inch increments of seat width, seat depth, and back height. They offer lots of personalized options to make each chair fit and function for each I-Want-What-I-Want customer *(2)*.

Are you frustrated by the amount of space required for your business's recordkeeping systems? Call Spacesaver. The Spacesaver Company designs and builds flexible bookcase and recordkeeping systems to fit each customer's available space.

Spacesaver's storage units are mounted on motorized recessed floor tracks that allow all the rows of storage units to be squeezed together, leaving only one aisle. With a touch of a button, the storage units move left or right, so the one movable aisle is positioned between any two storage units. Spacesaver is so efficient that a 16-foot wide room can contain seven 24-inch wide bookcases with only one 24-inch wide aisle instead of the normal six to eight aisles. While this type of system may seem expensive, many customers avoid the much greater expense of adding another building because Spacesaver builds their units into the customer's existing space *(3)*.

Ever wish your business had its own employee training program? It can. The Forum Corporation of Boston provides training programs tailored to each client's specific needs. The Forum meticulously studies the current skills and competencies that employees need. The Forum also studies the firm's growth strategies and expected industry changes to identify the employee skills and competencies that will be needed in the future. Then, the Forum designs a personalized training program to fit the I-Want-What-I-Want client's needs and finances *(4)*.

Do your employees know what they're doing? Osterlind & Associates of Columbia, Missouri, can answer that question. They use a Flexibility strategy to design certification and licensing tests to establish an employee's level of competence. For example, the Association of Money Managers and Investors asked for a certification program to test and qualify managers to handle clients' retirement funds. Osterlind's approach is to form a test development committee made up of the association's most experienced and accomplished money managers — the association's acknowledged experts. The experts then determine the level of knowledge that new money managers must have to be certified. Osterlind provides the expertise in question wording, customized test construction, and statistical verification of the test results. After the test's accuracy is proven and accepted, the test becomes the customer's employee certification instrument.

Then Osterlind administers the test, grades the test, and certifies new money managers on behalf of the association. Also, since money management techniques and systems change over time, Osterlind forms an association committee to guide them in updating the test.

Osterlind can use its Flexibility strategy to customize a certification procedure for any field, any industry, any mental task, and any physical task. They can certify your employees.

These examples show how small businesses use a Flexibility Enhancement Competitive Strategy. These small firms develop flexible skills and competencies and use flexible equipment, processes, and systems, so they can tailor each product and each service to satisfy the individual wants and needs of each customer. This strategy is used in both consumer markets and industrial markets.

Key Success Factors for Flexibility Enhancement

Flexibility Enhancement is another form of the Enhancement Competitive Strategy that is popular with small businesses. Like all competitive strategies, Flexibility Enhancement succeeds when the business excels in three key areas:

- Sales Triggers
- Cost Controllers
- Competition Limiters

Key Success Factors that Trigger Sales

One or more of the following factors trigger the sales of various Flexible Strategy firms.

Ability to Customize. The ability to customize triggers sales and is the major KSF that must be improved continuously. Customizing is the major KSF because each I-Want-What-I-Want customer's purchase depends on the business's ability to alter, personalize, and customize each service or product. The ability to customize is achieved through the use of flexible equipment, flexible employee skills, flexible processes, and combinations of the three.

Flexible Equipment. Flexible equipment is a KSF that triggers sales when it is the major resource that allows your business to produce customized products and services. The more flexible the business's equipment, the wider the range of alterations the business can make, which allows the business to trigger sales to a wider variety of individual customers. While most equipment is built for speed and limited adjustment, flexible equipment is built to maximize the range and ease of adjustment at the sacrifice of production speed.

Two types of flexible equipment are generally used: manual and computer adjusted. Manually adjusted general-purpose equipment is the cheapest equipment a small business can purchase. This type of equipment is often available as used machinery from other businesses, equipment dealers, and at auctions.

Computer-aided design (CAD), computer-aided manufacturing (CAM), and computer-integrated manufacturing (CIM) equipment is faster, more flexible, and more accurate than manually adjusted equipment. Such equipment is particularly useful for reducing the setup time required to change from the last customer's job to the next customer's job and minimizing mistakes in the early part of a production run. Computer-controlled general-purpose equipment is expensive, and because of its expense, computer controlled equipment is usually the second generation equipment purchased by growing firms .

Flexible Processes. Flexible processes are sales trigger KSFs when they are critical to producing customized products and services. Some small firms use flexible work processes to personalize their services quickly. For example, a flexible computer software program allows a policy consultant to choose the right policy statement quickly for each client. Or, a flexible process allows personal health consultants to make quick alterations in recommendations for each client. Since a process is simply the sequence of routine work steps used to perform some task, everything an employee does for the customer is the result of a work process. Flexibility is enhanced by altering the sequence of work steps to better fit each customer's needs, and only a flexible process will support easy and quick changes.

Flexible Employee Skills. Flexible employee skills are a KSF when they are the major resources required to operate either the flexible equipment or provide a flexible service. In flexible manufacturing, employees must often have both a wide range of product fabrication skills and a wide variety of mechanical skills to reconfigure the equipment for each job. These employees are highly skilled, highly creative, and well paid.

Similarly, flexible service businesses are often dependent on employees who possess a wide range of skills. Frequently, employees must have the marketing skills to work with a variety of temperamental individuals. Plus, employees must have the ability to alter each piece of equipment and each service procedure. And, most important of all, employees must have the confidence to perform each personalized service while the customer witnesses the whole operation. This is a demanding job that requires talented, confident, and flexible employees.

Customer Communication Skills. Customer communication skills are a sales trigger when complicated or complex customer ideas are involved. In complex situations, a high level of communication skill is needed to capture the mental visions and images that exist in the minds of customers who are often not product or service experts. Unlike dealing with knowledgeable buyers who have mastered the industry jargon, I-Want-What-I-Want customers are often novices, amateurs, or beginners who communicate with words and phrases that are unclear. In these situations, the ability to communicate accurately with your customers becomes a KSF. If key employees can decipher the confusing language of customers effectively, sales will surely increase because satisfied customers will tell others about your business. Often a good communicator, aware that the customer doesn't know the market's special vocabulary, quickly adopts the customer's vocabulary and adjusts to speak their language and use their symbols and gestures — sort of like quickly learning a foreign language. Good communicators use all the information available from the customer: words, actions, reactions, gestures, body language, and appearance when deciding what customers want.

One custom cabinetmaker created a communication KSF by making beautiful and accurate, three-dimensional drawings to capture the customer's vision. The unfortunate side effect was that the drawings were so good that unscrupulous customers used them to shop for cheaper prices with less talented competitors. The cabinetmaker/artist retaliated by keeping all copies of the drawings until the customer put down a deposit and signed the contract.

Key Success Factors that Control Costs

A Flexibility business faces an unusual array of problems that require unique cost-controlling abilities or competencies.

Work Scheduling

Work scheduling is often a KSF because it frequently determines the firm's productivity. Scheduling determines the number of jobs that the flexible small business can complete each day; great scheduling results in more jobs being completed in the same amount of time and with the same amount of labor costs. When each individual job is different, considerable skill and experience is required to arrange each day's job sequence to shorten the lost time between jobs or tasks. In other words, doing job A then job B then job C then job D, because that's the sequence in which the orders were received, may require twice as much setup time between jobs as doing job B then D then A then C. Minimizing setup time often means not doing the jobs in the order they are received, instead, it means doing jobs in the order that allows smaller, easier, quicker changes in equipment or in employees' work routines. Good scheduling can also minimize costly mistakes that occur by limiting the number of changes required to do the next job.

Limited Flexibility

Limited flexibility is a KSF when it significantly lowers costs by boosting productivity. Placing no restrictions on the type of customization your firm performs will maximize the number of orders received, but it lowers daily productivity. Limited flexibility means specializing in only those areas where your firm is especially skilled and efficient. Limited flexibility is achieved by establishing policies that avoid slow jobs and problem jobs. As a small business progresses from a start-up firm to an established business with healthy demand, it typically puts more restrictions in place to maximize productivity and profits.

One small furniture manufacturer restricted the number and type of modifications it accepted from retailers during the busiest time of the year. The firm's retailers asked customers to return with their complex modifications during the slow period between February 15 and June 15 when the manufacturer relaxed its restrictions. Most customers came back, which boosted both the manufacturer's and the retailer's sales in the off-season. For this firm, limiting flexibility increased sales and productivity in their busy season, and relaxing the same limitations increased sales and productivity in their off-season.

Low Overhead

Low overhead is often a KSF that controls costs. Because customized products and services are normally items that customers are willing to travel longer distances to get, the business is usually free to choose less expensive locations away from the high-priced commercial areas, thus cutting costs significantly.

Another way to achieve low overhead is to purchase used equipment, and lease-purchase financiers are a surprisingly good source of both used equipment and good financing. These financing firms put up booths at industry trade shows to assist new equipment dealers and their customers. However, when they repossess equipment, they become eager to get rid of it because they have a non-performing loan and are paying to warehouse the repossessed equipment. They become motivated sellers who will negotiate both pricing and financing. Get their business cards at the show, but wait till the following week to call them. Ask to be placed on their mailing list for used equipment.

Physical Layout

Physical layout of the workstations and work areas can be a crucial KSF for a flexible business. Unlike an assembly line layout where all work tasks can be arranged in a sequence and every job goes through the same sequence of steps, in flexible firms each service and each product often requires a unique sequence of work steps, so there is little uniformity in work flow. Instead of constructing an assembly line layout for services and products, flexible firms dedicate a different area in the facility for each type of work or task — called functional areas. Each job travels only to some of the functional areas, so each job is said to take a different route through the facility. Different routes mean any one job may go to one functional area then across the facility to the next functional area, and maybe cross back to yet another functional area.

For example, a custom cabinet shop is designed with functional areas for receiving, millwork, door making, drawer making, glass work, laminate work, assembly, sanding, finishing, and shipping. Not all jobs physically move through each functional area; if one customer orders doorless, unfinished bookcases, the shop uses only a few of the functional areas. Only jobs needing doors are routed through the shop area where doors are made and installed; likewise, only jobs needing drawers are routed through the drawer area. Each job physically travels a unique route through the facility.

Using different routes for each job is also common in flexible service businesses. For example, a small health clinic will have numerous areas: receptionist, waiting room, examination rooms, various laboratories for different tests, various treatment rooms for different patient problems, a few X-ray rooms, and minor surgery rooms. Each patient uses a different combination of the health care facility's designated areas. A poorly designed physical layout hurts overall service efficiency and clinic revenues while a good design boosts productivity and profits.

Total cost is greatly affected by the physical layout of any flexible work area because the layout determines how easily and how quickly an average job will flow through the facility. The best layout is the one that minimizes the time, trouble, and costs for the most common types of work performed. Choosing the best layout will maximize productivity, minimize costs, and maximize profits.

Unfortunately, the most common types of work performed may change over time, causing a previously efficient layout to become inefficient. Some forward-looking entrepreneurs have made their functional areas and equipment moveable. They rearrange their physical layout anytime doing so will significantly increase productivity or lower costs.

Programs like Total Quality Management, strict budgets, or Just-in-Time inventory controls can also be used with this strategy to control costs.

The Key Success Factor that Limits Competition

Flexibility Enhancement is a type of Enhancement Competitive Strategy; thus the KSFs that limit competition are the same. Please refer to Chapter 4 for a discussion of customer targeting.

Flexibility Enhancement Limitations

I-Want-What-I-Want customers make up only a small fraction of a community's consumers for any particular industry. Smaller communities will not have enough customers to support some types of flexible businesses.

Another limitation faced by businesses using this strategy is caused by diminishing returns. The term "diminishing returns" refers to the profit made on each item manufactured or each item or service sold. For example, profits increase as sales increase up to a point, but start to diminish past an optimum level of activity. Profits diminish if workers are pushed to exceed the optimum workload and start to make mistakes, get tired, are injured, or exceed 40 hours and start earning overtime wages. Profits diminish for many reasons for all types of firms when they exceed their optimum activity level, but that optimum level is reached more quickly by Flexibility businesses.

Typically, as the flexible firm grows, it encounters many scheduling problems. The largest scheduling problem involves bottlenecks. Each day's group of jobs places different demands on each functional area, and on any given day a different functional area will reach capacity and become that day's bottleneck. Unfortunately the mix of jobs varies daily, thus the functional area responsible for causing the bottleneck changes daily. If the same area bottlenecks the firm frequently, the firm can increase profits by expanding that area. However, expanding work areas that only occasionally bottleneck the business will increase overhead cost more than they increase revenue — a point of diminishing returns. Flexibility firms often encounter such a point.

As the small business grows, the number and variety of customized jobs grows, and eventually the scheduling complexities reach a practical limit. As the amount of work increases, more jobs are scheduled that have unique supplies, raw materials, material handling needs, setup problems, delivery requirements, and installation problems. Most small flexible firms discover they can only handle a certain number of orders before scheduling mistakes, problems, and errors start eating up profits — diminishing returns.

Diminishing returns create a limit on the amount of profit a flexible firm can make. If demand is hearty for the firm's goods and services, the flexible business usually limits some of its variety of customization to increase productivity and delay the effects of diminishing returns. In this way the firm can serve more customers with the speed gained by making fewer changes. Because of diminishing returns, most flexibility businesses will discover that their optimal size is limited and that expanding beyond that size will actually decrease their profits.

CHAPTER 7

Reduction Competitive Strategy

Another Very Small-Business-Friendly Strategy

THREE MAJOR TYPES OF CUSTOMERS exist in most markets: some Selective Shoppers wanting enhanced products and services, a lot of Prudent Shoppers wanting low-priced products and services, and some Bargain Hunters wanting cheap products and services. The Reduction Competitive Strategy targets the Bargain Hunters. Reduction and Enhancement strategies both provide important methods for the small business to avoid the aggressive competition of Low-Cost strategy corporations, but that's about all the Reduction and Enhancement strategies have in common. For instance, while an Enhancement strategy is used to operate a gourmet restaurant, an exclusive dress shop, and a Snapper lawnmower dealership, a Reduction strategy is used to operate an inexpensive All-U-Can-Eat buffet, a second-time-around dress shop, and a used lawnmower and repair business. In practice, Reduction is the opposite of Enhancement.

Both competitive strategies are favorites of small businesses, but big businesses sometimes use them as well. Consider two large corporations: Sony targets customers wanting highly advanced televisions using an Enhancement strategy with state-of-the-art, expensive technology. At the same time Goldstar targets customers wanting cheap televisions using a Reduction strategy with older, generic technology.

Perhaps one of the best-known big firms using a Reduction strategy to target Bargain Hunters is Perrigo Company in Allengan, Michigan, who makes the Equate line of over-the-counter pharmaceutical products found in discount department stores. Perrigo, compared to the well-known brand names, has reduced its image simply by not investing in expensive advertising and promotional programs to manipulate the image of their products in consumers' minds. Instead, Perrigo makes products that are chemically equivalent to the big brand name aspirins, antacids, and decongestant products on the market. By avoiding the high cost of image building, Perrigo can sell its products at cheap prices to Bargain Hunters and still make a good profit. Over time, Perrigo hopes that word-of-mouth testimonials from satisfied users will convince many Prudent Shoppers to become Bargain Hunters when shopping for these items.

The Reduction Competitive Strategy exists *relative* to the Low-Cost Competitive Strategy; Reduction prices are cheap when compared to the low prices of Low-Cost strategy firms. The Reduction strategy targets customers who reject the market's standardized, high-volume, low-priced products and services because the price is too high — they want a cheap price. Cheap is achieved through reduction; a reduction in the product's performance, a reduction in the number and quality of services offered, a reduction in the skills of the contact personnel serving the customers, and/or a reduction in the image of both the product and the business selling the product or providing the service.

In most ways reduction is the opposite of enhancement. But by being opposite, a Reduction strategy offers several unique advantages for small business owners, especially first-time business owners. The Reduction Strategy allows owners with limited skills, limited assets, and limited special abilities to avoid experienced competitors who are using either the Low-Cost or Enhancement Competitive Strategies.

Bargain Hunters Seek C-H-E-A-P Prices

Reductions are targeted at "Bargain Hunters." Bargain Hunters are extremely frugal, extremely price sensitive, and extremely tightfisted with their money. These customers view the industry's standardized product as too expensive and too extravagant. Bargain Hunters settle for stripped-down products, low-performance products, limited warranty products, and even no-warranty products.

In the new car industry, Bargain Hunters buy cheap, sub-compact cars when they can be enticed away from the used car market. In the lawn mower industry, Bargain Hunters buy used lawnmowers. In other industries they buy low-quality paints, generic products, tickets on no-frills airlines, salvage yard parts, and products at auctions, yard sales, and flea markets.

Bargain Hunters often buy from small, little-known businesses with no name recognition. They buy cheap cabinets from the community's newest, most inexperienced cabinetmaker. They buy rebuilt cars from the body shops that deal in salvaging wrecks. They buy furniture from small, unknown, regional furniture manufacturers.

Bargain Hunters are a mixture of low-income consumers, frugal middle-income consumers, and other price-sensitive customers. Many customers are Bargain Hunters for only some of their purchases because despite their incomes, they love searching for bargains. Situations can create Bargain Hunters; for example, customers forced to replace their car's battery while trying to sell the car will gladly purchase a cheap battery with no concern for how long it will last.

Reduction strategies are increasing in popularity. During the last decade, income distribution in the United States has become more bipolar; demographers say the U.S. is becoming a nation of "haves" and "have-nots" with fewer in-betweens. As the size of the "have-not" group increases, demand increases for stripped-down, no-frills products and services from small businesses using a Reduction strategy.

One reason a Reduction strategy favors small businesses is because big businesses often avoid the "have-not" customer segments for fear of tarnishing their "quality" image if they produce "low-quality" products and provide stripped-down services. Small businesses have been quick to take advantage of these opportunities. Increasingly, small stores are being opened to sell used sporting goods, used baby furniture, used toys, used high-quality clothing, and rebuilt cars. Even single engine airplanes are now available as relatively inexpensive build-it-yourself kits. Big business has attempted to fight back in factory outlet malls that have sprung up all across the U.S., but for identical merchandise, prices at factory outlet malls aren't really much cheaper than at regular department stores.

Small Businesses Using a Reduction Strategy

While Landmark Ford sells thousands of new, full-sized pickup trucks in Springfield, Illinois, every year, Ray's Auto Sales in Pawnee, Illinois, makes a fine living selling hundreds of used pickups to price-sensitive customers. Ray's is just one of the many small businesses using a Reduction Competitive Strategy to target Bargain Hunters with cheap, used trucks.

Used pickups are reduced every way possible: product, service, personnel, and image. Used pickups will have higher repair bills, a reduction in reliability and durability. Many used pickups are sold with no warranty, a reduction in service. All used pickups have a shorter expected product life, a reduction in product performance. The used pickup salespeople are less knowledgeable about their trucks than the factory-trained salespeople at the new truck dealership, a reduction in personnel skills. The used pickup lot has a lower image than the new truck showroom and so does the used truck with its older styling and signs of wear. Of course, the same four factors are reduced when selling used cars, used boats, used airplanes, used appliances, used furniture, and any other type of used merchandise.

A Reduction strategy is occasionally used to build large businesses. From the beginning, customers flocked to Southwest Airlines and its three airplanes, as the business expanded out of Texas. Southwest had tested its no-frills tactics while running its initial Houston-Dallas-San Antonio route. Southwest targeted Bargain Hunters with less comfort, no-meals, limited baggage handling, inconvenient ticketing, reduced cabin services, and cheap prices. In many ways, Southwest treats customers like cattle: the planeload lands, the herd is driven off through one shoot, a new herd is driven on via another shoot, luggage in the cargo hole is quickly exchanged, and in less than 15 minutes the cattle-plane is in the air again flying its herd to the next pen.

Gloomy, but Bargain Hunters accept such treatment, and they accepted Southwest's reductions and scrambled to fill their seats. Studies have shown that Southwest's tickets are so cheap that the company actually pulls customers away from Greyhound busses. Despite the cattle car criticism, Southwest has plenty of loyal Bargain Hunters and plenty of profits *(1)*.

The Southwest Airlines scheme was so successful that it was copied by the Morris Travel Agency. Morris set up a similar no-frills system to serve charter flight customers. Stripping services and charging low prices was just as successful for Morris *(2)*.

Bill Meadows used a no-frills operation. Bill had no background in horticulture; his only agricultural experience was operating a roadside vegetable stand in the summers. Then Bill got the idea to establish a discount price nursery, and Meadows Farms in Virginia was born. Bill's cheap prices were possible because he stripped away the standard guarantees, hired cheap labor to tend the plants, and bought big volumes of plants at reduced prices from other growers for resale. So many Bargain Hunters flocked to Meadow Farms that Bill has expanded to 21 retail locations *(3)*.

Nancy's Trade-a-Book doesn't have 21 locations, but it is a thriving small business in Columbia, Missouri, using a Reduction strategy. For a small transaction fee, Nancy lets Bargain Hunters swap their used paperback books for hers. A combination of used paperbacks and reduced overhead has served Nancy's well for 13 years.

The discount lumber and home repair centers such as Home Depot, Payless Cashways, Sutherland, and Lowes battle for the Prudent Shopper core of the do-it-yourself home improvement industry. Not Hoods. Located in the cheapest locations and buildings, Hoods has completely abandoned any pretense of image; they have stripped away all customer service; they stock only very cheap products such as factory overruns, products purchased at auctions, and stripped-down products. No attempt is made at merchandising, so Bargain Hunters shop in the atmosphere of a disorganized garage sale, which makes finding the bargain sort of like finding an Easter Egg in a clump of weeds. Hoods spares all expense, so all sales are final — handling returns would raise costs. Prices are *c-h-e-a-p, c-h-e-a-p, c-h-e-a-p,* but low-income customers, rental property owners, and other bargain hunters flock to Hoods.

During the 1980s, San Diego Design, a West Coast Furniture Manufacturer, sold huge tractor/trailer loads of standardized entertainment centers to retailers all across America. At the same time a small manufacturer, Arkansas Woodworks of Russellville, Arkansas, sold stripped down, look-alike entertainment centers. They shipped their furniture in a 24-foot trailer built at a local sheet metal shop and served retailers within a 250-mile radius of their plant to minimize freight costs. While San Diego Design's unit had all the bells and whistles like doors, drawers, TV swivels, and wheels, Arkansas Woodworks built open systems designed to let the customers display their attractive electronic gear. While San Diego Design purchased huge containers of supplies direct from Asian manufacturers at specially negotiated prices, Arkansas Woodworks purchased full bundles of wood from a wholesaler in Fort Smith, Arkansas, at a little off list price. San Diego Design went bankrupt; Arkansas Woodworks, using a Reduction strategy, didn't.

Key Success Factors for the Reduction Strategy

A Reduction Competitive Strategy is usually easier than an Enhancement Strategy for the owner/manager of a new small business to use. Employees need fewer skills, the business needs less equipment and less-expensive locations, and managers need fewer special competencies. Customers are less critical because they have reduced expectations about used products, very cheap products, or stripped-down products. They also have reduced expectations about the level of assistance they will receive from managers and employees.

However, the success of the Reduction strategy, like any competitive strategy, depends on the business's ability to build three types of strategic superiority:

- Sales Triggers
- Cost Controllers
- Competition Limiters

A Reduction strategy's keys to success are easy to grasp, easy to use, and all related.

Cheap Price — Key Success Factor that Triggers Sales

A cheap price is the major KSF that triggers sales. The price of a product or service is cheap *relative* to the low price of the standardized, high-volume product sold by the Low-Cost leader who controls the center of the market.

Cheap is determined by the amount of product, service, personnel, and image that's stripped away. For example, used cars are cheap relative to new cars, but there are markets for both $20,000 used cars with relatively few reductions in features and service life and $500 used cars with relatively huge reductions in features and service life. Bargain Hunters, like Selective Shoppers, are easily divided into customer segments according to their price and reduction sensitivities. What's perceived as cheap will depend on the expectations and desires of each segment of Bargain Hunters. Therefore, one segment of Bargain Hunters considers 1- to 3-year-old used cars cheap, another considers 4- to 6-year-old cars cheap, and another considers still older cars cheap.

Generic products are an example of reduction products. They are cheap relative to low-price products; however, generics are perceived as good products whose prices are very low because of reduced brand image and guarantees.

What's cheap is determined by your customer segment. Making the correct reductions and still satisfying your chosen target segment creates success. The correct reduction mix supports a cheap price while still giving customers what they want. Determining the correct reduction mix of product, service, personnel, and image is the principle job of the manager of a small business. The correct reduction mix is the SSF that allows the firm to charge cheap prices while still giving the customer sufficient value to trigger the sale.

Key Success Factors that Control Cost

The Low-Cost strategy's big cost advantages are gained through economy of scale, learning curve, and experience curve savings. However, the Reduction strategy's sales volume isn't large enough to accrue many economy of scale and learning and experience curve cost cuts; it targets fewer customers and doesn't generate sufficient sales volumes. A Reduction strategy depends on you stripping away additional portions of the product, service, personnel, and image factors to achieve big cost savings. Therefore, identifying and stripping away the most costly but least wanted portions of the four factors will slash costs and not hurt sales to your segment of Bargain Hunters.

Any of the following four factors or combinations of these four factors may be cost-controlling KSFs for your Reduction business.

Product Reductions that Control Costs

The factors that control the cost of a Reduction Competitive Strategy are the same factors that formed sales triggers for the Enhancement Competitive Strategy.

Performance Reduction. Performance is the major benefit of a product, and normally the most costly to provide. Therefore, finding acceptable ways to reduce product performance is frequently a KSF that controls costs. For example, a paint's coverage and blemish-hiding performance are reduced when costly ingredients such as titanium dioxide, pigments, and latex adhesive are reduced. The poorer paint's performance is acceptable to Bargain Hunters who only want a short-lived improvement in the appearance of their rented apartments in order to recover their rental deposits. A departing renter hardly cares about the 10-year performance of the paint, just let it last long enough to cash the landlord's check.

Here are some common examples of how the performance and costs of many products are reduced to make cheaper products:

- Smaller motors are used in cheap cars, trucks, airplanes, powertools, microwave ovens, and kitchen appliances.
- Noisier, less expensive motors are used in cheap ceiling fans.
- Color stability is reduced in cheaper clothes, and they fade more.
- Anti-corrosion undercoatings are eliminated on cheap vehicles.
- Operating efficiency is sacrificed when producing cheaper central air conditioners and heaters.
- Biodegradability isn't designed into cheap diapers.
- Weaker steel is used in cheap tools, and they break easier.
- Less labor and skill go into producing cheap shoes.
- Less precision is engineered into cheap razors.
- Older technologies are used in cheap dishwashers, requiring customers to do more pre-rinsing.
- Inexpensive fabric goes into cheap lingerie.
- Less user-friendly systems are used in cheap computer software programs.

Features Reduction. Features are frequently reduced to form a KSF that controls costs because Bargain Hunters expect cheap products to have fewer benefits. For example, big furniture manufacturers make fancy furniture with doors, drawers, glass, tambour, arches, swivels, and rollers. Small firms strip many of these expensive features to make simple, cheap look-a-likes which serve the same purpose, but are much less costly to produce.

Furniture is stained and varnished — well, not all of it. In the unfinished furniture industry, which is dominated by small manufacturers, stain and varnish are mere features to be eliminated for Bargain Hunters. Small furniture manufacturers often make nude or unfinished furniture in inexpensive, no-frills facilities. These small firms not only avoid the high cost of chemical finishes and finishing labor, but they escape the high investment costs required to add stain rooms, spray booths, and moisture-controlled drying rooms. They escape emissions inspections by OSHA and safety inspections by insurance companies and fire departments. They escape a multitude of compliance expenses. In this industry, feature reduction is a major cost-controlling KSF that allows the firms to charge the cheap prices that trigger sales.

The late Mr. Bich is famous for his Reduction strategy. Bich founded and grew the huge Bic Corporation by making cheap, reduced-feature versions of prestige products-knockoffs. Bich gave Bargain Hunters a stripped down plastic pen as an alternative to the fancy fountain pen, a stripped down 25-cent plastic razor as an alternative to the fancy chrome razor, and a stripped down plastic cigarette lighter as an alternative to the fancy metal lighters.

Reliability Reduction. Reliability is often reduced to form a KSF that controls costs. For example, power tools used by professionals have to be highly reliable, but the tool's reliability can be greatly reduced for homeowners who only occasionally use the tool. Homeowners who buy cheap power tools won't blame the product when it breaks after only 100 hours of use because it takes them 10 years to accumulate 100 hours of use. Hey, a tool that lasts 10 years is great!

Like the power tool market, many markets contain heavy product users, moderate users, and light users. Reliability is frequently reduced in products targeted to light users who only occasionally use the product, and, therefore, won't pay a lot of money for it and tend to be Bargain Hunters.

Consistency Reduction. Consistency from product to product is also reduced, especially for light-use or occasional-use customers. These customers usually don't possess enough product experience to recognize a reduced level of consistency from product to product, and they may not care.

Service Reductions that Control Costs

When searching for services to reduce to cut costs, study the Low-Cost firms in your market. You are looking for services they provide that your customers will allow you to reduce.

Free Labor. Free labor can significantly lower costs. Free customer labor is often substituted for employee labor in a no-frills business to form a KSF that controls costs. For example, instead of employees filling out the paperwork, customers can do it. Instead of employees writing up the customer's order, customers can do it. Instead of waiters and waitresses serving customers, customers can serve themselves and clean up after themselves too. Customers can bag groceries, fill their own gas tanks, wash their own car windows, carry their own luggage, and print their own copies on the copy machine then report the number of copies they made to the cashier. Customers can spend their time listening to the business's recorded phone options instead of talking to a knowledgeable trained receptionist. Lots of work done for customers by employees in other businesses can be done by customers themselves in Reduction businesses — free labor.

Stripping Services. Stripping services to form a KSF to control costs means more than just going from full-service to self-service, it includes reducing, eliminating, or charging for services such as:

- credit
- deliveries
- installation
- assembly
- merchandise returns
- adjustments
- repairs
- gift wrapping

Location. Location of the business greatly affects overhead costs. A no-frills business often forms a KSF that controls cost by choosing a less convenient, less attractive, less accessible, inexpensive location. Yet, this does not hurt sales because Bargain Hunters are conditioned to expect cheap prices in out-of-the-way locations. In fact, they search for them.

Cost-Effective Scheduling. Cost-effective scheduling can be used to form a KSF that controls costs by methods that seem unfair, much like the unfair scheduling used to increase productivity in firms using a Flexibility Strategy. A no-frills, Reduction Strategy firm schedules all customer work to achieve the lowest overall costs. Therefore, all similar jobs, orders, and delivery locations are grouped together to minimize the cost of switching from one type of job to the next. Customers should be reminded constantly that cost-efficient scheduling is used to keep prices cheap.

Personnel Reductions that Control Costs

Low Skilled Employees. Personnel reduction controls cost by operating the business with employees who have less work skills, experience, training, education, and social skills. Personnel reduction, the opposite of personnel enhancement, can cut costs significantly because less skilled employees are paid less, and payroll is normally a large part of any small firm's total costs.

To compensate for the reduction in employee skills, the workplace must be redesigned to overcome the employees' shortcomings. The physical work environment is organized so that experienced supervisors can maintain direct, visible, or audible control over less talented employees. Policies are carefully established to constrain and limit employee activities, behaviors, and decisions. Employees are trained to recognize which problems are routine and which are not routine. They are given guidelines for solving routine problems and are instructed to give non-routine problems to the trained supervisor. The supervisor solves all unusual and complex problems.

Finally, to cut costs further, many of the jobs are filled with part-time employees who receive no benefits.

Image Reductions that Control Costs

Prestige and status reductions cut costs simply by avoiding the expense of establishing an image. For example, McDonald's has spent lavishly on promotional campaigns, first to build up its family image, and more recently to create an image which would appeal to adults. By contrast, Rally Restaurants simply didn't spend those big bucks on promotional campaigns in order to control costs and support cheap prices.

Using a Combination of Reductions to Control Costs

Often all four types of reductions are combined to aggressively slash costs. Whittier Furniture provides a good example of combinations of reductions. It makes unfinished furniture (product reduction) that is unassembled (service reduction that substitutes free customer labor), and Whittier does no consumer advertising (image reduction). The combination supports cheap prices for good, solid furniture.

The Key Success Factor that Limits Competition

The same principles of customer targeting that were extensively presented in the Enhancement Competitive Strategy chapter apply to targeting segments of Bargain Hunters. Those principles begin with identifying and describing the customer segment being targeted, communicating to the segment, getting feedback from the segment, revising the description of the segment, revising the firm's knowledge of the trends and needs of the segment, and repeating the steps over and over. Please refer back to Chapter 4 if a targeting and customer feedback review is needed.

Reduction Strategy Limitations

Your success can create its own limitations. A successful Reduction business quickly attracts new competitors because businesses using this strategy are inexpensive to establish. New entrants can lead to an excess of competition, which limits growth and profits. For example, every community goes through cycles of too many and too few makers of cheap cabinets. When too few makers of plain, stripped down cabinets exist, prices climb and profits soar. At this point, employees from existing cabinet shops, employees from home construction companies, or guys that have built good home woodworking shops soon launch into business for themselves and begin to cut prices to establish their new businesses. With each new startup business, the already cheap market prices are pushed down until low profits and high operating costs cause losses and force some firms to shut their doors. Then the cycle begins again because a Reduction market is easy to exit as well as easy to enter.

Ease of entry often encourages new competitors to start up, which threatens the profits of existing businesses. Ease of entry ruined the once lucrative video rental business. Early video store owners enjoyed good sales and profits. Their video customers paid a $25 per year membership fee to belong to the video club in addition to rental fees for videotapes and equipment. The up-front membership fees were used to buy additional videos to rent to the new customers. An enviable situation — new customers providing a business with the cash flow it needs to serve them. Unfortunately, ease of entry encouraged lots of new video rental competitors to start up. As competition heated up, membership fees disappeared and rental fees dropped, causing profits to plunge. Overnight, most of the original video store businesses, saddled with high overhead for premiere locations, closed their doors. The original owners might have been more cautious about the long-term expenses they were incurring if they had considered how ease of entry might eventually affect them.

Ease of entry can sometimes be limited by signing exclusive agreements with suppliers, so new entrants don't have access to needed supplies. New entrants can also be discouraged by hiding some of the visible signs of a small business's success. Perhaps it's best for a Reduction business owner or manager to claim hard times even in the best of times.

Success can also lessen the owner's motivation to struggle with costs, to put up with spartan offices, and to deliberately operate a frugal, tight-budget organization. However, the day the owner parks a new Cadillac out front is the day employees line up for raises, suppliers announce price increases, and a new competitor springs up.

CHAPTER 8

Constructing a Competitive Model

Applying What You've Learned

CONSTRUCTING A MODEL OF YOUR small business's competitive strategy and Key Success Factors is the best way to conclude the first half of this book. Instead of reading several summarizing pages or concluding remarks, your assignment is to put all you've learned to work by building a competitive model of your business in your mind or on paper.

Taking pen in hand and actually writing down your business vision isn't necessary. Strategic visions that include competitive strategies, target customer descriptions, Key Success Factors, and more, can be mentally formulated and used to guide decision making. Nevertheless, written plans have advantages. First, the process of writing a plan forces you to clarify your thinking, to realize precisely what you know and don't know, and to focus your energy on collecting any missing information that could ensure your success. Second, committing a plan to writing greatly improves your ability to communicate your strategic vision to those people whose help is vital in achieving your vision. A written plan is easier for employees, managers, suppliers, loan officers, and potential investors to understand, implement, and consistently support.

Still, a strategic plan that exists only in your mind is quite workable. First try completing the following model in your head, after which you can consider drawing up a formal model.

A Key Success Factor Model

Your first model-building task is to complete the Key Success Factor Model, shown in Figure 8.1, for your business. First, you must identify your chosen competitive strategy.

This is the point where many owners and managers of small businesses realize they don't have a clear vision guiding their choice of products and services. Suddenly, managers realize they don't have a concise mental image that describes all the things they offer. The description of their competitive position takes more space than that short line in Figure 8.1 allows. Perhaps the business has some enhanced products, stacked next to low-priced products, all placed across from a bargain bin of cheap sales items. Or, maybe your business offers a wide range of low-scale to high-scale products and services, making it hard to form a concise mental picture of the few, general benefits offered to customers.

FIGURE 8.1: Key Success Factor Model

Key Success Factor Model

Competitive Strategy ______________________________

Target Customer Segment ______________________________

____

____

____

Key Success Factors

Sales Triggers

KSF 1: ______________________________

KSF 2: ______________________________

KSF 3: ______________________________

KSF 4: ______________________________

Cost Controllers

KSF 1: ______________________________

KSF 2: ______________________________

Or, maybe your business has elements of several different competitive strategies. But does it really matter if you can't form a clear vision about your firm's competitive purpose?

Unfortunately, the lack of a concise vision around which to mold and construct a business profoundly affects customers. Customers are busy people, and as studies show, they increasingly feel rushed and short on time. Customers size up a business by listening to friends and co-workers, viewing advertising messages and promotions, getting a strong hint about the business from its location, viewing its product assortment and mix of services, judging the business's atmosphere and pricing. Customers put all this together into a short, descriptive image of the business, and they store that image in their memories. When they need or want a product or service, they match up their needs with their images of various businesses, and they go to the one they think will fill their need. For example, customers have formed and stored a mental image of Wal-Mart as having "everyday low prices" for "good, ordinary, standard products." So, customers go there when that description fits the items they want to purchase.

Jiffy Lube is "a fast place to get your oil changed." McDonald's serves "good, fast, low-priced food in a clean, convenient facility." Such images stored in customers' minds guide their decisions. If customers need a quick oil and filter change, they know where to go. If customers are on vacation and want to get off the Interstate Highway for a quick meal, they know where to go. Customers use their mental images comparing various businesses to guide their shopping decisions. Customers need to be able to form a clear mental image of your business if they are to include your business in their shopping plans. If you can't easily identify a dominant operating strategy that separates your business from your competitors, you can be sure your customers are confused about your business. And, *if you confuse customers, you lose customers.*

Also, keep in mind that competitive strategies aren't about individual products and services. Competitive strategies describe your overall, general products and services, not the exceptions. For example, Wal-Mart may have a few items that aren't consistent with its Low-Cost Competitive Strategy, but those are the exceptions. Wal-Mart's use of a Low-Cost Competitive Strategy has been consistent enough that customers have formed a clear mental image that guides their shopping decisions. Your goal is to consistently use your competitive strategy to plant the right mental image of your business in the minds of your target customers.

Returning to Figure 8.1, next describe your target customers. The more descriptive details you know about your target customers, the more space you'll need to describe them.

Next, identify, *in the order of importance,* the few critical factors that trigger sales to your target customers. If you serve several customer segments, complete

FIGURE 8.2: Example Key Success Factor Model

Little Italy Frozen Food Company
Key Success Factor Model

Competitive Strategy *Enhancement Strategy*

Target Customer Segment *Busy lovers of gourmet Italian food who need the convenience of frozen foods. Customers are time-starved, high % are dual income couples, socially active, and live in the N.E. U.S.*

Key and Support Success Factors

Sales Triggers

KSF 1: *Product Quality (taste and attractive appearance)*

KSF 2: *Distribution (to attain shelf space advantages)*

KSF 3: *Packaging (to trigger in-store impulse sales)*

KSF 4: *Advertising & Promotion (to build brand and company image)*

SSF 1: *5% Pricing rule — Prices must be maintained at 5% above industry averages for comparable products to maintain a high-quality image.*

SSF 2: *Product development — Nine new products are targeted for development in the next three years (see attached budgets).*

SSF 3: *Sales training — Each new sales representative will travel with an experienced sales person for 30 days and pass an oral product and services examination, before being assigned a territory.*

Cost Controllers

KSF 1: *TQC (to minimize waste and maximize efficiency)*

KSF 2: *Financial budget system (to control the cost of Enhancement projects).*

a model for each segment because different factors trigger sales to different segments. Finally, identify your major cost-controlling systems.

After your first attempt at completing Figure 8.1, you'll probably discover it's harder than you think. It may take some weeks or months to accurately complete a satisfactory business model that you can enthusiastically defend, but along the way, you'll better understand your customers and their needs.

Figure 8.2 demonstrates a sample Key Success Factor model for a small frozen food producer. Pay close attention to the sales trigger KSFs in Figure 8.2; after each KSF the continuous improvement goals are provided to identify exactly how each KSF is to be continually enhanced or improved to trigger additional sales growth. The sales trigger KSFs are listed in their order of importance, so KSF 1 is more important than KSF 2 which is more important that KSF 3, etc. However, we don't know how much more important KSF 1 is than KSF 2; it could be a little more important or five times more important. The more important a KSF, the more effort you must expend improving it.

Figure 8.2 provides an example of a KSF model that has been expanded to include important Support Success Factors (SSFs) and their support levels. Identifying the support level of a factor or activity keeps the firm from overspending or straying from its winning success formula. Improving these factors above the support level won't trigger more sales. Also, establishing support levels keeps these factors from diminishing and harming sales.

Figure 8.3 shows a second Key Success Factor model example for a rent-to-own retail business. Notice the target customer description. Even though some rentals are expected from fraternity houses and some big screen TVs are expected to be rented for parties and pay-per-view neighborhood get-togethers in more affluent parts of town, the target customer description ignores these fringe groups and focuses on the major segment of customers the firm has chosen to serve. This is where the bulk of sales will be made if the firm is successful.

Constructing a model like Figures 8.1, 8.2, or 8.3 helps you to focus on what isn't known about target customers, sales triggers, and controlling costs. Constructing a model will motivate you to gather more information, watch customers more closely, ask more questions, send out customer questionnaires, and read magazines, like *American Demographics*, to improve your ability to identify and describe your target customers. You'll start questioning customers specifically about their main reasons for buying products and about what influence various marketing factors and product attributes have on their purchase decisions. You'll form theories about sales triggers (KSFs) and supporting factors (SSFs) and indicators of performance, and you'll test your theories. You'll study the cost-controlling techniques of successful businesses. You'll form a new set of questions for suppliers, friendly competitors, and trade association

FIGURE 8.3: Example Key Success Factor Model

Rent to Own Furniture and Appliance Key Success Factor Model

Competitive Strategy *Enhancement Strategy*

Target Customer Segment *Low income households with limited access to credit. Primary target customers are in the Brewer area bounded by Walnut, Hickory, 2nd, and 31st streets.*

Key and Support Success Factors

Sales Triggers

KSF 1: *Easy credit — Credit is approved on the basis of the customer's likelihood of staying in the community, so we can repossess the merchandise if they fall behind in payments.*

KSF 2: *Low weekly payments — Customers are more concerned with the amount of payments than the number of payments.*

KSF 3: *Fast deliveries — Same day delivery and installation.*

SSF 1: *Merchandise — Equivalent to Low-Cost strategy furniture and appliance stores, which are good products, but not the best.*

SSF 2: *Advertising — 60% of yearly budget will be used to increase customer awareness of the store. 20% will target slow-moving merchandise. 20% will fund contests to build direct mailing lists.*

Cost Controllers

KSF 1: *Financial Budget System — Every functional area is budgeted, monitored, and controlled.*

representatives. The process of constructing a model of your business can help you become a better decision-maker.

A Simple Competitive Model

Since customers have to choose between competing stores, competing products, and competing services, you would like to build a simple model that resembles the customers' decision-making process. This would primarily be a way of looking at the business from the customers' point of view and measuring the appeal or strength of each competitor's sales triggers. With a little embellishment, the simple model can be slightly expanded to identify each competitor's *relative* targeting and cost-controlling strengths and weaknesses which can guide a manager's improvement plans. Toward this objective, the Key Success Factor Model in Figure 8.1 is now upgraded to become a Simple Competitive Model in Figure 8.4 that compares all "real" competitors' KSFs — remember, "real" competitors are those targeting the same customers with the same competitive strategy. When a "real" competitor makes a sale, you lose a sale.

A Simple Competitive Model, such as the one found in Figure 8.4, cannot be constructed until the Key Success Factor Model in Figure 8.1 is finished, because the Simple Competitive Model uses the KSFs from the previous model. Simple Competitive Models are a lot more work because they require gathering detailed information about competitors, which is a difficult and time-consuming task. Constructing a Simple Competitive Model requires such things as conversations with customers about their competitive choices, asking suppliers' representatives to compare your business and its products and services to your competitors, talking to bankers, questioning trade association representatives, and being prepared with the right KSF questions should a competitor's employee apply for a job.

The Simple Competitive Model in Figure 8.4 compares three firms: "Our Firm," Competitor A, and Competitor B. Assume this is a local market with three real competitors, and the manager has identified the KSFs that trigger sales by completing a Key Success Factor model. After collecting as much information as possible on each competitor's strengths, a manager subjectively assigns "Superior," "Good," and "Weak" ratings to represent the best educated guess about each firm's relative strengths.

In Figure 8.4, each competitor's targeting expertise is rated in the "Targeting Strength" section. "Our Firm" was rated Superior (S) while both competitors were rated Good (G) because "Our Firm" is believed to have a better understanding of target customers. For example, "Our Firm" has developed a good direct mailing list, a good demographic profile of target customers and a

FIGURE 8.4: A Simple Competitive Model

A Simple Competitive Model

Competitive Strategy *Enhancement*

Customer Segment (Targeted by all competitors)* *Dual income households with $40,000+ combined income in the Aberdeen shopping area.*

Rating of Targeting Strength

Our Firm = S
Competitor A = G
Competitor B = G

Key Success Factors

		Ratings	
	Our Firm	**Competitor A**	**Competitor B**
Sales Triggers			
KSF 1: *Product Performance*	*S*	*G*	*G*
KSF 2: *Store Image*	*G*	*S*	*S*
KSF 3: *Personal Selling Skill (i)*	*S*	*G*	*G*
KSF 4: *Advertising/Promotion*	*S*	*W*	*G*
Cost Controllers			
KSF 1: *Strict Budgets*	*S*	*W*	*G*
KSF 2: *TQM*	*G*	*NA*	*S*

**The businesses rated are as follows:*
Our Firm
Competitor A
Competitor B

***The rating system used is as follows:*
S = Superior Competitive Strength
G = Good Competitive Strength
W = Weak Competitive Strength
NA = Not Available
(i) = Indicator of Performance

good understanding of customers' media habits. This relative strength advantage will be used by "Our Firm" to get feedback from target customers to guide further sales trigger enhancements. If new customer trends emerge, customer feedback will allow "Our Firm" to spot them first.

The sales trigger section of Figure 8.4 is the heart of the Simple Competitive Model. This section tries to duplicate the few most important comparisons the typical customer makes when deciding which of the three firms to buy from. The most important sales trigger is enhanced product performance. Customers' buying decisions are most influenced by getting the exact product improvements they want, and "Our Firm" scored superior because it has the largest variety of the most wanted enhancement choices. Next, customers sales are influenced by store image and prestige and Competitors A and B each scored a "Superior," while "Our Firm" only scored a "Good" because "Our Firm" has been reluctant to match the large expenditures made by Competitors A and B to enhance their images.

Personal Selling Skill, KSF 3, is the third most important sales trigger. However personal selling skill can be a KFS for different reasons. Personal selling can be a KSF because customers need a salesperson to explain each product's performance and to help match customer needs to the right product choice. Personal selling can be a KSF if it is used to skillfully close sales. Or, personal selling can be a KSF because it is a vitally important indicator of performance. "Our Firm" has determined that personal selling skill is primarily an indicator of performance, thus it has enhanced the traits of its sales force to more effectively signal enhanced performance. The (i) at the end of "Personal Selling Skill (i)" is used to denote it's an *indicator*. "Our Firm" scored a superior. Furthermore, "Our Firm" doesn't believe that competitors truly understand the real role of personal selling skills in this market.

Finally, "Our Firm" scored another superior for KSF 4, Advertising/ Promotion. This superiority is the result of "Our Firm's" vast customer knowledge that allows it to reach more target customers with effective promotions.

Two cost-controlling KSFs were scored. Competitor B and "Our Firm" use strict budgets more effectively, and Competitor B has a stronger TQM program. Competitor B is the best at controlling costs to generate a good profit, which gives them the best opportunity to use those profits to overcome their current KSF weaknesses. Competitor B appears to be "Our Firm's" closest threat, and they must be watched more closely than Competitor A.

Overall, "Our Firm" has the most "Superior" rated sales triggers. This is an overall rating system and doesn't mean that each and every product or service in "Our Firm's" store is superior to the competitors'. Also, both competitors have spent more money enhancing their image, and target customers do value the prestige and status that image creates. This explains why competitors have good sales volumes.

The Simple Competitive Model is a snapshot of today's relative strengths and weaknesses. Tomorrow's strengths and weaknesses will be determined by the firm that makes the best enhancement decisions and the wisest investments today. The more you know about which factors you must continuously improve, the more likely that your firm will make the right choices, resulting in a long-term competitive advantage. By constructing a Simple Competitive Model, you'll identify which competitive weaknesses you need to overcome and which competitive strengths you need to protect.

Complex Competitive Models

Until you've completed the first two models, and that will take a good while, this section should be skipped or at least read over quickly. Model making can get complicated, much more complicated than even this section would suggest. However, sometimes there are reasons to go to the trouble to build more and more realistic models of a business and its interaction with customers and competitors.

One type of Complex Model is a weighted and scored model which more accurately depicts both customers' decision making and the relative strengths of competitors. Let's make a weighted and scored model of just the sales trigger

FIGURE 8.4: A Simple Competitive Model

Key Success Factors

		Ratings		
		Our Firm	**Competitor A**	**Competitor B**
Sales Triggers				
KSF 1:	*Product Performance*	*S*	*G*	*G*
KSF 2:	*Store Image*	*G*	*S*	*S*
KSF 3:	*Personal Selling Skill (i)*	*S*	*G*	*G*
KSF 4:	*Advertising/Promotion*	*S*	*W*	*G*

section of the previous simple competitive model. First, let's bring back just the Sales Trigger section of Figure 8.4.

Next, let's convert the superior-good-weak (S-G-W) rating system to a numerical scoring system using these guidelines:

Previous Rating	New Score
Superior	10 or 9
Good	8 or 7
Weak	6 or less

By using numerical scores, we can have different levels of Superior, Good, and Weak. Similar to the difference in school between making an "A" with 90% or an "A" with 98%, we can now make finer distinctions between relative business strengths. Of course, we'll have to collect more accurate information to do so.

Now, suppose "Our Firm's" manager has subjectively converted the sales trigger ratings to numerical scores to more accurately depict the differences between the three firms.

Next, suppose that KSF 1 is still more important than KSF 2, but the manager feels that importance is marginal. In other words, these two have almost the same impact on customer decision making. However, the manager of "Our Firm" is sure that KSF 1 and KSF 2 are twice as important as KSF 3 and KSF 4, and KSF 3 and KSF 4 are almost equal in importance.

These assumptions can be used to make a weighted average score that better represents customers' real decision-making process. To do this, just multiple

FIGURE 8.5: Comparing Sales Trigger Comparisons

Key Success Factors

		Ratings		
		Our Firm	Competitor A	Competitor B
Sales Triggers				
KSF 1:	*Product Performance*	*9*	*8*	*8*
KSF 2:	*Store Image*	*8*	*9*	*10*
KSF 3:	*Personal Selling Skill (i)*	*9*	*7*	*8*
KSF 4:	*Advertising/Promotion*	*9*	*6*	*8*

FIGURE 8.6: Scoring Competitive Sales Triggers

Key Success Factors

			Ratings	
		Our Firm	**Competitor A**	**Competitor B**
Sales Triggers				
KSF 1:	*Product Performance*	*9 x 2 = 18*	*8 x 2 = 16*	*8 x 2 = 16*
KSF 2:	*Store Image*	*8 x 2 = 16*	*9 x 2 = 18*	*10 x 2 = 20*
KSF 3:	*Personal Selling Skill (i)*	*9 x 1 = 9*	*7 x 1 = 7*	*8 x 1 = 8*
KSF 4:	*Advertising/Promotion*	*9 x 1 = 9*	*6 x 1 = 6*	*8 x 1 = 8*
	Grand Score	*52*	*47*	*52*

the KSF 1 and KSF 2 score by 2 because their scores are twice as important as the other two, then we'll add up a total score for each competitor (see Figure 8.6).

The results are quite different from those shown in the Simple Competitive Model. By scoring each KSF from 1 to 10, by weighting each KSF according to how important it is believed to be, and by adding up a grand score, "Our Firm" and Competitor B are now tied in the customers' minds. Don't forget, Competitor B had better cost-controlling techniques and should have better profits. The whole competitive relationship is altered.

A Complex Model is important in certain situations. In the beginning, a manager constructs a Simple Competitive Model to help guide decisions about which KSFs to improve in order to maintain a competitive advantage. Suppose the manager of "Our Firm" discovers by talking to suppliers that "Our Firm" and Competitor B have roughly the same level of sales, even though the two have quite different sales trigger strengths. This is not consistent with what would be expected from the Simple Competitive Model. The manager might then feel a compelling need to build a more complex model that might explain this more complicated relationship before deciding which sales trigger KSFs to improve and by how much.

This is exactly why more and more complicated models are built. The Key Success Factor Model is built because it improves a manager's ability to operate the business. The Simple Competitive Model is built because it improves a manager's ability to control competitive rivalry. A Simple Competitive Model tells a manager which crucial factors are relatively weak and must be improved and which are relatively strong and must be maintained — this information guides budget decisions. A Complex Competitive Model is built *only if* the Simple Competitive Model doesn't answer all the important, competitive questions, and the manager believes that getting the answers is worth the additional trouble. If you ever build a complex model, it will be after you have completed the first two models, have gained great benefits from the first two models, and believe you can gain even greater benefits by building a complex model.

If you attempt a complex weighted and scored model, keep in mind that the weights are arbitrary. You can assign any weight you think best describes the situation. For example, you might decide KSF 1 is five times more important than KSF 4, then you'd multiple the KSF 1 score by 5. Your weighting decision is a profound decision because it should affect budgets for improvement projects. If KSF 1 is five times more important than KSF 4 in triggering sales, it should get more funding for continuous improvements. As you can see, model building can and should affect the way a business is run. The more accurate the model, the more profound its affect on a manager's decision-making.

A word of caution, if you decide to construct a Complex Model, never combine targeting, sales trigger, and cost controller KSF scores into an overall grand score. Always analyze each area separately, because each area represents a different type of short- and long-term competitive advantage. First, the competitor with the best "targeting strength" KSF score will have a big advantage in spotting emerging customer trends and in knowing when to make changes. This competitor is likely to become the market leader in the future.

Second, the competitor with the best "sales trigger" KSF score should be able to generate the most immediate sales — a big advantage in building long-term customer loyalty.

Third, the competitor with the best "cost-controlling" KSF score should be able to generate the most profits to invest in improving any KSF weaknesses. Analyzing the relative strengths and weaknesses in each of these three competitive areas gives managers a more complete understanding of their competitive position than comparing grand scores.

Even sales trigger grand scores like those just calculated for "Our Firm" and its two competitors make sense only part of the time. Such grand scores should be used only when customer decision making is compensatory. Compensatory means the customer considers both the benefits and negative consequences from each sales trigger and buys the best overall competitive product or service. In this case, a firm's KSF weakness can be overcome by its KSF strengths.

For example, customers make compensatory purchasing decisions when they buy complex items like automobiles, cameras, and stereo systems. When buying an automobile, the customer shops around and compares each vehicle's pluses and minuses. The customer will like some product attributes on any one car, and dislike other attributes. A dislike can be offset, or compensated for, by the features the customer likes a lot. So, good styling, good gas mileage, and a low price may offset a small trunk and a poor stereo. While the customer doesn't like the small trunk and inexpensive stereo, the attractive features compensate for the unattractive features. If you're selling products or services where the customer's decision-making process is a compensatory process — they add up pluses and minuses — making a model with a grand sales trigger score is useful because it best resembles the thought process used by customers.

Non-compensatory means the customer doesn't add up the plus and minus benefits of each competitive product or service, so a model that provides a grand sales trigger score wouldn't resemble the customers' thought pattern. Non-compensatory purchases are usually for less complex items, like women's shoes. A woman may go into a store planning to purchase a pair of shoes that matches her dress. If she finds three different pairs that match the dress color, she may then decide to buy the pair that is the most comfortable. If two pairs are equally comfortable, she may then decide to buy the pair that's least expensive.

As this example shows, a non-compensatory purchase is most often triggered solely by the top priority sales trigger. If the woman had only found one pair of shoes matching the color of her dress, she would have bought those shoes and never considered the next sales triggers. If customers' purchasing decisions are normally controlled by one or two very important KSF sales triggers, and if the decision is only occasionally influenced by other, minor, KSFs then a four-KSF model with a grand sales trigger score shouldn't be used. Each sales trigger should be examined individually.

This will undoubtedly confuse readers who have never thought of making a KSF model of any type, but the point is that sales trigger models are meant to mirror the decision-making process of customers. If customers value some benefits more than others, or if customers value some benefits only in certain situations, the model must be designed to reflect those troublesome realities. Now you see why this section is titled "Complex Competitive Models." Complex models can get darn complex.

CHAPTER 9

Competitive Strategy Limitations

BEFORE LAUNCHING INTO GROWTH strategies, a few black holes need to be navigated. First, how are organizations and businesses without competitors affected by the concept of competitive strategies? Second, since all businesses exist in a market stage that can be described either as emerging, growing, mature, declining, or dying, how does each market stage affect the use of each competitive strategy? These issues are briefly examined before we shift to stimulating your sales and boosting your profits.

Competitive Strategies for Businesses with No Competitors

The primary reason for you to adopt a competitive strategy is to minimize competitive rivalry by developing specialized skills, assets, and competencies that provide your business a competitive advantage with one, targeted customer type. Without competitors, owners and managers are free from the self-imposed restriction of tightly focused specialization and can concentrate on a wide variety of growth strategies. They can choose to provide as many different groups of customers with as many products and services as they find economically feasible, or choose to provide general products and services for all customers and avoid targeting the specific needs of various groups of customers. However, not having competitors is not the same as not expecting competitors. A business in an emerging market may not initially have competitors, but it expects competitors and must prepare for an inevitable competitive contest for sales dollars.

However, some firms, both for-profit and not-for-profit, actually have no direct competitors. Surprisingly, this situation creates many complications for management. For example, a state association of school boards, or any other similar professional association, usually doesn't directly face competitors or expect to face competitors. Of course, there are competitors for some of the individual services the association offers members, but overall the association doesn't have competitors.

In this case, a competitive strategy isn't required to target a particular customer segment or to limit the rivalry from competing associations. The organization is free to focus on the general needs of all of its customers. However, the down side of this situation is that the firm's customers or members seldom have homogeneous needs. Customers should still be grouped into segments with similar needs and, to maximize their satisfaction, each segment's needs should be individually served. At the same time, segmenting will force the firm to develop a variety of KSFs required to trigger sales to each segment, and these triggers can be very diverse. Without competitors, the firm will likely sell to segments of Selective Shoppers, Prudent Shoppers, and Bargain Hunters. The conflicting efforts to please such diverse segments places great pressure on management to both serve each type of customer and develop ways to control many diverse costs.

Even though management doesn't face the pressure of competitors, the job of management without competitors has plenty of other complications. For instance, management often has to challenge their organization to simultaneously develop three levels of products and services — cheap, low-priced, and enhanced — to serve all three types of customers. This requires contradictory systems that stress efficiency when serving frugal customers and stress enhancements when serving selective customers. It requires contradictory assets that support different price levels without unduly burdening frugal buyers. It requires contradictory competencies that can efficiently produce a basic product or service quickly and turn around, slow down, and shift to producing an enhanced product or service. Added to these complications, costs must not only be controlled but also allocated fairly to each customer type and segment; unfortunately, cost fairness often disappears in businesses without competitors. Success still depends on management knowing what few critical factors should be improved continuously for each customer type and knowing what other factors should be maintained at support levels for each customer type and segment.

This is a complex and daunting job that no manager is prepared or trained to handle. For example, a well-run school board association targeting a wide range of customers should try to separate its membership into individual segments. Perhaps rural, suburban, and city segments each have unique product and service needs. Perhaps elementary and high school boards have unique product and service needs. Perhaps there are unique needs in poor, affluent, ethnic, or high-crime area segments. The purchasing behavior and needs of school board members in each segment will vary from some Bargain Hunter segments, to a large number of Prudent Shoppers, and to some Selective Shopper segments. Management of any business without competitors should try to serve the divergent needs of each customer type and each customer segment.

The key to serving diverse segments is good customer feedback — not from customers in general but from each customer segment. Good segment feedback is necessary to guide the development of products and services at prices fair to each. Instead of collecting customer feedback, some managers mistakenly substitute their beliefs about what products and services customers need then they direct their organization to develop and offer those new products and services to their customers. However, managers in markets without competitors should resist the temptation to dictate to customers. Monetary success is driven by customer satisfaction, and customer satisfaction cannot be maximized without the guidance of customer segments.

Managers of businesses without competitors must avoid two customer feedback traps. First, they must avoid combining all customer feedback into one, general response instead of examining feedback by segment. Soliciting general customer feedback is all right, but the responses should always be evaluated to identify the unique needs of each segment. Managers must keep in mind that products and services designed for all their customers might not please any customer segment.

Second, managers must not be fooled by inherent customer feedback limitations. As already presented, there are three types of customer feedback: basic, *articulated,* and *exotic.* When customers are asked what product and service improvements they most want, they mention only a few needs — *articulated needs.* They don't mention their *basic needs* because they assume those are already understood. They almost never mention *exotic needs* because most customers are not creative and visionary *(1).*

With the absence of visionary customer feedback to guide new product and service development, managers in markets without competitors often mistakenly assume customers don't have exotic needs because they don't express them. These managers try to fill the creative void with their own new product and service visions. However, consumer research proves that while customers don't dream up exciting product and service improvements, they are very capable of evaluating a manager's new and exciting ideas and indicating which they most value. Managers should test new ideas with customers. Without competitors, there is no excuse for management not to thoroughly test customers' responses to proposed product and service ideas with each customer segment before funding their development. In contrast, a manager in a highly competitive situation might choose to solicit less feedback and risk an occasional market mistake in order to maintain competitive secrecy, but without competitors, a failure to obtain customer segment feedback is a clear sign of management's hubris.

Finally, businesses without competitors can easily get into financial difficulties because of the "pass-it-along" attitude. Without competitors, the entire organization operates without any competitive limitations on prices, which greatly lessens every employee's resolve to control costs. This predicament can lead to bad decision making and even financial hardships because the firm's money is wasted. Managers of businesses without competitors should vigorously establish KSFs to control costs. They should adopt TQM, Just-in-Time, tight budget controls, or other cost-controlling systems to force their organizations to use resources efficiently, avoid waste, and control costs. They should strive for fair prices for each customer type and each customer segment and avoid the unfairness of one-size-fits-all thinking.

Competitive Strategies for Different Market Phases

Some businesses compete in old, well-established industries, referred to as a mature market phase. Other businesses compete in new industries, referred to as an emerging market phase. The effectiveness of competitive strategies differs by market phase.

The Emerging Market Phase

One situation without competitors is a pioneer business in an emerging industry, like the first manufacturer of an ultralight airplane, the community's first video rental store, the first computer store, or the first microbrewery. While a pioneer business has no direct competitors, it expects competitors and expects intense rivalry for customers to emerge in the future. In the beginning of a new market, a competitive strategy isn't useful because the market's standard product or service hasn't been chosen by customers, so the concept of either an enhanced product or a reduced product makes no sense. For example, the pioneer microwave oven first offered to customers was a massive machine with multiple power settings, timers, defrost cycles, and a meat probe. Of course, the standard microwave that became so popular turned out to be a small contraption with one defrost cycle and one heat cycle that was used to heat leftovers, warm coffee, and occasionally thaw frozen foods. As the microwave market was emerging, no one could have predicted what product version customers would eventually choose as the industry's standardized product, much less predict what an Enhancement or Reduction product might realistically look like. Market confusion is why alternative strategies should be formed after the marketplace chooses its low-price, standard product or service.

Emerging markets are in chaos, several product varieties will exist, and no business will know which new product version will win the hearts and minds of customers and dominate the market. Therefore, it's unwise for a business to over-commit a lot of limited resources too early in an emerging market. It's unwise to over-commit to high-volume production systems and expensive promotion campaigns because you think you have the winning product version. Most early product promotions, while promoting the pioneer firm's new product, should also stress the business's special pioneering role. This image of an innovator will be long remembered by customers as the new product and new industry undergoes many changes.

The tendency of managers of small businesses to over-commit is due to their mistaken belief that they possess some superior insight into the emerging market, when in truth, they are blind to a seldom acknowledged type of business hazard — unknown risks. Business managers face several types of known risks. They know the risks they face any time they expand a business with existing products and existing services in an established market. They can cope with the risks of expansion encountered when trying to grow in order to serve more target customers because most of the risks they face are known risks.

Also, business people face many known risks anytime they expand an existing business with new products. New product risk is usually judged by looking backwards, so, if in the past only 30 percent of new products in an existing, mature industry have been successful, a manager assumes there is only a 30 percent chance that today's new product will be successful. Constrained by known risks, managers are duly cautious.

Most managers of small businesses haven't thought about the existence of unknown risks, though they've encountered them in the past. The term "unknown risk" describes a hidden risk. Such risks can be discovered only as your business gains practical experience. For example, in the 1970s the U.S. automobile industry faced an unknown risk — they didn't know how quickly gasoline prices could escalate and affect car sales. For automakers this was an unknown risk they discovered only through experience. If gasoline price volatility had been a known risk, automakers would have developed and introduced a few gas-efficient cars in the early 1970s to protect their huge investments. This demonstrates the invisible nature of unknown risks. You don't see them, so you can't consider them. Or, as one manager described them, "unknown risks are risks you don't know you are taking."

Likewise, Sony invented the first video recorder and began a new industry; they used a BETA system because it provided the best sound and picture quality. Sony's unknown risk was that they didn't know customers would soon be able to choose between Sony's high-quality BETA and a low-priced VHS competitive system, and Sony didn't know the majority of customers would prefer a low price. (Of course, they should have, since a low price always establishes the industry standard.) As the VCR pioneer, Sony faced a lot of unknown risks, and, as is the nature of unknown risks, Sony didn't know the risks existed.

Similarly, the first video rental store owners in communities everywhere didn't understand the concept of unknown risks. They later encountered many business surprises (unknown risks) that unfortunately drove many of them out of business and some into bankruptcy.

It's important for managers to realize that the early days of any emerging market are dominated by unknown risks. No one knows what product attributes will become the standard of the industry. No one knows which of the multiple product features offered by various competitors will be the most popular among customers. No one knows what trade-offs between performance, service, personnel, and image the majority of customers will eventually accept to get a lower price. No one knows which new competitors will enter the emerging market. No one knows what new technologies will soon be invented, and, perhaps most important of all, no one knows what questions they should be asking.

When the manager of a small business in an emerging market is developing the first business plans or developing an initial business vision, he or she should accept that many unknown risks exist. Admitting the existence of unknown risks, the first business plans will be more financially cautious, which will position the new business to cope with the unknown. Successfully entering an emerging industry requires a balance of optimism and prudence. And to the point, until some of the unknown risks about customer preferences and competitive actions are discovered, it's too early to pursue any one competitive strategy.

In emerging markets, a manager should simply form a preference for one competitive strategy. Managers should know which strategy they would prefer to use as the competitive battle heats up and the new market enters a rapid growth stage. However, the preferred competitive strategy shouldn't be implemented until the industry's standardized product emerges. Until that time the firm's goal should be to maintain flexibility.

In marketing, ideal flexibility is offering a variety of new products or new services with the widest possible mix of performance, features, and services, so the firm can fully participate in helping customers evaluate a wide range of new benefits. In production, ideal flexibility is to use flexible equipment to make small runs of different product versions with a wide range of performances and features until the market sorts itself out and customers' likes and dislikes become more clearly understood. When the firm is ready to commit itself to a permanent competitive strategy, the flexible equipment is replaced with permanent production equipment as the firm implements its chosen competitive strategy.

Ideal location flexibility is for the firm to sign a short-term lease for its facilities, perhaps with an option for a long-term extension or purchase. Then, as customer location needs become clearer, the firm has the option to relocate to better satisfy customers.

Ideal distribution flexibility is achieved by using multiple distribution chains, so cheaper products will find their way to low-price retailers while enhanced, high-price products will get to specialty retailers.

Ideal flexible advertising and sales promotion is to stress the business's pioneering position and market leadership more than its new products and services. This builds name recognition and business loyalty that will eventually boost the firm's market share when industry growth accelerates.

Flexible positions are replaced with more permanent positions that establish the firm's preferred competitive strategy 1) as quickly as the customer's purchasing preferences can be understood, 2) as quickly as the strengths and weaknesses of competitors are understood, and 3) as quickly as the strengths, weaknesses, and behavior patterns of suppliers, manufacturers, distributors, and retailers are understood. Of course, ideal flexibility isn't achievable, but the business should maintain as much flexibility as possible.

Early in an emerging market, unknown risks are at their highest level. A business should maintain maximum flexibility for as long as possible. This approach helps a new business to avoid getting prematurely locked into specific products, services, images, production equipment, distributors, and promotions. Until the fog surrounding customers, competitors, and the industry's standardized product or service starts to lift, a business shouldn't commit to one competitive strategy.

The Growth Market Phase

The growth phase of an industry begins when one of the many variations of new products or services in a new industry can be identified as emerging from the pack as the most popular choice of customers. At this point in the new industry's growth, one new product or service begins to emerge as the standardized, high-volume leader. The firms producing, distributing, or retailing the winning product or service will seize the moment and move quickly to accumulate the big economy of scale, learning curve, and experience curve cost advantages that are available to the winners. These advantages will be used to further lower their price and gain a significant price advantage with Prudent Shoppers. Now, all smart competitors should choose an alternative competitive strategy and begin to distance themselves from the growing power of the firm using the Low-Cost Competitive Strategy.

The market growth phase is like the mid-point in a horse race; the initial chaos and uncertainty inimical to the emerging industry swiftly fades as customers' wants, needs, and behaviors become known, as one version of the product or service emerges from the pack. Prudent Shoppers, Selective Shoppers, and Bargain Hunters become increasingly knowledgeable about the benefits of the new industry's products and services. Industry sales accelerate and sales to each customer type and each segment increase, but sales to Prudent Shoppers grow the fastest. With overall industry growth soaring, as more and more first-time customers are attracted to the new industry, competitive rivalry is low among Enhancement and Reduction businesses because they can increase their sales without having to steal customers from competitors.

In the early growth phase of a new market, a business doesn't have to choose a competitive strategy to make a profit. However, without one, as the growth continues and the market begins to mature, any business without a competitive strategy will wobble around in the market, unfocused, seeking business from all types of customers and not develop the specific strengths to satisfy any one customer type. The unfocused firm will not develop a loyal customer base. Over time, an unfocused firm will lose the customers who want cheap products because they will buy from Low-Cost and Reduction firms. Over time, the unfocused firm will lose customers who want enhanced products because they will buy from competitors who specialized in state-of-the-art products. The unfocused firm's struggle to remain profitable will intensify throughout the growth phase, and its future will become increasingly shaky.

The Mature Market Phase

During the growth phase, most competitors experience sales growth, as lots and lots of new customers are attracted to the new industry. When overall industry sales growth slows down, the industry enters its mature phase, and it feels like someone applied the brakes. The good news is that total industry sales remain at all-time high levels, but the bad news is that sales growth stops. In the mature phase, most firms keep sales steady with replacement sales to past customers or repeat sales to current customers, as new sales to virgin customers decline significantly.

Most sales growth is now achieved by robbing customers from other businesses. Unlike the growth stage where all firms have growing sales because the market is expanding rapidly, total sales (the combined sales of all competitors) stops growing in the mature stage. Industry sales remain at a high but stagnant level, and, without industry sales growth, a business can increase its sales only by taking sales away from a competitor. Obviously, competitive rivalry greatly increases, and this combined with the faltering industry growth rate kills off the unfocused firms that didn't develop ways to minimize the effects of competitors by building a loyal customer base.

In the mature phase, firms that chose a competitive strategy and firms that developed in a fashion consistent with one of the competitive strategies are the survivors — they have developed the special skills, assets, and competencies to satisfy one customer type or segment. Competitive strategies don't have to be deliberately chosen, a clear competitive strategy can emerge from a consistent pattern of management decisions and competitive tactics without a manager or owner being aware of the existence of competitive strategies. However, deliberately choosing a competitive strategy will more likely lead to success than will leaving the matter up to chance.

Surprisingly, new opportunities for small businesses often accompany the mature market phase. Early in the mature phase is often a great time for a small business to enter a market with a Reduction Competitive Strategy. For example, Southwest Airlines entered the mature airline industry as a no-frills airline with only three planes and grew rapidly. Wal-Mart entered the mature department store industry as a discounter with only one store in the small town of Rogers, Arkansas, and grew rapidly. The stripped-down microwave appeared in the early mature phase and captured significant sales. Generic and private brand products aren't introduced until the market enters the mature phase.

One caution, industries can develop in peculiar ways, so not all competitive strategies will exist in every industry. For example, in most medical markets, customers don't want cheap or stripped down services and procedures. In addition, governments may forbid or restrict the use of some competitive strategies. The Canadian government has in the past set minimum retail prices for beer to control tax revenues, and those restrictions effectively eliminated the use of both the Reduction and the Low-Cost strategies. Therefore, Canadian brewers have had to compete on the basis of performance, service, personnel or image enhancements.

The Declining and Dying Market Phases

Some industries decline and even die. It's more common to witness the decline and death of a product or a service when a replacement product or service is introduced, but it can happen to whole industries as well.

For example, the blacksmith industry died, in comparison to the robust industry it was in 1900, when the automobile industry began. The black-and-white television industry died, for all practical purposes, as the color television industry grew. The vacuum tube industry has approached death as the transistor industry has grown. The carbon paper industry has been on life support ever since the birth of the copier industry.

However, declining sales don't automatically lead to the death of an industry. The coffee industry's sales are in decline as fewer and fewer people drink coffee, but no one believes the industry is dying, only declining to a lower plateau of industry sales. The sports fishing industry is entering a declining phase because of the nation's high divorce rate. Studies have blamed the decline on absent fathers and single mothers who aren't teaching their children to enjoy fishing, but the industry is only declining, not dying. Fishing, the industry will be glad to hear, will continue.

Competitive strategies remain viable and effective in declining industries, but this relationship isn't true for dying industries. In dying industries, the market center begins disintegrating as sales of the low-price, standardized product sag badly. Fortunately, not all the customer segments of an industry decline at the same time or same rate.

With a decaying center, the dying industry begins to resemble an emerging industry because neither has an established market core. Similar to an emerging industry, competitive strategies aren't useful if the center of the market disappears. As the standardized product dies, the structure of the market becomes weakened with the withdrawal of some major competitors and some major suppliers. As some competitors withdraw, their customers and customer segments are left for the remaining competitors. Therefore, mixed with the turmoil and chaos of terminal decline is the opportunity to refocus a small business on the few remaining profitable customer segments. At this time, the small business should carefully target the remaining profitable segments and drop unprofitable and marginally profitable ones.

For example, Arkansas Woodworks Manufacturing company, a small regional business, was able to raise prices and enjoy steady sales on one product line as the industry leaders withdrew from its market. The shrinking market left some ideal small business segments which were too small to attract large competitors but were stable and profitable because the aggressive low pricing of Low-Cost competitors had disappeared.

Firms that remain profitable during the dying phase do so by targeting the few remaining healthy customer segments and aggressively pruning away the high-cost customer segments. Unfortunately, the pruning step may mean discarding accounts where long-term friendships exist, which is difficult for many small business owners to do.

In a dying market, significantly reducing operating costs is vital to remaining profitable. A customer segment that requires expensive installations is discarded while another customer segment that doesn't involve installation is kept. Another segment is unprofitable because it requires special deliveries, and it's dropped. Sometimes customers can be separated into zones according to distance from the business. Farther-off zones that are costly to serve are dropped.

Marketing expenses frequently separate customers into profitable and unprofitable segments. In healthy industries, the expense of attracting new customers is generally five times the cost of keeping existing customers. In a dying market the cost of attracting new customers is even higher. Therefore, in a dying market a firm often drops all outside, field sales aimed at developing new accounts. Instead, the firm concentrates on serving existing customers with catalogs, 800 numbers, Internet web sites, and with only an inside sales staff. Some companies eliminate small orders and concentrate exclusively on large customers who are more cost-efficient to serve.

When a dying product's sales trends become erratic and unstable, retailers often shift to smaller suppliers who can make relatively fast and frequent deliveries. This allows the retailer to minimize the risk of getting caught with large, unsellable inventories and still not miss any sales opportunities.

In Conclusion

While competitive strategies aren't much use in emerging and dying markets, the overwhelming majority of small businesses compete in the growth and mature market phases. In these two phases competitive strategies are more effective in limiting competition because competitors are more numerous and rivalry is more intense.

Looking Forward to Growth Strategies

As you begin the growth strategy section of this book, you'll discover many new growth opportunities. The few you choose to pursue should be influenced by your competitive strengths and by your competitive weaknesses, and not by your wishful pursuit of profits. The best opportunities are those within your competitive reach, and your reach is determined by the skills, assets, and competencies that your business develops by implementing its competitive strategy. As you identify new growth opportunities in the following chapters, let your competitive strategy guide your decision making about which to pursue.

CHAPTER 10

Small Business Growth Strategies

How to Increase Your Sales and Profits

AT LEAST ONCE A YEAR EVERY SMALL business owner and manager must escape the shackles and frustrations of day-to-day operations and focus exclusively on developing a plan to grow sales and profits. Probably the most productive time for this creative exercise is after the annual Income Statement and Balance Sheets are prepared. Fresh financial report cards always motivate a manager to improve, to grow, and to set higher sales and profit goals for the coming year. Success challenges you to create a bigger success. And if the last business year was disappointing, reading the latest financial reports will definitely put you in the mood to formulate a better growth plan. Whether you're up or down, this half of the book will help you find new ways to grow.

It's time to draw a new map to success. It's time to learn a few simple growth strategy secrets. It's time to learn a few new management skills. In this half of the book, you'll learn how to make a systematic search to identify all the possible growth opportunities for your business. You'll learn how to determine which growth opportunities are best for your business and your situation. You'll put together a great growth plan for this year, and you'll learn what information to collect during the next year to improve your growth planning effectiveness. Each year's growth plan should get better because each year you get smarter about which techniques work for your business and which don't, smarter about spotting emerging trends that create and support new opportunities, and smarter about analyzing your strengths and your competitor's weaknesses. Each year you must take charge of your future and make yourself and your key employees plan for growth —*finding new ways to grow must never cease.*

Growth strategies must be tailored to each business. Even if two businesses in the same industry developed identical lists of potential growth opportunities, the best opportunity for each to pursue would likely be different. After all, most businesses have developed their own success formulas that are made up of different competitive strategies, strengths and weaknesses, levels of investment cash, management skills, equipment, facilities, and suppliers. Each business's differences create unique advantages and limitations that determine which growth opportunities are best for it to pursue.

Your growth choices are affected by the amount of money you can invest, but regardless of the amount of money you have, there are growth opportunities for your business if you know where to look. There are growth opportunities for struggling businesses, businesses in dying industries, businesses in unstable industries, and businesses in various competitive positions.

Regardless of your business's growth circumstances or limitations, one assumption is universally true. Limited resources will keep you from chasing every good growth idea, so you need to make prudent choices. Pursuing some growth opportunities means not being able to pursue others — an opportunity lost. Once you make your choices and invest in one group of growth opportunities, you lose the ability for some period of time to invest in other growth opportunities. Therefore, it's important to make a systematic search to find all your growth possibilities, so you can make the best choices.

Managers of Small Businesses Need Help Increasing Sales

The next few chapters provide an exhaustive system to help managers of small businesses systematically search for growth opportunities, so they can find all their opportunities to grow, not just the obvious ones. A systematic search is one that examines one facet of your business at a time. So, you'll focus on finding opportunities to increase sales and then you'll focus on finding opportunities to increase profits. One at a time, you'll explore 14 different ways to expand your business with 14 different growth strategies. You'll learn how to examine your business's growth potential from three separate business perspectives: one marketing viewpoint and two management viewpoints.

A manager of a small business especially needs this type of systematic, one-compartment-at-a-time approach to overcome the significant disadvantages of being small. You're disadvantaged because you're forced by your small business size to be a generalist. By contrast, big businesses have department specialists searching for growth opportunities in each functional area — marketing, operations, finance, personnel, shipping, research, etc. Unfortunately, these jobs are combined in a small business — you may head up each area by yourself. All too often you solve a marketing problem at 9 A.M., an operations problem at 10 A.M., and meet with the bank loan officer to discuss financing at 11 A.M. The problem is that these roles are still mixed together when you sit down to plan for growth. While the big business has a specialist assigned to each functional area who can focus exclusively on that area and identify all its growth opportunities, managers of small businesses, like you, lack that type of narrow focus. But, that type of narrow focus is built into the systematic search procedure you're about to use.

Sharpening Your Focus on Growth

Finding every opportunity to grow depends on limiting your focus to one perspective at a time. First, you'll use a marketing perspective to identify all your marketing growth opportunities. You'll put yourself in the position of a marketing specialist like a director of marketing or vice-president of marketing. Then you'll limit your growth search by analyzing products, services, consumers, markets, customer segments, replacement products, and complementary products. One at a time you'll work your way through the four ways marketing can be used to grow sales:

1. Concentrated Growth
2. Industry Development
3. Product and Service Development
4. Marketing Diversification

Working with each of these four strategies will help you to discover many new ways to increase sales.

Second, you'll use a management perspective to find all your opportunities to grow by shifting your focus to that of a Chief Executive Officer (CEO). CEOs of every size business are enthusiastically involved in marketing's growth opportunities, but as the CEO of a small business, you have a unique sales growth perspective that is not shared with marketing. A successful CEO must see his or her business through its financial statements. Analyzing the financial condition of your firm will help you to discover additional ways to grow sales that would never be considered by a marketing manager. For example, unlike a marketing manager, a CEO is keenly concerned with the way the firm is using its people, equipment, and facility resources. Inefficiencies glare up from the business's Income Statements in the form of expenses that are too high. The cost of operations, expense of delivery vehicles, or expense of the sales force will appear too expensive when they are underutilized or inefficiently used. Such problems drive the CEO to find sales growth opportunities that will use the idle resources. When the CEO is successful at putting idle resources to work, the business gains two new profits: one from the extra sales and one from lowering costs on existing sales.

The CEOs sales growth perspective is broader than just financial, it also involves 1) examining other markets and other industries, 2) analyzing developing local and national trends, and 3) analyzing the latest changes in the attitudes of consumers. Since a CEO's perspective is much broader than a marketing manager's, CEOs are able to increase sales with four Management Sales Growth Strategies:

1. Management Related Diversification
2. Opportunistic Diversification
3. Forward Integration
4. Horizontal Integration

Third, after you've discovered all the ways you can increase sales wearing first the marketing manager's hat then the CEO's hat, it's time to narrow your focus to increasing profits with another management perspective. It would be an understatement to say that CEOs were concerned with profits; *CEOs are much more concerned with growing profits than with growing sales.* In fact, the small business CEO is willing to cut sales anytime it will increase long-term profits. A CEO is always willing to look beyond sales in order to increase profits. To increase profits, a CEO will explore consolidating employee tasks and laying off some employees. To increase profits, a CEO will work to re-invent a work process to speed it up, improve productivity, and cut costs. In fact, many important CEO profit-building strategies don't involve sales; they involve changing the way work is done.

Six management profit growth strategies have evolved from the CEO's unique focus on increasing profits:

1. Backward Integration
2. Process Re-Invention
3. Divestment/Reinvestment
4. Revitalization
5. Retrenchment
6. Liquidation

All totaled, these three perspectives provide you with 14 growth strategies. These strategies are so compatible that 13 of them can be used at the same time. However, expanding with 13 strategies is impractical because no small firm has enough money or people for such a grand and ambitious plan. However, your business will be able to pursue several different growth strategies at the same time. In fact, some of your profit growth strategies will likely generate the money needed to fund some of your sales growth strategies.

Finding Your Best Opportunities to Grow

Since your small business is only going to be able to pursue a few growth opportunities, it's important that those few be the best ones for your business and its situation. To help you find the best, each of the 14 growth strategies will be defined, explained, and explored separately. Practical examples of businesses using each strategy will be provided to help you understand each strategy. Then, you'll be asked to stop and apply each growth strategy to your business by creatively searching and identifying opportunities to use each strategy in your business. Each time you identify a way to use a strategy, you'll jot it down on your growth opportunity's list. As you progress from one strategy to the next, you'll build an exhaustive list of all your potential growth opportunities. After you finish all 14 strategies and have a list of all your opportunities to grow, you then focus on choosing the best opportunities for your business to pursue.

It's important that you're highly motivated when you begin the search for growth opportunities and that you have the right attitude — a creative attitude. Being creative involves an activity called brainstorming. Brainstorming is a fancy term that business gurus have invented that describes an active mental state without normal inhibitions. Inhibitions come from the little voice inside your head that tells you *it's not proper to be silly or goofy*, but inhibitions stifle creativity. Jotting down a silly idea often triggers an ingenious idea which is refined into a brilliant idea. Under normal circumstances, a person is too somber to write down a humorous growth idea during a deadly serious strategy session, but brainstorming requires some lightheartedness. For example, writing "Run away, Run away" on your retrenchment strategy list may help you to realize you need to cut your losses and finally get rid of an old product line. So, loosen up.

Another key to finding all your growth opportunities is to buy copies of this book for all your key employees and have them make their own independent lists of opportunities (*this is also great for book sales!*). Then schedule a group session to discuss and combine the lists; more opportunities will emerge from the group interaction. However, avoid convening a group session until everyone has done his or her homework, and everyone has something to contribute. Otherwise, they'll all wait for you to speak, and they'll feel compelled to support the boss. Be sure to get them all in a brainstorming attitude by demonstrating your lightheartedness in your instructions and requiring it at the group session. Your goal is to promote an open, wide-ranging discussion of growth ideas so you can build an exhaustive list of opportunities for your business to grow. Once you get the exhaustive list, you can toss out the unworkable or bad ideas and narrow the list, with the aid of the last chapter, to the few best growth opportunities for your business.

Improving Your Motivation: Eleven Reasons Why You Should Pursue Aggressive Growth

All this sounds like a lot of work. You want to grow, but you aren't sure how aggressively to pursue growth. It's time to pump up your motivation.

The best-kept small business secret is that many owners and managers of small businesses aren't trying to maximize profits or sales. Instead, they're trying to maximize control over their own lives while they make a respectable income. To these business people, fighting tooth and nail to grow sounds like the oppressive work environment they tried to leave behind when they quit their jobs and started their own businesses.

Accept the premise that owning and operating a small business is often a balance between the quest for wealth and the desire to control one's own life. Too much customer demand and too much growth could severely reduce your freedom. You could start to feel like an employee working for a boss, but this time the boss would be demanding customers, suppliers, and banks. It's true that too much growth might have some negative side effects. Unfortunately, your business has to grow as fast as possible.

Either your business grows or a competitor's business grows. A quick peek at the upward trend of the Gross National Product shows that customer demand is increasing year after year. Therefore, you have a choice. Either try to protect your lifestyle or seek your share of the growth aggressively. You can either try to control your life or you can lie awake at night and worry about the shifting balance of power between your business and your competitors' businesses. The simple fact is that if your business doesn't grow aggressively, you're encouraging a competitor to grow, and that competitor could eventually steal your customers and your lifestyle. Growth is necessary to protect your way of life, and here are eleven more reasons why you should seek growth aggressively.

1. Bigger Profits Let You Enlarge Your Competitive Advantage

The additional profits earned through growth can be invested 1) to create an even larger competitive advantage, 2) to maintain your *relative* Key Success Factor

(KSF) advantages in a highly competitive market, or 3) to overcome your competitive weaknesses. Because the KSFs that enable you to successfully target customers, trigger sales, and control costs are *relative* strengths, not absolute strengths, the ability to stay ahead of competitors requires constant investments and continuous improvements which are paid for from profits. The more profits you make, the more improvements you can afford to make. Don't rest on your laurels, your business may have a superior KSF today, but if your competitors improve their KSF while yours stays the same, you will lose your *relative* superiority and your sales will fall. In other words, you can fall behind by standing still. The only way to keep a business strong is to grow bigger and bigger profits and to keep investing additional money in your KSFs to keep your *relative* strengths.

2. Protect Your Business from Cross-Subsidization

Growth protects your business from the nasty cross-subsidization tactics of new competitors. Aggressive competitors typically use cross-subsidization to establish themselves in new markets. Cross-subsidization occurs when a competitor outside your geographic area expands into your market with massive loss-leader prices supported by profits from their other areas. The new competitor's goal is to operate at a loss in order to steal your customers, and those losses are subsidized by their profits from their other locations. Typically, the new competitor opens and announces low, low grand opening prices that are below your costs and below their costs. Nevertheless, the competitor's grand opening prices continue until they capture enough market share to establish their business in your market. After they've mugged you, they'll raise their prices up to normal levels.

Aggressive growth can protect your business from cross-subsidization. As your business grows, its ability to fight back increases. With higher profits, you can instantly retaliate against a new competitor by either matching their introductory prices or by expanding into the aggressor's established territory with your own low introductory prices. This reduces the new competitor's ability to produce profits in the other area and funnel them to your market.

Aggressive competitors are less likely to attack your market if they think you can launch a counterattack that will make their new venture unprofitable. They'll avoid your area and instead search for another area where retaliation is not expected.

3. Growth Can Add Two Profits

Growth allows your business to push its per product and per service costs down, increasing profits (see Economy of Scale, Chapter 3). As sales grow, so do your purchases from suppliers which qualifies your business for additional price discounts. Buying bigger quantities from suppliers lowers your incoming freight costs per product. Growth allows you to install high-tech equipment to lower labor costs per product or per service. Shipping out larger quantities to customers lowers out-bound freight costs per product. Advertising costs per ad decline when you purchase in bigger blocks. Growing larger makes it affordable to purchase more efficient computer systems to streamline various internal processes, boost productivity, speed up customer response times, and cut costs. The rewards of aggressive growth are 1) additional profits from additional sales plus 2) additional profits from cutting overall costs.

Increasing profit margins achieved through economy of scale growth puts your business in a stronger competitive position, makes it more capable of surviving price wars, and more capable of counter-attacking aggressive competitors. Lowering costs simply improves the business's ability to survive.

4. Growth Attracts Better Suppliers

Sadly, the best suppliers with the highest quality, lowest prices, and fastest service avoid smaller businesses because they don't buy enough products to offset the cost of selling, servicing, and delivering. If you're lucky, the best suppliers will ship your business through a network of distributors and wholesalers, but they charge higher prices. As you grow, the best suppliers finally knock on your door and offer you some wonderful competitive advantages. However, if the best suppliers believe you're highly likely to grow, they'll seek you out sooner and be willing to bend their size rules to build a relationship with your growing business. Of course, this makes it easier to grow.

Often the best suppliers maintain a "Fast Track" list of small accounts they expect to grow. Such lists are usually developed from attendance records, sign-in sheets, and booth registrations at your industry's National Trade Shows. To get on such a list, attend national conventions and national trade shows and sign in at each and every booth. Suppliers assume that only aggressive, growth-hungry managers of small businesses attend these national events, so they add those business names to their "Fast Track" lists and give them special attention.

5. Sales Growth Creates More Sales Growth

Growth improves a small business's image in the minds of potential customers. Growth enhances the business's image which is an *indicator of performance* that customers substitute for actual product and service performance (see Indicators of Performance, Chapter 4).

Consumer behavior researchers explain that customers have conscious thoughts that they express when they think, talk, and write. Customers also have feelings that are moods or emotions that have never reached the conscious level of thinking, talking, or writing. And, a business's image affects the way customers *feel* about your business.

Customers will *feel* (not think) that business growth signals better products, better service, and better personnel. Being lazy creatures, many customers will *feel* comfortable trusting the image created by growth instead of actually comparing your products and services to those of your competitors. Understandably, when customers *feel* good about your business, they are more likely to trust your promotional messages and sales claims. This is how growth creates more growth because growth signals success, success creates the image of better products and better services, a good image improves the effectiveness of your promotions, and your promotions attract even more customers.

6. How to Run a Bigger Business with Less Inventory

A growing business can often reduce its inventories. Suppliers have minimum order quantities that force the smallest businesses to purchase more inventory than they actually need and to receive shipments of those goods at the supplier's convenience. At times, suppliers act as though they are doing the small business a favor by supplying them at all. This attitude forces a small business to increase inventories anytime upcoming shortages are even rumored, since suppliers are likely to divert goods in short supply to larger accounts.

As the business grows, power shifts from the supplier to the small business. As you grow, suppliers try harder to comply with your business's needs, ship the quantities you request, and deliver them at the date and time you request. Suddenly, supplier delivery routes are altered to make frequent shipments of small volumes that arrive just when your growing small business wants them to arrive.

Many small business owners discover that as their businesses grow they can reduce inventory levels because suppliers make adjustments to serve their needs. Reducing inventories increases cash flow that can be used to finance further growth.

7. The Best Employees are Attracted to Growing Businesses

Employees with superior education, training, and experience want to work for growing businesses where career opportunities are more likely to open up.

Talented employees with drive and ambition want advancement opportunities that are only possible at growing businesses. In fact, these skilled people start knocking on your door when your small business is noticeably growing.

The corollary is also true. Your most talented employees often leave when they realize there is no opportunity for advancement. The old joke is really true, "How do you identify the brightest employees in a stagnant small business? They're the ones who are leaving."

Growth helps you keep the good employees and hire the more talented applicants, which makes your business easier to manage.

8. Growth Makes the Best Technology Affordable

State-of-the-art technologies are expensive, and smaller firms often can't afford them. A business has to reach a certain size before it can afford to acquire the technologies to make the highest quality products and services, achieve the lowest costs, significantly speed up services, or allow greater flexibility. Not only do growing businesses have more profits to reinvest in new technologies, aggressive equipment suppliers frequently offer them easy financing plans. For example, one small firm reported that their highest quality equipment supplier offered to co-sign the small business's bank loan in return for permission to show its equipment to potential customers. Not only did the equipment supplier want to showcase his equipment, he was sure the small firm's growth would continue, and the equipment supplier's reputation would be enhanced if that growth occurred with their equipment.

9. The Best Locations are Reserved for Growing Businesses

Landlords and city governments often compete to attract an expanding business. Small communities frequently offer location incentives to attract small manufacturers. The incentives include favorable interest rates, city-backed loans, subsidized land in industrial parks, and subsidized employee training.

Similarly, landlords struggle to attract growing retail firms in hopes they will increase the consumer traffic to the landlord's commercial facility. Increased consumer traffic helps other retailers in the complex grow and profit, which stabilizes the landlord's income. Landlords also know that growing firms are more likely to be long-term tenants, so they are more willing to make concessions to lure a growing business to their location.

All this adds up to a significant location advantage or cost advantage for growing businesses.

10. Don't Let Your Business Become a Prison

As many owners have discovered, a small business can sometimes turn into a prison where the owner is required to continue working days, weeks, months, and years with little time off until burnout occurs. Your personal prison is built when you invest your life savings in a small business, become the business's only manager, and perform a significant amount of the business's total productive work. Then, anytime you try to take a little time off, the business is deprived of all its management and a large part of its labor — productivity plummets, costs rise, customers are inconvenienced, and profits drop. The owner is trapped and can't afford time off.

The effects of no time off are brutal. Owners need to take time off for extended holidays and vacations to recharge their creative batteries, rejuvenate their attitudes, and gain fresh perspectives that only come from looking back at the business from afar. Without time off, burnout is inevitable.

Growth is the only acceptable way to extricate the owner from the work-yourself-to-death trap that drives many owners into voluntary liquidation.

11. Keeping Score

Beyond these ten logical reasons to aggressively grow, add an emotional reason — keeping score. Sooner or later, most small business owners report feeling like a competitor on an athletic field or a student in a classroom. Profits become personal scores or grades. Most owners like to compete and want to win, and profits become an easy and accurate way to measure one's competitive achievement. Profits are an easy way to keep score among competitors.

These 11 reasons are meant to motivate you, not only to read the remainder of this book but also to put considerable effort into applying the growth concepts in the next four chapters. Use each of the three growth perspectives. Read, understand, and apply each growth strategy. Get in a creative, lighthearted, brainstorming mood. And along the way, think about the information you want to collect for next year's planning session so it will be even more productive.

How to Find All Your Business's Growth Opportunities

So here's your assignment. Every time you reach a point in the next three chapters that's titled, "Finding Your Growth Opportunities," read that section and follow the instructions. You'll be asked to think of opportunities to use each growth strategy in your business over the next few years. Don't be cautious, be creative. Propose both silly and serious ideas. Tell yourself that the goofy ideas are the catalysts that drive the mental reactions that trigger great ideas and wonderful new opportunities. Also, don't worry about financing until you've finished compiling your list. Some of the profit growth opportunities you'll devise in Chapter 14 will generate the cash you need to bankroll some of your sales growth opportunities.

After you've finished all 14 small business growth strategies and amassed a long list of opportunities, you can shorten and prioritize the list, and then choose your best and most realistic opportunities to pursue.

CHAPTER 11

Marketing Sales Growth Strategies

DON'T CONFUSE MARKETING STRATEGIES with marketing tactics. Marketing strategies are similar to overall plans for a major military battle while marketing tactics are more like minor plans to get ammo, food, and supplies to the troops. Supply lines are a vitally important part of waging a battle, and marketing tactics are vitally important parts of implementing a marketing strategy. However, a growth strategy is a big growth plan, a tactic is an element used to implement that plan. This book is about strategies.

Marketing tactics involve putting an eye-catching display in a store window, placing an effective advertisement in the Sunday paper, and devising a killer closing technique that increases the effectiveness of your salespeople. Tactics have significant influences on sales. For example, consultants constantly educate retail clients about the tactical advantage of using the proper colors. They've discovered that blue and green inside a store can calm customers down in tense situations, exterior use of yellow and red can attract customers to the store, but using too much red and yellow inside the store can cause customers to become tense, which can kill the sale *(1)*. However, using the right color isn't a strategy; it's a tactic. Another tactic is to combine the correct interior design, colors, music, and appropriate appearances to build an atmosphere that subtly builds customer trust. In fact, product, price, promotion, and place are all part of an important mix of marketing tactics that influence sales.

Tactics are used to implement growth strategies, and if a small business doesn't have the ability to perform or purchase a necessary tactic to implement a marketing strategy, the strategy will fail. However, marketing, like every field, has its little parts and its big parts, its micro components and macro components. This chapter is about the macroscopic marketing components called marketing sales growth strategies — the big picture. Macroscopic marketing is about making the big growth choices, like which type customers to target, which segment within a customer type to target, and which product and service benefits to offer.

Microscopic marketing tactics are important. Just as no four-star general ever won a battle without good discipline, food for the troops, and spare parts for equipment, no marketing strategy every worked without good merchandising, good advertising and promotions, good pricing, good locations, the right return policies, on-time delivery systems, and so on. Tactics rightly consume most of your daily work. However, a manager of a small business has to occasionally step back and develop growth visions and plans to guide the future development of the business. But the decision sequence is obvious; a business manager develops a growth strategy and then develops the tactics necessary for implementing the strategy.

The Logic of Marketing Strategies

Where do marketing strategies come from? Marketing strategies are developed from a few simple facts.

Fact One: *A business's marketing personnel can only increase sales with existing products and services or new products and services.*

Existing products and services are those your business now sells. New products and services are those you could sell. Dividing products and services into two groups leads to the development of two types of marketing strategies: growth strategies for existing products and services and growth strategies for new products and services.

Fact Two: *A business can only increase sales with existing customers or new customers.*

Dividing customers into two groups leads to the development of two more types of marketing strategies: growth strategies for existing customers and growth strategies for new customers.

However, customers can be further separated into markets, customer types, and customer segments. For example, a business could target a market — the Home Furnishings market. A business could target a customer type within the Home furnishings market — Selective Shoppers (see Chapter 1, Customer Types). A business could target a customer segment within the customer type — young, married, dual income customers. Then, the business might choose to expand by targeting other customer segments in the same market or by targeting other markets.

Subdividing products and services and customers gives the marketing manager of any sized business six macro components to use in formulating growth strategies. These are the six macroscopic marketing components from which all marketing sales growth strategies are devised:

1. Existing products and services
2. New products and services
3. Existing customer segments
4. New customer segments
5. Existing markets
6. New markets

These six macroscopic components are used to form the four major marketing growth strategies shown in Figure 11.1.

As you read this chapter, your job will be to identify all the opportunities to expand your business with each of these four marketing strategies:

1. **Concentrated Growth:** increasing sales of existing products and services to existing target customers in your existing market.

FIGURE 11.1: Four Marketing Sales Growth Strategies

	Existing Products and Services	New Products and Services
Existing Customer Segments and Markets	Concentrated Growth	Product Development 1. Replacement Products and Services 2. Complementary Products and Services
New Customer Segments and Markets	Industry Development 1. Segment Development 2. Market Development	Marketing Diversification 1. Segment Diversification 2. Market Diversification

2. **Industry Development Growth:** selling existing products and services to a new customer segment or a new market.
3. **Product Development Growth:** adding new products and services for existing target customers. There are two types of new products and services that you can add: replacement and complementary. When a modified or new product or service with new benefits for target customers replaces an old one, it's called a *replacement*. When another product or service is added for customers to purchase at the same time they purchase existing ones, it's called a *complementary product or service*.
4. **Marketing Diversification Growth:** selling new products and services to a new customer segment or a new market.

These marketing strategies don't overlap; they are mutually exclusive. A product or service is either new or existing — if it isn't being sold at this time by your business it is new and if it is being sold at this time by your business it's *existing*. Likewise, customers are either existing or new — if they are being targeted at this time they are existing and if they aren't being targeted at this time they are *new*.

For a manager of a small business, the fact that these strategies don't overlap and are mutually exclusive means no potential opportunities to expand sales will be missed by narrowly focusing on just one marketing growth strategy at a time. Focusing on one strategy at a time and brainstorming to find all your opportunities to use that one strategy will produce an exhaustive list of all your business's growth opportunities. No great ideas to expand are going to slip-between-the-cracks. So, put yourself in a creative mood, and let's get started.

CHAPTER 12

Marketing Growth Strategies for Existing Products and Services

IN THE LAST CHAPTER, YOU DISCOVERED that all marketing sales growth strategies fall into two categories: 1) strategies to increase sales with *existing* products and services, which is the focus of this chapter, and 2) strategies to increase sales with *new* products and services, which is the focus of the next chapter. Just so there is no confusion, existing products and services are those your business currently offers customers plus modifications to your existing products and services that are *not expected* to generate significant new sales. *New* products and services are those your business is not currently offering customers plus modifications to existing products and services that *are expected* to generate significant new sales. These definitions are easy for an owner and manager to use because if you think a modified product is the same old product, it is. If you think your modifications have created a new product, you have. Just call it like you see it.

You can't make a mistake when classifying a modified product as an existing or new product because, with this book's system, you'll still find all your opportunities to grow. All opportunities to increase sales to existing customers, new customers, and new markets will be carefully considered for existing and then for new products and services. That's the advantage of this book's growth opportunity search system — you can focus on one growth strategy at a time without missing any of your opportunities to increase sales and profits.

We begin the search for your opportunities to grow with marketing strategies to increase the sales of existing products and services because they are more important than other growth strategies to the average small business in the short-run. These strategies can be implemented faster, and cheaper, and they boost profits more quickly than other strategies. For that reason, they're presented first.

Concentrated Sales Growth Strategy

A Concentrated Sales Growth Strategy is a tactical plan to increase sales of existing products and services to existing customers. In short, doing what you're doing now, but doing it better. Studies show that for the average business, 65 to 70 percent of current sales and profits come from products and services the firm was selling 3 to 5 years ago *(1)*. Therefore, you should expect, on average, that two-thirds of your sales and profits in the next several years will come from products and services that are presently sitting on your shelves. Even among aggressive firms who are adding new products and expanding into new markets, existing products will likely be important to sales and profits for years to come.

Therefore, devising ways to grow the sales of current products and services has tremendous potential for your business. Concentrated Growth is an important strategy that is worth a considerable effort to develop. Finding ways to grow with Concentrated Growth will make two-thirds of your future products and services produce greater than expected sales and profits. Also, Concentrated Growth is an easy starting place for group planning sessions because everyone knows the most about this topic and are eager to contribute their ideas.

Your final growth plan will likely contain several types of growth strategies, but regardless of what additional growth strategies you decide to pursue, Concentrated Growth will almost always be in the mix. This strategy, unlike the others, deals mostly with marketing tactics that are effective in increasing sales. It involves identifying the best ideas for increasing your sales to existing customers.

The term "existing customers" refers to the customer segment you are currently targeting. For example, your existing target customers might be a segment described as upscale, 45 to 54-year-old men who primarily purchase one type of service from your business. In addition to that segment, you might also target a second, smaller segment described as upscale, 55+ year-old men who primarily purchase a different type of service from your business. ***Exceptions to these segments by definition are not existing customers,*** so if a few women, a few young people, and a few customers of modest income also purchase your services, they don't qualify as existing customers for strategy purposes, even though they are handing you their money, because they are not target customers. You'll focus intently on them with the next strategy, and they may become target customers at that time. To maintain the mutually exclusive nature of this growth search system, *existing customers* are only those you are deliberately targeting, not incidental customers who pleasantly surprise you by making purchases.

This growth strategy focuses only on your targeted customers and your existing products and services; finding all your growth opportunities requires that you examine each growth opportunity separately and exhaustively. Now that you're focused, let's look at some of the fundamental ways that other small businesses have grown with a Concentrated Growth Strategy. Maybe some of these examples will generate a few valuable growth ideas for you. If so, stop and jot your ideas down.

Concentrated Growth Examples

No business sells to all of its target customers, just a portion of them. Perhaps your business only sells to 30 percent of your targeted customers. Customer turnover also occurs, so at any given time some target customers stop buying from your business while others begin buying. Turnover occurs when customers move, change their habits, or switch to your competitor. Most businesses constantly lose some individual customers while they are struggling to gain additional target customers.

Jan Powell states the obvious when she says that it's easier to grow if you lose fewer customers. She says, if you want to grow, make sure you're retaining all your present customers while you're adding new ones. Jan wanted her business, Ads Infinitum in Raleigh, North Carolina to grow rapidly, and she knew it would grow faster if it didn't have to continuously replace lost customers. That's why Jan installed a computer system to track and monitor every detail of each customer order to make absolutely sure every customer remained highly satisfied. And, she says that highly satisfied customers are walking, talking, free advertisements providing free and persuasive word-of-mouth advertising that stimulates growth (2).

Jan's good business sense is supported by consumer research. One consumer products company made the surprising discovery in a market research study that 44 percent of its satisfied customers later switched to a competitive product (3). They learned that many customers who said they were *satisfied* still switched to a competitor, but customers who said they were *highly satisfied* could be counted on to remain loyal and not switch. How fast you grow with Concentrated Growth may depend on your ability to turn your satisfied customers into highly satisfied customers. If any ideas about how to achieve this transformation come to mind, they are your first opportunity to grow and should be written on your Opportunities List.

The people running The Delta Dental Plan of Massachusetts understand the concept of highly satisfied customers, and how it affects their sales growth. Delta sells dental insurance plans to businesses. Each business then assigns an administrator to manage the dental plan. The employees use the dental plan, and the dentists are paid by the plan after they submit their claims to Delta. To grow continuously with their existing service and with their targeted business customers, Delta needs all three groups — businesses, customers, and dentists — to be highly satisfied. To achieve their goal, Delta routinely gathers feedback from each group to measure satisfaction and to be sure all problems with their service are promptly eliminated. To do this, both administrators and employees are surveyed four times a year, and dentists are surveyed once a year. On top of that, groups of participating Delta dentists are frequently assembled to help the company improve its dental plan *(4)*.

Another Concentrated Growth success story concerns Home Depot. Home Depot has grown into a large corporation because it has been able to increase customer satisfaction continuously. Management loves to brag about the customer-oriented culture they've created in which employees truly care about each customer.

Of course, Home Depot has a big financial reason to keep customers highly satisfied. Looking at the averages, Home Depot's management says that each customer spends an average of $38 every time they visit the store, and they visit 30 times a year for 22 years. Management sees each customer as a lifetime money stream, and that stream could be cut off if the customer isn't highly satisfied each time they visit Home Depot *(5)*. So Home Depot solicits lots of customer feedback about how to improve customers' shopping experiences.

As you can see, a Concentrated Sales Growth strategy requires searching for opportunities to improve customer satisfaction and that involves *listening* — not talking — to customers. Stew Leonard, Sr. and Jr., can teach every manager of a small business a lesson about how to listen to customers. The Leonards have pioneered the use of in-store chat groups to help them better understand the feelings of their customers.

Once a month, the Leonards pay a dozen customers $20 apiece to attend a one-time, one-hour talk session. Everyone sits down in comfortable chairs to talk with the Leonards about their likes and dislikes in the Leonards' grocery stores. The Leonards know they could hire consultants as facilitators to run a fancy focus group and provide them with written reports of their findings, but they believe customers are the experts, so they hire the customers to help them find ways to increase the sales of existing products to existing customers.

Not surprisingly, the Leonards have stunned the grocery industry. They were the ones that started the fish on ice displays all across America. In one of their customer chat sessions, they asked the group of customers why fish sales were slow. That evening's participants responded that they didn't view the fish as fresh enough. The Leonards could have defended the freshness of their fish, but they didn't try to convince those 12 customers of the truth about how extremely fresh those fish actually were. No, the Leonards are *listeners*, and they were much more interested in *customer perceptions*, so, one of the Leonards asked, "What does a fresh fish look like?"

The subsequent discussion boiled down to the customer opinion that fish in plastic trays covered with shrink-wrap were like green beans in tin cans. Fresh fish should lie loose on ice in the fresh fish department just like fresh green beans lie loose in the produce department.

Instead of arguing, the next day the Leonards took their fish out of the plastic trays and laid them in an attractive setting on a bed of ice at the end of the meat department. Fish sales doubled. The Leonards are good listeners *(6)*. Are you missing opportunities to grow because you don't *listen* to your customers? Do you know the truth instead of the way your customer's *perceive* the truth? Are you a great talker, great at explaining things, and a poor listener?

Promotions generate sales, and great promotions generate more sales. Concentrated Growth plans often involve devising better promotional techniques, which is often easy to do, since you have last year's experiences to build upon. After all, you've accumulated new insights into what works and what doesn't, you've watched your competitors' promotional successes and failures, and you've listened to suppliers talk about the experiences of businesses like yours in other parts of the country. What have you learned? How can you use what you've learned to increase sales? More opportunities!

Conbe Inc. grew by designing a better promotional plan to improve the "reach" of its promotions. Conbe makes hair-care products for older men, and Conbe spotted a place that was a gold mine full of potential customers — the Senior PGA Tournaments. These tournaments are restricted to pro-golfers over 50 years of age, and the audience is loaded with the same aged men who want to see their old favorites compete for prize money. This presented Conbe with a Concentrated Growth opportunity. It decided to set up booths at the tournaments and give away free samples. Potential customers have eagerly taken the samples, liked the products, and begun purchasing Conbe products. The sales promotion tactic has been a success *(7)*.

"Reach" is an important promotional tactic. Reach refers to the number of target customers who receive your advertising or promotional message out of the total who are exposed to it. The more target customers in your advertising audience, the better your "reach." For example, suppose you've been running advertisements in the sports section of your local paper because 22 percent of your target customers read that section. If you conducted a study and found that 42 percent of your customers read the cartoons every day, advertisements placed on or opposite the cartoon page would have greater "reach." Therefore, your goal is to identify opportunities to improve the "reach" of your promotions in order to improve your sales.

For example, one small nursery realized it could improve its promotional reach by supplying temporary flowers, shrubs, and trees for free to selected events, like Garden Club picnics, where its best potential customers gathered. Of course, each free flower display contains a sign identifying and promoting the nursery.

Like all small businesses, you're only selling to a portion of the people in your target customer segment. One way to develop a good Concentrated Growth plan is to find new tactics to attract more target customers. For example, one small brewery in New York knew that its current, best customers loved music, especially live performances. These customers filled the brewery on nights that bands played. So, the owners devised a new plan to attract more "best" customer types. The brewery began sponsoring band contests. To build community awareness, they gave away free tickets. Free tickets brought lots of new customers into the brewery. The result was a significant growth in sales *(8)*.

Often Concentrated Growth involves a plan to expand geographically — reaching out to serve more target customers in new areas. But, small business people have figured out many different ways to achieve geographical expansion.

John Chuang demonstrates the most common form of geographical expansion. Believe it or not, Chuang ran out of room to grow in New York City. In 1988, he started a rather simple small business that specialized in providing New York businesses with temporary workers who were skilled at operating Apple's Macintosh computers. Other firms were already targeting businesses that wanted IBM-PC temporary workers, so Chuang targeted the smaller Apple temp segment and avoided competing with the big firms — a typical small business customer targeting tactic.

Growth eventually slowed, so Chuang sought additional customers by expanding to other cities. Chuang's Mac-temp service is now in 21 cities. His last performance figures counted $21 million in revenues and approximately 5,000 temporary employees, all with Concentrated Growth through geographical expansion *(9)*.

A second form of geographical expansion doesn't involve new locations. Jim Kelly's small business, Rejuvenation Lamp & Fixture of Portland, Oregon, saturated the local market, and Jim craved more growth. Jim began advertising his specialty in various magazines and eventually built up a mailing list of 80,000 names. Then, Jim practiced Concentrated Growth by introducing a catalog, which greatly expanded his territorial boundaries and put sales back on an upward, well-lighted slope *(10)*.

A third form of geographic expansion involves services. Thanks to our electronic age, geographical expansion of a service can be accomplished without adding any new facilities. Nancy Friedman of St. Louis, Missouri, demonstrates the tactic. She founded a telephone manners consulting firm called the Telephone Doctor. Nancy soon filled up her calendar with consultations and seminars designed to teach companies how to portray a positive mental image to customers in the first six seconds of phone contact. Using a Concentrated Growth Strategy seemed impossible when Nancy's time was completely booked up. However, she expanded with a slight modification of her service — she cloned herself by making Telephone Doctor Videos. Distributing videos has stretched her services to 27 countries. Nancy certainly knows how to be in more than one place at a time *(11)*.

Another sales growth opportunity is loading customers up — getting them to purchase more products at a time so they can't occasionally buy from competitors. Loading also is accomplished by getting customers to purchase your services more frequently. That's the idea behind the movement to unisex pricing by a few dry cleaners. Unisex pricing means the cleaners charge the same for men's shirts and women's blouses, men's pants and women's pants, and they charge the same extra price for pleats in women's skirts and in men's pants. Unisex pricing boosts sales for two reasons. First, it encourages women to make more trips to the cleaners which boosts sales. Second, women most often bring other family members' clothes with their own, which further boosts sales.

Changes in remote trends can create new opportunities for Concentrated Growth. If your target customer segment is expanding, this expansion favors making investments in Concentrated Growth. For example, if you target customers who are college graduates and if the population of college graduates in your area is growing, you have a good opportunity for successful Concentrated Growth. The better you can describe your target customers, the easier it is to track their trends and to make wise growth strategy and investment choices.

Changing customer attitudes are important to monitor because shifting attitudes can create additional opportunities for Concentrated Growth. For example, if you sell exercise equipment and consumers in your market are becoming more interested in pursuing healthy lifestyles, you would want to develop promotions that link home exercise equipment and health improvements. Attitudes in your market are important to monitor because attitude shifts always precede changes in sales.

Likewise, there can be favorable economic, technological, political, and environmental trends that favor a Concentrated Growth Strategy. For example, changing technological trends favorably affected Front Porch Computers. The evolution of on-line services like CompuServe, Prodigy, America Online, and the Internet allowed the small home-based firm to expand nationwide into a $4 million business without leaving its front porch *(12)*.

Even bad trends can occasionally be friendly for a small business. For example, Arkansas Woodworks Mfg. Company, a small regional furniture manufacturer serving retailers within a 250-mile radius of its mid-Arkansas plant, produced, among other things, simple oak computer tables. As the customer demand for oak computer tables declined in their sales territory, retailers sought to avoid the high volume requirements of their major suppliers and began searching for suppliers who would ship smaller quantities. The small manufacturer spotted the growth opportunity and responded with a new personal selling message that stressed the firm's ability to deliver any quantity of oak computer desks, from one to a truckload, to retailers in its territory. The small business was even able to raise its prices while it increased its sales.

Concentrated Growth is a wise strategy choice because it uses your small business's existing strengths. It's less risky because management and employees know and understand the current business. Concentrated Growth uses the wealth of knowledge you've acquired about how to operate your business and about customers, suppliers, and competitors. And, there are always ways of improving the way you do business. For example, you can collect additional customer feedback and use it to reduce your lost-customer rate, to increase customer satisfaction, and to improve your promotional programs. You can grow by expanding the area you serve; you probably already know the best geographical areas for expansion. You already know many of the important trends affecting your market. You know the major sales triggers for existing customers and how to use those triggers to boost sales. You understand your business's costs, risks, and technologies. For most small businesses, Concentrated Growth is wise because there are few unknown risks.

How did you get this knowledge? You bought and paid for it with money and hard work, so you owe it to yourself to develop a growth plan to get as much return on that investment as possible. You owe it to yourself to discover all the opportunities to profit from a Concentrated Growth Strategy.

Finding Your Growth Opportunities

Your first assignment is to identify all your opportunities to use a Concentrated Sales Growth Strategy — this involves identifying all the major marketing tactics you might use to boost sales in the next few years. "Might" means you're considering them, not that you're committed to them. At this point, you aren't committing your business to use any of the opportunities that you jot down. You're only committing yourself to consider them, rank them, prioritize them, and later choose the best opportunities from a master list assembled after working with all

14 growth strategies. Right now, just be creative and conjure up opportunities. The serious part about commitment comes later.

What would an opportunity look like? What is an opportunity? For example, one opportunity that might appear on your list would be to build a profile of your target customer's demographics — age, sex, income, occupation, place of residence, etc. over the next four months. Then in the following four months, design a new promotional program to reach all customers with matching demographics in a 50-mile radius of your business. In the last four months of the coming year, you'll try to measure which of the surrounding areas had the highest response, so you can develop a new plan to better "reach" the most responsive areas during next year's growth strategy session. The four-month timetable should be shortened or lengthened to fit your available time.

Here are a few more suggestions:

- Devise possible opportunities to increase the sales of existing products to existing target customers by borrowing and improving the ideas in the examples you just read.
- Develop a plan to reduce the rate of lost customers.
- Develop a plan to improve customer satisfaction.
- Develop a plan to use customer chat sessions like the Leonard's to improve your firm's products, promotions, indicators of performance, services, product displays, business image, personal selling techniques, pricing, financing, warranties.
- Develop a plan to build on your most successful, proven promotional campaigns.
- Develop a plan to expand your business geographically by adding new locations, catalogs, videos, or using new media.

Borrow ideas from the Competitive Strategy section of this book. Such as:

- Develop a plan to study the "Indicators of Performance" discussed in Chapter 4 during the next six months and implement any needed changes in the subsequent six months.
- Examine your KSFs. Develop a plan to overcome any weak sales trigger.
- Examine your SSFs (see Chapter 2). Are any support levels too low? Develop a plan to improve any deficient SSFs.
- Develop a Competitive KSF Model in the next three months and plan to develop a tentative budget for KSF improvements suggested by the model in the following three months.

You're now in a reflective mood and should be looking back at the past marketing tactics that boosted sales as well as those that failed. Do past efforts suggest an opportunity to make a good marketing tactic even better? What did you learn from the marketing tactics that failed last year — yours and your competitors' — that should influence your marketing efforts in the coming year?

Ask yourself questions about your current business. Probe, question, analyze, think, be creative, be lighthearted, be silly, be serious, but examine every aspect of selling your existing products and services to your existing customers in your existing markets. Your goal is to build a list of every opportunity to grow with Concentrated Growth.

Industry Development Sales Growth Strategy

An Industry Development Growth Strategy increases sales by targeting existing products and existing services to new customer segments in your current market or by selling existing products and services in an entirely new market.

"New customer segments in your current market" are any groups of customers that are not being deliberately targeted with your Concentrated Sales Growth Strategy. A new customer segment would obviously be one that has never purchased from your business; however, it's more likely to be one whose members have made occasional purchases, just not enough purchases to catch your attention unless you're actively searching for new growth opportunities. Often, incidental customers who occasionally purchase from your business are members of customer segments that you are not deliberately targeting. Sales can be increased by targeting them with special promotions.

For example, P & G was targeting Noxzema Skin Cream at a segment of young women as a skin cleanser when the company discovered, through a simple survey, that some older women were purchasing the product and using it as a moisturizer. P & G seized the opportunity to increase sales by targeting and promoting Noxzema to the older segment. The company continued its regular advertisements which stressed the product's cleansing benefits in young women's magazines. The company added new advertisements which stressed the product's moisturizing benefits in older women's magazines — an Industry Development Strategy. The product remained the same, an additional segment of customers was targeted with promotions aimed directly at them, and, as a result, sales and profits for Noxzema increased *(13)*. The company was able to spot this existing product growth opportunity only because the firm had developed a description of its currently targeted customer segment. Knowing who was suppose to purchase Noxzema drew immediate attention to the non-targeted customers when they were discovered making purchases. Next, the company interviewed the older women to identify the benefits they sought and developed their Industry Development growth strategy.

Industry Development is also used to target entirely new markets. The term "new markets" simply refers to additional markets for the same products and services. For example, aspirin has long been sold in the headache relief market, but because of new medical studies, aspirin is now also sold in the heart attack prevention market. Likewise, baking soda was first sold in the cooking ingredients market, and then a second market was targeted, the refrigerator deodorant market. Customers were encouraged to place an open box of soda in the back of the refrigerator to remove odors.

One small retailer discovered she could sell lots of her store's products to schools — a public school market. Although she sold lots of products to the new market, profits in that market were low, so total profits from sales to schools were small. However, the combined volumes from both retail and public school sales allowed the business to qualify for additional price discounts from its suppliers — an economy of scale cost advantage. Price discounts from suppliers greatly increased her retail store profits.

It is common for an Industry Development strategy to boost sales, add new profits, and lower overall costs. Frequently, the business's per product or per service overhead, labor, and material costs decline. Industry Development allows small manufacturing plants to cut costs by operating the plant at a higher capacity and increasing the productive use of their warehouses, trucks, and sales force. Industry Development can generate many economy of scale cost reductions (see Chapter 3) for both retailers and manufacturers.

Two Types of Industry Development

The Industry Development growth strategy encompasses two mutually exclusive growth strategies: Segment Development and Market Development. These two strategies are mutually exclusive because one focuses on your existing market and the other on your new market. This natural division allows you to make a more thorough search for your opportunities to grow because you can focus intently on one market at a time.

Segment Development Sales Growth Strategy

When customers other than those you deliberately target purchase your services or products, a Segment Development opportunity is born. For example, with record numbers of women owning small businesses and with record numbers of women in the work force, lots of small businesses who formerly targeted men have increased their sales by adding a women's segment — a

Segment Development Strategy. Briefcase advertisements, once targeted solely at men, now show up in women's magazines as firms target professional women. Car dealerships have hired consultants to help them target and communicate with women. Automobile parts houses have put women behind their counters to help them target the small but growing female fix-it-yourself segment.

One auto parts store targeted a new segment of customers — nervous non-customers. These are people who don't do their own repairs because of a lack of experience and confidence. The store's promotional technique was to offer a free class to teach repair techniques to budding do-it-yourself home mechanics.

When some travel agencies took a closer look at the demographics of their customers, they realized that gays and lesbians were a lucrative segment that could be targeted. Demographic profiles showed that gay and lesbian customers traveled in pairs, were unencumbered by children, were highly educated, and most often professionally employed. Best of all, they had higher than average incomes and, without children, much higher than average disposable incomes. Many agencies took active steps to target this customer segment *(14)*.

One do-it-yourself home improvement store targeted a new customer segment — the deaf. It had employees learn sign language, so they could communicate with the hearing-impaired. No product modifications were necessary, just an added employee skill to serve a special customer segment. Deaf customers turned out to be unexpectedly numerous, understandably appreciative, and very loyal.

Finding Your Growth Opportunities

The most common opportunity to use Segment Development is to target a new type of customer you discover buying your business's products and services. For instance, you're targeting older women and discover some younger women buying your products. Or, you're targeting young adults and find middle-age men occasionally buying your products.

Unfortunately, many managers of small businesses don't realize that an incidental customer may represent a group of similar customers. A good way to identify new customer segments is to carefully study the different types of customers purchasing from your business. Classify them by demographics (where they live, sex, age, family life cycle, education, occupation, race, etc.), social class, personality, opinions, attitudes, lifestyle, rate of purchase, or other attributes you believe are important to your business. If you've never thought about who your business is targeting, separate customers into your best customers and other customers. Call your best customers your "targeted" customers. Then, separate the "other customers" into various groups. Finally, decide which of the "other customer segments" you should attempt to target — these are your new opportunities to grow. List these on your growth opportunities list.

Don't overlook groups of customers who have been buying from your business for a long time, even though you have never targeted them. Maybe you've taken them for granted. Now it's time to seize the opportunity to target them. Add these groups to your opportunities list.

You can also use Segment Development to target a new customer segment that doesn't presently purchase from your business. Perhaps an ethnic, religious, professional, or some other type group in your community has been growing in numbers, and it's time to target them with some trial promotions. Develop these opportunity ideas and add them to your list.

To develop any new segment opportunity, 1) search for the common needs of customers making up the new segment which you'll use in your new promotions, 2) determine the size of the new segment, 3) decide how to reach the new segment with your promotional messages, and 4) forecast the new customer segment's potential sales and profits. No doubt you'll discover that some segments can be targeted easily and cheaply. Other segments will be too small, too difficult to reach, or too expensive to reach. But put unfeasible segments on your opportunity's list anyway, so you can reconsider them during next year's growth planning session to see if something has changed that would let you target them.

Next, study the groups of people in your geographical area who don't buy your products and services at all. To develop these new segment opportunities, gather the same four types of information mentioned in the last paragraph. Add to the list any of these customer segments you think your business should consider targeting.

Finally, prioritize the segments on your growth opportunities list according to their potential sales and profits and according to the trouble and cost of appealing to them. For more information about segmenting, see Appendix A.

Market Development Growth Strategy

The second type of Industry Development involves finding new markets for your existing products and services. Opportunities to serve new markets are discovered in two ways. First, customers in other markets and other industries will occasionally contact your business with requests and inquires. Such outside contact is more likely when supply in the other market is inadequate, which means such inquires usually represent excellent opportunities to expand. So, if your business makes farm pond liners and you receive an inquiry asking if your business makes sanitation liners, the request may represent a valuable growth opportunity. Too often a telephone receptionist, secretary, or even an inside salesperson quickly dismisses such requests with a simple "No, I'm sorry, we don't," and your opportunity to grow through Market Development quickly disappears.

The second way to discover new markets is to actively search for them. A manager can list every market that uses a product or service like those offered by his or her firm. Then, analyze the market to 1) determine if that market has common needs, 2) determine the size of the new market, 3) determine how to reach customers in the new market with promotional messages, and 4) forecast the market's potential sales and profits.

For example, a small bookcase manufacturer who was targeting the home furnishing market with sturdy and attractive oak bookcases conducted a simple search for new markets and discovered another market that needed sturdy and attractive bookcases — the office supply market. Only a slight modification in stain colors was required to satisfy the business customers who purchase from the office supply market. Sales to the new market increased the productivity of the existing bookcase manufacturing facility because the small firm was able to make longer production runs. The small manufacturer made additional profits on the additional sales to the new market while it lowered the costs of all the bookcases it produced.

Market Development is an important growth strategy for many small businesses. Maury Island Farm is a small business making gourmet jellies under its own brand name for specialty food shops. It discovered a new market when a large department store called to ask them to provide jellies under the store's private label. The private label market sent sales soaring, and the only product modification required was the label *(15)*.

Judith McDowall is president of a Little Rock, Arkansas, technical writing business with annual sales of $837,000. Her firm, Biotechnical Services, Inc., was serving the Little Rock community when she decided to try targeting the federal government market. Her efforts landed a two-year contract worth $1 million with the National Institute of Environmental Health Sciences — a 60 percent increase in annual sales revenue through Market Development *(16)*.

Market Development rescued The James Clem Corporation of Chicago from the jaws of bankruptcy. James Clem founded a firm to manufacture pond liners. Clem's Claymax liner system was intended to replace traditional clay pond liners to keep ponds from leaking and going dry. Unfortunately, Clem's sales to this market were dismal.

Then James joined the U.S. Commerce Department's International "Matchmakers" program. An export specialist helped James get a trial in a different market with an Italian firm looking for a landfill liner. Success came quickly and sales soared as Claymax became an international waste containment product — the same existing product targeted at a new market *(17)*.

Here is a typical, broad breakdown of the types of markets into which you might expand. Each market can usually be subdivided in many different ways for different products and services. Your business is presently operating in one of these markets and can likely expand into one of the other markets.

1. Consumer Markets (many, many different ones)
2. Business Markets (lots of these)
3. Reseller markets (plenty of these)
   - wholesalers
   - distributors
   - private packagers
4. Government Markets
   - Federal
   - State
   - Local
   - Schools and Colleges
5. International Markets

Expanding into another consumer market may require identifying how your product or service can be used for a different purpose. For example, an unscented cold cream used in the cosmetics industry can be used as a hand cleaner in the automotive market. Epoxy glue used in the automotive market can be used as a high gloss finish in the furniture market. A liquid car wax can be used as a plastic shower and bathtub cleaner.

Resellers such as wholesalers, distributors, and manufacturer's representatives can help you identify new consumer markets for your products and services. The small Everett's Restaurant & Lounge chain developed a salad dressing that was a hit with customers. Everett's then used a reseller to bottle and distribute its salad dressing to the grocery store market. Without the reseller's distribution capabilities and access to valuable shelf space in grocery stores, Everett's Market Development could never have succeeded.

Small businesses serving consumer markets often expand by targeting business markets. After all, businesses also purchase automobiles, bookcases, cleaning solutions, lawn services, foods, and a host of other consumer type products and services.

The Federal Government is the single largest purchaser of goods and services in the United States, primarily because they purchase for the armed services *(18)*. Importantly, the Federal Government actively solicits small business products and services through its Procurement Automated Source System (PASS). To get listed, contact the U.S. Small Business Administration, PASS, 409 3rd St., S.W., Washington, D.C. 20416 *(19)*.

The Federal Government reserves some of its purchases for small businesses in order to encourage them to grow and provide increased competition in the future. Such special government set-aside programs for small businesses helped Claudette Weber's construction business to become the largest woman-owned general contracting firm in the U.S. *(20)*.

State governments also have special programs to help small businesses develop. Most states give a 5 percent price allowance to in-state small businesses bidding on their state's contracts. This means your price can be 5 percent higher than an out-of-state firm, and your business will still get the contract. Before submitting a bid, get copies of the previous years' winning bid proposals which will help you prepare your bid. Past winning bids become public records and are free for the asking.

In addition, if you're a female owner of a small business bidding on an in-state contract, many states give an extra 5 percent price allowance. The state usually adds another 5 percent price allowance if you belong to a minority. For example, if you are an African-American woman and own 51 percent or more of a small business, you could get a 15 percent price allowance. All small businesses should explore their opportunities to sell to their state government when trying to expand sales and profits.

International market assistance, private and public, can help you to identify foreign opportunities for your products and services. To enter a foreign market, you'll need help to produce foreign language promotions, to design packages for each target country, to find foreign technical writers, and to produce foreign presentation films tailored to each target country. For example, YAR Communications, a private consulting firm in New York City, has contacts in over 100 countries to help you *(21)*. Another source of international help is The American Chamber of Commerce, a public firm, maintains offices in many countries. Telephone the Washington D.C. Chamber office 202- 331-8696 and ask for publications about exporting. Also, contact the U.S. Commerce Department's Trade Information Center at 1-800-872-8723 and ask for assistance.

Finding Your Growth Opportunities

Finding new market opportunities begins by following up on the queries received by your business in the past from customers of other industries and other markets. Talk to your employees and make a list of the inquires your business has received. The interesting possibilities should be added to your growth opportunities list.

Next, search to discover new markets where your type product or service is purchased. You should expect the new markets to use your type products or services in a different manner. Add any interesting possibilities to your list.

Then, contact purchasing agents for your federal, state, or local governments and inquire about opportunities to sell your products and services to them. Add any interesting possibilities to your list.

Finally, contact the private and public groups who can help you discover your opportunities in international markets. Add any interesting possibilities to your list.

Most Market Development opportunities require you to spend some time and effort to study the new markets before deciding which new markets to enter. At this time, you'll probably want to develop a timetable for specific Market Development actions you will take in the next year. You'll need to collect initial information, evaluate it, and plan subsequent steps. On your growth opportunities list, establish a timetable for contacts and list the questions you want to ask. Then set a date for evaluating your discoveries.

CHAPTER 13

Marketing Growth Strategies for New Products and Services

THIS CHAPTER IS DEVOTED TO the second way that the marketing function of your business can grow sales — with strategies to sell *new* products and services. For growth planning purposes, "new" doesn't refer to a recently introduced product or service in your industry. A "new" product or service is defined as *any product or service your business isn't selling right now.* Other businesses in your industry may already offer the product, but for planning purposes it's new when your business decides to add it because the product is new to your business. Previously discontinued products and services are new when they are later reintroduced. For example, nostalgic products are old products that are reintroduced many years later when demand re-emerges, so nostalgic products are considered new even if your firm stocked and sold them in the past.

Finally, significantly modified versions of existing products and services become new products and services because they are expected to generate significant increases in sales. Slightly modified products and services are classified as existing products and services because they are not expected to generate significant increases in sales; they are expected to keep sales from declining.

Product Development Growth Strategy

A Product Development Growth Strategy is a plan to sell new products and new services to existing customers in the market where your business now competes. Studies show that for the average business, 30 to 35 percent of sales and profits come from products and services the business didn't offer 3 to 5 years earlier *(1)*.

Therefore, the average small business should expect that as much as one-third of future sales and profits will likely be generated by this growth strategy.

Product Development opportunities originate from ideas gathered from many sources, but the best source is customers themselves. Always ask customers what improvements they want. Also, prepare a list of proposed new product and service ideas or proposed new benefits and ask customers which they most want. If the list is long, ask them to indicate their top three choices by placing 1, 2, or 3 beside their preferences.

Customer requests are valuable sources of new product and service ideas. You should keep a list of requests. Make sure your employees are adding customer requests to your opportunities list. Review the list frequently and always review the list at planning time.

Don't ignore customer complaints, they're a gold mine of Product Development ideas. Contrary to common practice, you should encourage complaints, make complaining easy, collect complaints then study them. Be aware that research studies have concluded that only a few upset customers will bother to complain, most will simply switch to another business, product, or service. Because complaints are such a wonderful source of improvement ideas, you must design a simple, easy, customer-friendly complaint system.

Always try to separate both customer requests and complaints into two types: those from target customers and those from "other customers." Target customer feedback should be used to generate Product Development ideas. "Other customer" feedback should be used to generate Segment Diversification ideas; we'll cover this area later.

Managers and employees need to become sensitive to customer requests. Customers don't often walk up to an employee and state, "I have a request!" Most customers make offhand remarks like these:

"I wish your store carried ..."
"Could I pay someone to ..."
"I wish your product didn't ..."
"It broke because ..."
"I wish your product would ...
"Do you deliver?"
"I wish I could get a snack while I waited."
"I'm going to run across the street and get a soft drink while you finish that."
"Is there a pay phone around here?"

Customers often struggle with a business's products and services, and an idea that would eliminate that struggle would be a good Product Development idea. Instead, managers and employees, who have become experts at using the business's products and services, often say derogatory things like:

> "I can't understand why customers don't ..."
> "Customers don't understand that product."
> "Customers are so dumb, they believe that ..."
> "Why don't customers know about our service?"
> "Customers are so misinformed, they think ..."

You should insist that any employee uttering such comments be required to submit a Product Development idea designed to eliminate known customer problems and misconceptions. After all, the analysis of any one of these statements may lead to a new product or service idea, or it may help customers understand and purchase your existing products and services.

It's not uncommon for customers' problems to be in their heads. Unfortunately, sales are depressed anytime customers have the wrong ideas in their minds about your product or service. One part of product development is changing what customers think about your products and services with repositioning. When customers are confused about a product or service or when customers don't believe some of your truthful promotional claims, it may be time for a Repositioning strategy.

While customers are the source of the *best* Product Development ideas, employees are the source of the *most* Product Development ideas. Employees, yes even yours, are an endless supply of creative thoughts that you should nurture and encourage. One study reported that employees contribute 55 percent of all new product and service ideas *(2)*, so employees' ideas are important to the future of your business and its growth. Of course, most employee ideas are triggered by the customer comments they hear, which makes employee contributions particularly important. One manager couldn't believe his ears when a production employee began telling him what improvements customers wanted. It seems the employee's friends, who used the firm's products, frequently gave the employee their analysis of the products' good and bad points.

About one-fourth of all improvement ideas come from analyzing the benefits and shortcomings of competitors' products and services. Many of your competitors guess at what customers want. The result is a product with many attributes, each providing some arbitrary level of benefits. You can introduce a better product if you can determine which benefits customers want improved and which they would trade for a lower price. Your analysis of competitive products should be designed to discover if customers want more of certain benefits and less of others. One company analyzed a product that a competitor discontinued and only had to improve one attribute to make the product a success.

Don't forget to ask suppliers for new product and service ideas. True, they usually give you their ideas whether you want them or not, but when you're involved in an annual planning session, be sure to ask them for suggestions. Tell them you're planning for the upcoming year and that you want to know what new offerings they expect to introduce in that time frame.

Two Types of Product Development

Finding all your opportunities to use a Product Development Strategy is easier when the strategy is divided into smaller, more manageable pieces. Product Development involves two sales growth strategies: 1) Replacement Products and Services and 2) Complementary Products and Services.

Replacement Products and Services Growth Strategies

Replacements are improved products or services that replace existing ones. With technological advancements, the impossible becomes possible and the unaffordable becomes affordable. New benefits customers have long wanted can be added, benefits once too expensive can now be added economically, and new equipment allows services to be upgraded inexpensively. A non-ending cycle of invention is largely responsible for the four product life stages whereby a product or service is introduced, sales grow, sales mature, and sales decline as the next generation of improved products and services steals sales from existing ones.

For example, the black & white television, the 8mm-movie camera, and the dot matrix computer printer have traveled through Introduction, Growth, and Maturity life cycle stages. Then, sales of each declined with the introduction and growth of sales of color televisions, camcorders, and laser printers.

Replacement products are common; managers search for them; customers crave them. Consumers marvel as computers are continuously created that outperform existing models, and computer retailers eagerly anticipate the next generation of faster and better products because customers are waiting to grab them and rush to the cash registers. For the same reason, new cars are introduced each year as are new clothing styles. Replacement products are everywhere. Cereals are improved, tennis shoes are improved, and even pork is improved to be leaner. In fact, customers in many industries are conditioned to expect new, improved replacement products, and their satisfaction levels decline if a product or service isn't occasionally upgraded. Most customers look forward to change.

Customers' desire for change can be satisfied in two ways: 1) with actual product and service improvements and 2) with positioning improvements, using a Repositioning Growth Strategy. Either type, real or seemingly real, may create significant opportunities for your business to increase sales.

a) **Actual Product and Service Development Growth Strategy:** Actual improvements are physically or technically improved versions of existing products and services. The needs of target customers change and alter over time, forcing your business to modify existing products and services to better satisfy your customers. Technological advances allow a firm using an Enhancement Competitive Strategy to offer more advanced products and services with improved or totally new benefits for Selective Shoppers (see Chapter 4). Technological advancements allow a firm using a Low-Cost Competitive Strategy to offer Prudent Shoppers (see Chapter 3) benefits at a reasonable price that once were only available in enhanced products at high prices. Technological advances allow a firm using a Reduction Competitive Strategy (see Chapter 7) to design cheap substitutes and generic products and services at cheap prices that were not previously possible.

Replacement decisions should be driven by customer needs. For example, in the furniture industry, businesses targeting homeowners with wooden entertainment centers to hold televisions and stereo equipment physically alter their furniture designs to accommodate the changing needs of their customers. When customers began purchasing stereo receivers and equalizers, entertainment centers were redesigned to house them. When customers replaced turntables with cassette players and recorders, entertainment centers were redesigned. When customers began accumulating cassette tapes, cassette storage drawers were added. When compact disc players became popular, entertainment centers were redesigned. Entertainment centers were redesigned for VCRs and then again for VCR libraries. The latest entertainment furniture redesigns are to accommodate the shrinking size of stereo equipment and increasing size of television screens.

Surprisingly, in recent years replacement services have evolved even faster than replacement products. For example, services have been repeatedly redesigned to take advantage of the benefits of computer technology. From grocery store checkout scanners to bank ATMs to gas pumps with television screens that take credit cards, existing services are rapidly being replaced with improved services.

Almost all purchases involve a combination of products and services. Since the two are inseparable, improving either the product or one of the services creates a *new* replacement product because customers receive *new* benefits. For example, an automotive parts house sells a car battery with a service warranty.

The service warranty prorates benefits over the expected life of the product, so if you purchase a battery with a 48-month guarantee and it fails in its 24th month after purchase, the parts house gives you back half what you paid. The parts house would be using a Product Development Replacement Strategy if it improved only its service warranty. The parts house might offer a free replacement battery if the customer's battery fails in the first 24 months, and prorate the battery thereafter. The combination of the same battery with an improved service warranty provides customers additional benefits — peace of mind, added confidence in the product, and financial protection in the first 24 months.

Some small businesses design special systems to collect customers' improvement ideas, but one small furniture company devised an interesting low-cost system. The firm added a furniture modification system with guidelines for retailers. When the retailer's customer, the homeowner, requests a furniture modification that fits within the guidelines, the retailer telephones or faxes the request to the small manufacturer who quickly quotes a price for the special order. By building special orders, the small manufacturer is able to monitor the changing needs of its target customers. And frequently requested modifications become the next generation of replacement products. The small manufacturer calls the program its Poorboy's Market Research Program.

Improved products and services generate sales growth. Customers look forward to new benefits, modified benefits, and to the elimination of old problems. They often reward the business that is first to offer replacement products and services with increased loyalty.

Finding Your Growth Opportunities

The best sales growth opportunity for replacement products or services occurs when customer satisfaction begins to decline. For example, if you track and plot the monthly or quarterly sales of a typical product, sales will increase month after month, peak at a high level, and begin to decline some time in the future. If you could similarly track, measure, and plot customer satisfaction with the same product, satisfaction would take the same trip — climbing, leveling off, and declining — but satisfaction would begin to decline before sales began declining. The optimum time to introduce a replacement product, if you had the needed feedback from target customers, would be just as customer satisfaction begins to decline but prior to the decline in sales of the existing product. Using your crystal ball, you might be able to pinpoint the exact point in time to introduce a new product or service.

However, since crystal balls are both scarce and somewhat undependable, it's best to know that you can't expect customer satisfaction with a product or service to remain high forever, it won't. You can monitor customer satisfaction and work hard to find replacement products and services for introduction sometime after a product's sales level off.

Also, keep track of changes in remote trends — demographic, economic, political, technological, societal attitudes, and ecological — because they will create the need for replacement products with altered benefits. For example, the number of men over 50 years old will increase by 40 to 50 percent between 1995 and 2005. Sixty percent of men over 50 years of age experience a problem with enlarged prostrates, and doctors advise them to eliminate caffeine from their diets. This creates opportunities for businesses in the beverage industries to develop caffeine-free replacement beverages for men over the age of 50.

To find your opportunities to grow, write down every product and every service improvement, enhancement, or alteration that would increase sales if introduced in the coming years. When constructing your list of potential changes, think about how changing remote trends will likely affect your target customers and study the changing needs of customers. Remember, remote trends often cause customer dissatisfaction with existing products and services.

Next, consider the additional benefits allowed by new technologies. Consider that customers often expect previously unaffordable benefits to become economical; after all, color TVs, microwave ovens, computers, and camcorders were once expensive and are now affordable and have additional features. Customers are conditioned to expect and look forward to such changes. From your list of potential changes, identify the realistic changes that could be made to trigger additional sales to existing customers in the next few years. These are your new growth opportunities.

For each opportunity on your list, get feedback from customers to determine which changes and what level of changes they want, forecast the sales potential of each change, determine the actions your business must take to influence the development of each replacement product or service, and project the cost for each replacement opportunity. Finally, indicate the likelihood of your business's success for each opportunity, and prioritize your list of opportunities.

Repositioning Growth Strategy: Sometimes, to increase sales, an existing product or service needs only to be improved in the minds of your customers — the place where the decision to purchase is controlled. Once customers have the right information in their minds, sales can be robust. Consumer researchers have determined that customers form and store in their memories a short message comparing your products or services to those of your competitors. That short comparative message is called a "position message." If you asked customers to compare your product to competitive products, using only a few words, you'd be hearing their position message. When customers have a need or a want and decide to purchase a product or service, they often rely heavily on the position message in their minds to tell them where to shop and what to purchase. Therefore, the position message in your target customers' minds can have a huge effect on their buying decisions.

Smart businesses can greatly influence sales by formulating and planting a favorable positioning message in the minds of their target customers through their promotions. For example, 7-Up's highly effective positioning message is that it's the "Un-Cola." Managers at 7-Up understand that even the most loyal Coke and Pepsi drinkers occasionally want soft drink variety, and they have positioned 7-Up in customers' minds as a break from colas. Tide's positioning message is that it's an "All Family Detergent." Tide may or may not be any better as an all purpose family detergent, but Tide's product managers want their target customers to store in their minds a short, comparative message that Tide is unique because it will clean father's grease, mom's cooking splatters, son's little league stains, and daughter's crayola marks, all at the same time — the "All Family Detergent." The folks at Volvo want customers to store the thought that Volvo's "The Safe Car" because Volvo targets customers worried about safety. All of these companies have deliberately and successfully planted their positioning message in the minds of their target customers.

Unfortunately, customers sometimes store the wrong "position message" in their minds. When the wrong message is hurting your sales, the position message in customers' heads needs changing. That's when the business uses a Repositioning Growth Strategy. Repositioning is accomplished by 1) making some trivial change in your product or service or even just in your packaging and 2) making a major change in the positioning message you formulate and use in advertisements, promotions, and personal sales pitches.

Repositioning is constantly occurring all around you. Products you purchase in the grocery store are often repositioned to take advantage of current trends. For example, in recent years more and more consumers report an increased interest in eating healthier foods. Some fruit drink companies, whose products always contained some real fruit juice, have responded 1) with the trivial change of enlarging the picture of fresh fruit on their labels and 2) with the major change of promoting their products as healthy foods that contain real fruit juice — one such drink actually contains only one percent real juice, but it has a picture of three big oranges on its label. Simply by altering their package and altering their promotions, the fruit drink firms repositioned their drinks in the minds of target customers.

For the same health trend reasons, companies making cereals containing oats created new cereal box designs and promotions emphasizing the oat content to reposition their products as healthy choices in customers' minds. When using a Repositioning Growth Strategy, your product or service either doesn't change or it slightly changes, but your packaging, personal selling messages, and promotional messages change to support your new positioning message.

Finding Your Growth Opportunities

Few small businesses can afford expensive marketing research to measure the actual position message stored in target customers' minds. Therefore, your assignment is to think about the "position message" of your key products and services in minds of target customers. In conversations with customers, have too many of them expressed wrong opinions about your business or any of your key products or services? Do you hear target customers making false statements about your product, service, or business? Do you need to alter your business's positioning message or the positioning messages for any of your products or services to make them more compatible with emerging trends?

Many owners and managers of small businesses never fully appreciate the impact of the catchy, short messages that larger firms use, like Wal-Mart's "Everyday Low Prices" message. In this hectic, busy world where consumers never have enough time, Wal-Mart wants to position itself in customers' minds as a store with low prices everyday. That way, consumers can avoid running from store to store shopping advertised specials to save money. Your goal is to actively attempt to plant the positioning message you've formulated in your target customers' minds. You want them to know when to come to your business instead of shopping around with your competitors.

Identify your opportunities to increase sales by repositioning a product, a service, or your entire business in target customers' minds. Prioritize your list by sales increase potential, cost of repositioning, and likelihood of success.

Complementary Products and Services Growth Strategy

Complementary products and services are those that customers will purchase with your existing products and services. Most complementary items are connected to items customers are already buying. For example, a dress shop adds a line of belts, scarves, purses, and shoes that complement its existing line of dresses. Women will purchase these complementary items when they purchase new dresses. They often want to buy these items at the same time, so they can all be color and style coordinated. Furthermore, many women want the convenience and speed of one-store shopping.

Many lawn care businesses first offered customers basic lawn maintenance services. They soon discovered they could grow sales by adding complementary services like tree, shrub, and flower maintenance. These complementary services were purchased by existing customers.

Bookstores increased sales by adding bookmarks, book holders, and sweatshirts with pictures of authors — all complementary products. Barnes and Noble, the bookstore giant, even added a coffee shop.

For some small businesses, long-term growth has been achieved by continuously adding complementary items. Donna and Joseph Dubé started up a cheese shop in Wickford, RI, in 1981. Before long, some of their customers asked them to do catering, so they added a gourmet food catering service. Then some customers asked if they could purchase the same gourmet foods in their store, so they began selling gourmet foods and spices in their store. Next, customers asked for specialty coffees and fresh baked goods, and those complementary items were added. Later, customers showed a keen interest in the pots and pans the Dubés used, so they added a line of cookware and table accessories. Complementary products have been the Dubés' road to success *(3)*.

By adding a number of complementary products and services — beer, wine, liquor, video games, and pool tables — some enterprising entrepreneurs have transformed their mundane washaterias into a profitable form of singles' entertainment. Doing the laundry has become a way to make social connections.

Where do complementary product and service ideas come from? Talking to customers, listening to employees, analyzing competitors, and talking to suppliers. The best ideas come from customers, either directly or indirectly. If customers ask for a particular item, they obviously think your business should be selling it. Maybe you should.

However, complementary products and services don't have to be connected to your existing items. The simplest, non-connected example is a soft drink vending machine at a hair salon. Customers don't go to the salon for a soda, but they'll buy a soda while they wait. Likewise, customers don't travel to your oil and lube business to play video games, but many of them will play the games while waiting for their car to be serviced. Equally important, while they're poking money into your video game machine, they won't be complaining about waiting. Customers may not ask for non-connected, complementary items, but you can make a list of proposed items and ask customers to pick which they want.

Finding Your Growth Opportunities

Your assignment is to brainstorm — this is a good place to inject humor, to lower your inhibitions — about complementary products and services your target customers might purchase while they are at your business. Begin by listing items that are connected or related to your existing products and services.

Next, list the non-connected products and services that might be added. You may need to get some customer reactions to these ideas before you can assess each idea's impact on sales.

Prioritize your list by sales potential, cost, likelihood of success, and the effect each new item might have on your business's image. Inappropriate complementary products can cause the sales of other products to decline, so be sure to consider the interactions. For example, adding condom machines in the bathroom at a neighborhood bar would be appropriate and another source of profits, but adding condom machines in the dressing rooms at Nordstrom's Department Stores, while they might generate a few new sales, would harm Nordstrom's image and drive some customers away from the upscale department store.

Marketing Diversification Growth Strategy

Marketing Diversification is a growth plan that increases sales by selling new products or new services to new customer segments or to customers in entirely new markets.

Marketing Diversification is divided into Segment Diversification and Market Diversification. Segment Diversification is selling new products and services to new customer segments in your existing market. Market Diversification is selling new products and services in new markets. In general, Segment Diversification is the easier of the two to implement, but, like all generalities, exceptions abound. Actions of competitors, effects of remote trends, the growth phase of your industry, and your competitive strategy can combine to make either type easy or hard.

Segment Diversification is generally easier because it occurs within the existing market that you know well, and it likely involves new products and services that are modified versions of existing products and services. Therefore, costs, risks, and unknown risks are minimized. For example, employment opportunities at the Tyson chicken plant in Clarksville, Arkansas, have attracted a large number of Mexican-Americans and Mexicans with work visas to the community. Grocery store managers have added new products targeted at the new Hispanic segment, and video stores have added videos in Spanish — both examples of how easy Segment Diversification often is.

Market Diversification usually involves more investment and more risk. Risk is higher because less is known about the new market's various customer segments, business practices, and competitive structure. Such unknowns represent hidden risks. For example, one small, unfinished furniture manufacturer that supplied a network of unfinished furniture retailers decided to enter the conventional furniture market with a line of finished furniture. The manufacturer invested in finishing equipment and hired and trained additional employees, all with no clearly targeted customer segment in the new market. The small business had limited knowledge of the unique business practices in the new market and an incomplete list of competitors in the firm's territory. Not surprisingly, sales in the new market grew slowly.

New markets are easier to penetrate when a customer from that new market invites you in. For example, if a small water ski manufacturer is asked by a distributor to make a line of snow skis, the water ski producer will get a much needed helping hand while getting familiar with the competitive environment of the new market.

The best Segment and Market Diversification ideas usually come from the marketplace — from customers and from requests made by businesses, distributors, wholesalers, and resellers. Segment Diversification ideas often come from customer complaints, which is why you were advised in the Product Development section of this chapter to separate all customer feedback into *target customer* feedback and *other customer* feedback, this is where you use the *other customer* feedback. Requests and complaints from other customers are a gold mine of Segment Diversification ideas. It's not surprising that products and services made for your target customers would fall short of satisfying customers in non-targeted segments. And, since those other customers don't know who you're targeting, they assume you'd like to know what your problems are so you can fix them. By making requests or complaining, they're giving you the Segment Diversification ideas you need to make or add a new product or service for their segment.

On the other hand, Market Diversification opportunities are easy to ignore or prematurely dismiss. Usually, someone from another market telephones with a question like, "Do you have ...?" or "Do you make ...?" Employees say no and don't record who called, from what business, with what request, and how to call them back. So, the Market Diversification opportunity is lost. If you're lucky, some day the employee will say, "I bet I've had 50 calls asking for that in the last six months." If you're lucky you'll wake up and suddenly become aware of the new Market Diversification growth opportunity.

If you want to make sure your business doesn't overlook diversification opportunities, make sure that every employee in contact with customers — even the receptionist and repair person — is instructed to listen carefully and intently for any and all new product and service ideas, requests, and complaints. They should make written notes, and someone in your organization should be collecting them. The list should be reviewed frequently, and the list should be studied during your annual growth planning session.

Segment Diversification Growth Strategy

Segment Diversification is used to grow sales in a business's existing market. A manager spots an opportunity to expand sales and profits by offering a new product or service to a new customer segment. A good example comes from the diet food industry. By talking to customers, diet food manufacturers were pleasantly surprised to discover that a sizeable number of their current customers weren't dieters. These *other customers* ate diet foods because they were healthy foods. The manufacturers realized they could target the new customer segment with healthy foods by modifying their products, changing their packages, and designing promotions targeted at the new *health food segment* of customers.

Like diet foods, healthy foods are low in cholesterol, high in fiber and nutritional value but only reduced in fat content, instead of being low-fat or fat-free like diet foods. Healthy foods can taste better since these customers want to maintain their weight, not lose weight. By modifying diet foods to deliver the benefits wanted by healthy food customers, by formulating the appropriate positioning message, and by targeting promotions at the new segment, sales grew rapidly.

The healthy food segment was closely related to the existing diet food segment. Both belong in the same overall "convenience food market." Both segments could be served with the same competitive strategy. The production and retailing of both types of products required compatible skills, assets, and competencies. The KSFs that triggered sales to dieters and to health-conscious customers were related, compatible, and synergistic. All these similarities made the two product lines easy to manage.

You can also use Segment Diversification to successfully target customer segments with no current connection to your business. However, it is more likely you'll use Segment Diversification when you discover incidental customers (non-targeted customers) occasionally purchasing from your business who need and want a modified version of your existing product or service — a *new* product or service.

To find non-targeted customers, separate your existing customers into target customer segments and other customer segments, and then study the unique needs, wants, and behaviors of the other customers. Don't expect a large number of customers from other segments to be shopping at your business; your current products and services probably aren't capable of fulfilling their needs. Your goal is to identify new segments to whom sales would greatly increase if your business modified an existing product or service to provide the special benefits they want. Then to accelerate sales, you'll need to devise a new promotional campaign that's targeted at the new segment.

How to Separate Current Customers into Customer Segments

Segmentation techniques are simple and straightforward. Current customers can be segmented in many ways. You can separate consumers into segments by simply thinking about the different needs of consumers in your market. Do the needs of women differ from those of men? Do single people, married couples, and married couples with children all have different needs? Perhaps you've been so busy operating your business that you've not taken the time to study the differing needs of various segments of customers in your market; take the time.

Another segmenting method is to divide current customers into two groups: best customers and occasional customers. Then, study and compare the needs of each group in order to discover any unique needs of the occasional customers. Those unique needs represent growth opportunities.

Another simple segmentation method is to separate current customers by dividing them into groups according to the amount of products and services they purchase from your business: heavy buyers, moderate buyers, light buyers, occasional buyers, first-time buyers, ex-buyers, or even non-buyers. Then you can compare the needs of each segment to those of your heavy buyers to discover any unique needs of each segment. Those unique needs represent growth opportunities.

Another common way to identify all your Segment Diversification opportunities is to divide current customers into many different groups according to their significant demographic and lifestyle differences (see Appendix A). Then study and compare the needs of each segment to identify growth opportunities.

As presented in the Competitive Strategy section, demographics are the descriptive characteristics of customers such as age, gender, family size, family life cycle, income, social class, occupation, education, religion, race, nationality, place of residence, and other counting variables. A demographic variable can be any customer characteristic you think may be important. If you think age is a significant determinate of what various customer segments purchase or want to purchase, you can establish age ranges for current customers like 0 to 10, 11 to 20, 21 to 30, 31 to 40, and so forth, and count how many current customers fall into each age range then study each age groups' purchases and needs. Most products and services sell best to one age range, and most other age ranges need significantly modified products and services.

Likewise, you can count how many of your current customers fall into various income ranges, gender categories, sexual preference categories, family size categories, nationalities, drive pick-up trucks versus cars, listen to different types of music, and so forth. The needs of each customer segment may differ according to one demographic variable, or a combination of several demographic variables. A combination of variables is called a demographic profile. For example, in the clothing market a number of customer segments can be identified by combining the variables of age, income, occupation, wearing occasion, and gender. This creates different segments who want and need their own sizes, styles, and types of clothing.

In the marketplace, different demographic profiles exist for customers who buy different types of beer, cars, televisions, furniture, and services.

When you separate your current customers into various segments according to their demographic differences, you may discover that some of those groups have unique needs. Offering a significantly modified product and service to more fully satisfy a newly found customer segment will increase your business's sales.

A business manager can easily separate customers into demographic segments and think about the changes that might increase sales to each group. For example, it's easy for an auto parts business owner to mentally separate customers into a male segment and a female segment and imagine ways to grow with each segment. The same owner can separate customers into different occupations, income levels, social classes, or geographically by the subdivisions where they live. Then consider changes to existing services and even existing products that would boost sales to each group.

Another simple way to separate current customers into customer segments is by their lifestyles. Because people live their lives in different ways, they have different needs as consumers. One lifestyle segmentation technique is to separate customers into groups according to how they earn their living, their hobbies, vacation habits, club memberships, favorite sports, etc. Then study the needs of each group. You would expect the product and service needs of customers with professional jobs who garden for a hobby, take overseas vacations, and maintain a country club membership to differ significantly from factory workers who repair cars for a hobby, take fishing vacations to a nearby lake, and maintain a VFW membership. It's common for customers with different lifestyles to buy houses in different areas, to eat different foods, wear different clothes, and buy different accessories. The wants and needs of various customer segments will likely vary according to their lifestyle differences.

Lifestyle segmentation also involves segmenting customers by the interests they have: family, home, recreation, food, media, etc. Take just one example; it's common for customers with different media interests to purchase different products and services. Obviously, you'll have to reach each media segment with a different promotion delivered through the media each uses. You may want to segment your customers into heavy TV watchers, heavy newspaper and magazine readers, heavy radio listeners, and heavy Internet users. Then, study the needs and wants of each media segment.

Lifestyle segmentation can involve segmenting customers by the opinions they hold about politics, education, culture, social issues, ecology, etc. For example, a lawn care business might segment prospective customers according to their ecological attitudes and design unique services for each segment. If enough environmentally conscious customers were discovered, the lawn care firm might design an organic lawn service. Or, if enough bird-loving customers were discovered, the lawn care firm might design a lawn service for their needs.

Publishers of *The Farm Journal* expanded their sales through aggressive use of Segment Diversification. With the aid of their computer, they identified 1,134 different farm segments based on the geographic location of each farm and the type of farming each did. They put an apple farmer in Washington state in a different segment than an apple farmer in northern Alabama, because each faces a different set of problems and needs different information. Then, they decided to produce a different version of each magazine issue for each segment. Today they publish 1,134 different editions of each magazine *(4)*.

Blackie's restaurant and dance club of Springfield, Virginia, opened in 1988 featuring Top 40s music. As a Segment Diversification experiment in early 1992, Blackie's tried a one-time country music night. Business increased by 60 percent, and Blackie's eventually switched completely to a country music format *(5)*.

Unfortunately, the task of actually dividing customers into various segments, though simple, can be tedious for a manager of a small business. Segmenting is time consuming because there are so many segmenting alternatives. A manager might segment customers by income, study the needs of each segment, and get nothing useful out of that effort. A manager might try many segmenting schemes before finding one that reveals a new growth opportunity. But, while tedious, segmenting is a simple skill that can be developed easily with practice. Just remember, if you've tried one segmenting scheme and it didn't work, you're one scheme closer to finding the one that does work.

Some information about the success and failure rates of businesses using Segment Diversification has been gathered. One study by the Association of National Advertisers in 1984 found that 46 percent of new products introduced into new categories (segments) failed *(6)*. The good news is that 54 percent of the attempts were successful, an astounding success record. It would be interesting to count the number of failures where the failed product was inconsistent with the firm's competitive strategy. More failures would be expected if the firm didn't have the necessary skills, assets, or competencies to support their Segment Diversification choice.

Finding Your Growth Opportunities

The more accurately you can profile the characteristics of your business's target customer segments, the quicker and easier it will be for you to recognize "other customers" that might become targets with new products and services. Segmenting is a skill that's acquired through practice; a competency that develops as a manager works to improve continuously his or her ability to create a descriptive profile of various customer segments. Begin developing your skills by building a clear customer profile of your best customers, then proceed to describe other customers.

Your goal is to find new customer segments to target with new products and services by studying "other customers," who occasionally purchase from your business and potential customers who don't purchase from your business. Practice segmenting all customers into different groups by sex, income, social class, or any of the other appropriate characteristics for your business and be sure to review all of the segmenting characteristics in Appendix A. Then, study and compare the wants, needs, and behaviors of each of the segments to identify how they differ from your best or targeted customers. When you recognize any special needs of a new customer segment, you've discovered an opportunity to grow with Segment Diversification. Write it down on your list of growth opportunities.

Next, examine your community, or the area your business serves, to identify any emerging people trends. Just as Clarksville, Arkansas, retailers saw an increasing number of Hispanics moving to their community that they could target, you may spot changes in the mix of people in your trade area. Some trends may be too subtle to visually spot, so get copies of the last few census bureau studies of tracts in your trade area. These can show that changes in income levels, family size, types of homes, racial makeup, etc., are occurring. Your local library, congressperson, or college can help you acquire the right census track profiles. When you identify emerging people trends, study their needs to determine what new products or services will be needed to satisfy them. Add your discoveries to your growth opportunities list.

Finally, for each growth opportunity on your list, study the size of each new segment, determine how to reach each new segment with your promotional messages, and forecast each new segment's potential sales and profits. Prioritize your opportunities from best to poorest.

Market Diversification Growth Strategy

Market Diversification is the most difficult of the marketing growth strategies. It often requires entering new markets with new products and services and at the same time adding new technologies. A firm may find itself adding new equipment, new business processes, and new employees in order to produce or sell new items into an unfamiliar market that contains new competitors it doesn't yet understand. Therefore, Market Diversification can be risky.

For example, a water ski manufacturer making a high performance ski targeted at non-professional water skiers faces a risky situation when it decides to make a moderately priced snow ski targeted at middle-income snow skiers. This involves a new market, a new product, new customers, new technology, new distributors, new retailers, and new competitors. The comfort that management initially feels because both products are skis will fade as it faces all the new challenges and problems. It's easy to understand that the best Market Diversification growth opportunities are the ones most compatible with the firm's existing business because they involve the fewest new challenges.

Just as water skis and snow skis are both skis, most Market Diversification strategies involve entering a new market that has something in common with the firm's existing market. Knowing the firm's existing strengths, a manager can often search for other markets where those strengths might be used. Likewise, customers from other markets will search for new suppliers in your market if they believe your market is related to theirs. For example, if moderately priced snow skis were in short supply, a snow ski distributor would likely call a water ski manufacturer with a good reputation and ask them to consider making a line of snow skis.

Marketing Diversification growth opportunities can be discovered in lots of ways. For one company, a joke led to a new growth opportunity. Biofoam Inc. in Phoenix was formed to make a foamed snack food made from grain sorghum. Then someone joked about the product looking like those foamed plastic peanuts used as packing material. Management suddenly realized its grain sorghum peanut could replace plastic peanuts. With a little study, Biofoam discovered that those plastic shipping peanuts take 500 years to biodegrade while their foamed sorghum peanuts dissolve instantly. Heck, sorghum foam is so environment friendly, it can be eaten.

Biofoam stripped the nutritional content out of the sorghum and introduced a cheap, biodegradable packing material that could be disposed of by dissolving it in water, composting it, feeding it to the dog, or eating it with your favorite salsa *(7)*.

Guilford Mills felt it needed to diversify. Guilford was making material for lingerie manufacturers, but wanted to diversify so it wouldn't have all its eggs in one basket. The company's search for a way to use its existing strengths and existing materials in other markets resulted in making materials for car roof liners. Now Guilford's profits come from two unrelated markets: the lingerie market and the automotive market.

Your opportunity to use a Market Diversification strategy may be the result of a deliberate search for ways to broaden your business to unrelated markets, but, more likely, it will come from a customer request. That's what happened to Peter and Judith who own and operate the Maury Island Farm and sold fresh fruit. A Seattle restaurant chain that purchased their fruit asked them to consider making jellies. That customer request caused them to diversify into the gourmet jelly market which has become a vital and profitable part of their growing business *(8)*. Similarly, Alphatronix created the optical-disk integrated computer storage system because of customer requests *(9)*.

Customer requests brought a new market opportunity to Marc Kreiner's door. A few rent-a-car customers began asking to rent cellular phones, and Marc Kreiner saw his chance to diversify. He immediately realized that renting cars and renting phones were similar. His firm would use the same skills and competencies to find customers, qualify their credit, issue invoices, and provide service. On top of that, Kreiner's employees had the extra time to spend renting cellular phones. After diversifying, Kreiner discovered that running the two businesses was cheaper. He was able to spread his overhead costs among more products thus improving his economy of scale *(10)*.

Finding Your Growth Opportunities

Market Diversification opportunities are uncovered in two ways: through customer queries and through deliberate searches. First, you should ask every employee to recall all requests for any product or service your business doesn't sell. In the future, make sure every employee understands that when they respond to an inquiry by saying, "We don't have that," or "We don't stock that," or "We don't do that," or "We can't get that," that those inquiries represent opportunities to diversify into other markets. Tell your employees to document each request: name, business, address, phone number, and the request. Then the requests should be reviewed often to determine their Market Diversification potential.

Imagine the lost sales and profits if a receptionist for the Maury Island Farm had told the Seattle restaurant chain, "We don't make jellies," and sent the caller away. Or, imagine Kreiner telling his employees to get some business cards for area cell phone businesses and give them out when customers asked about renting cellular phones. Unusual customer requests can lead to major opportunities to expand sales and profits. If you're interested in expanding, you should collect unusual requests and study their potential.

Make a list of the diversification opportunities customers have offered your business in the recent past and follow up to determine the potential of each.

Second, deliberate searches for Market Diversification growth opportunities begin by identifying your strengths and weaknesses. After careful consideration, you may find that your strengths differ from the KSFs needed to trigger sales to your present customer segments. In fact, a good reason to use Market Diversification is because your business has strengths that are not important in your existing market and could be put to a more profitable use. Therefore, you initiate a search for another market where your strengths will generate bigger profits.

Examine each portion of your business. For example, identify any strengths or weaknesses you have in receiving, operations, shipping, marketing, service-after-the-sale, purchasing, personnel, technology management, finance, cash flow, credit, or general management. Then search for other markets where your strengths are valuable and your weaknesses aren't important. Advertise your strengths in business publications. Contact business brokers and tell them you're looking for a business where you can use your strengths. Even if you don't purchase a business from the brokers, the suggestions they come up with may help you to identify a more profitable way to use your strengths. Read small business magazines. Network with other business owners. Put out feelers. Add your discoveries to your Market Diversification list of growth opportunities.

Finally, study the size of each new market, the competitors in each new market, and the intensity of competitive rivalry in each new market. How likely are existing competitors to fight your entry into their domain?

Study substitute products and services in each new market. The price of substitute products and services creates a price ceiling for your new product or service. If the price of your product or service in the new market is too high or becomes too high, customers will buy the substitute. For example, steel cans can be substituted for aluminum cans. If the price of aluminum cans rises too high, customers will switch to steel cans. So manufacturers of aluminum cans have to monitor the activities of other aluminum can manufacturers and the activities of steel can manufacturers. Since most products and services have substitutes, you need to study the substitutes in the new market.

Study the power of customers in the new market. Lots of customers making lots of small purchases is usually much better than a few customers making a few big purchases. The latter is normally risky. The same is true of suppliers. If you'll need new suppliers for the new market, lots of suppliers are better than a few suppliers. The latter is normally risky.

And as always, you'll need to determine how to reach target customers in the new market with your promotional messages. Forecast potential sales and profits and prioritize your list.

CHAPTER 14

Management Sales Growth Strategies

OWNER, PRESIDENT, CEO (Chief Executive Officer), and Boss are a few of the official titles that top managers in small businesses give themselves; more colorful titles are occasionally invented by employees. Regardless of the title, a small firm's top manager has a unique perspective on sales growth that's broader than a marketing perspective. Even if the business is so small that you perform both jobs, President and Head of Marketing, you'll discover additional opportunities to increase sales when you examine the business strictly from a CEO's viewpoint.

All too often managers of small businesses view their firm only from a marketing perspective and wind up spending most of their efforts trying to expand immediate sales to current customers. The remainder of their growth strategy effort consists of working with suppliers to choose new products and services to promote. Rarely does a manager take the time to look beyond the firm's current marketing efforts and search for new opportunities to increase sales.

From the perspective of a small business CEO, you have a wider purview that's influenced by the bottom line on the Income Statement. You stop being the marketing manager who has to generate sales, and you start being the CEO who has to generate profits. You stop being a marketing manager who's disturbed by customer complaints, and become a CEO who's disturbed by overhead expenses that take too big a bite out of each sales dollar. A CEO is distressed when any of the business's resources are too often idle. It's the CEO who searches for ways to lower the cost of things like idle equipment, empty office space, or underutilized employees. It's the CEO who searches for opportunities to grow sales in specific ways that will get the business out of its current efficiency problems.

A marketing manager's growth ideas are influenced by customers' praise, suggestions, and requests, as well as by complaints. The small business CEO's growth ideas are influenced not only by customers but also by operating problems, by financial statements, and by opportunities discovered at community functions, social functions, and industry meetings. A CEO's growth ideas should be influenced by reading a large variety of business publications. As CEO, you should be in your community's rumor loop. There you may learn about a business that's for sale, though not advertised, or about an outside firm that's contacted the local Chamber of Commerce asking for help finding a local business to represent its products. As CEO, you have different information sources than a marketing manager, which will make you aware of different ways to grow.

The novel perspective of a CEO leads to the formulation of four additional sales growth strategies.

1. Related Diversification
2. Opportunistic Diversification
3. Forward Integration
4. Horizontal Integration

Forget about marketing for a while and look for additional growth opportunities by examining your business strictly from a CEO's viewpoint. You'll discover different growth opportunities because you're looking for different growth opportunities in different areas and in different ways.

Related Diversification Sales Growth Strategy

Related Diversification and Marketing Diversification are both diversification strategies, so they are similar. Both refer to strategies to sell new products and new services to new customer segments or in new markets. Yet the two strategies differ. Marketing strategies are developed to respond to customers' needs. Related diversification strategies are developed to respond to the business's needs. While marketing managers are responding to customer requests and market needs, CEOs are responding to the business's need for higher sales and profits. When marketing strategies can't generate the sales and profit growth your business needs, Related Diversification is the first management strategy a CEO explores when looking for alternative ways to grow.

Related Diversification opportunities are favorites of small business CEOs because they are relatively easy to implement. Related opportunities use skills, assets, and competencies the firm already possesses, or ones that are similar to those the firm possesses. There are two types of Related Diversification: Efficiency Diversification and Compatible Diversification. Each type is pursued for different reasons. Efficiency Diversification is used to expand sales in order to reduce costs, which will increase profits. Compatible Diversification is used to expand sales to directly increase profits.

Efficiency Diversification: A Type of Related Diversification

Efficiency Diversification is used primarily to compensate for burdensome overhead costs caused by specific inefficiencies. A small business CEO discovers such inefficiencies by 1) observing idle resources and by 2) reviewing the cost of items shown on the firm's financial statements.

Efficiency Diversification is typically used in two ways. A manager can add new products and services that will use the firm's idle resources. Or a manager can rent, lease, or subcontract the firm's idle resources to offset their cost to the business. For example, renting a piece of equipment to an area business would show up as additional sales on your next Income Statement, and the rental revenue stream would offset the high overhead cost of the idle equipment.

Head Ski, a successful snow ski manufacturer, demonstrates how adding new products can combat the inefficiency that accompanies a seasonal market. Management at Head Ski diversified into summer sporting goods and clothing because summer sales would add profits and would absorb the company's off-season overhead expenses. Prior to diversification, the entire year's management, warehouse, sales force, computer system, and equipment costs were charged to its snow ski business. After the diversification, a large portion of the overhead costs could be charged to summer business. Thus, the snow ski business costs would drop significantly, and the company's profits would increase as long as its summer business at least broke even *(1)*.

As the Head Ski example demonstrates, a CEO's best use of Efficiency Diversification is to identify a growth opportunity that will permanently put idle resources to work and add additional profits. This is healthy growth because it is a long-term solution to a recurring problem.

Efficiency Diversification can be used a second way. By leasing, renting, or subcontracting the idle resources, the business can offset the cost of those resources. For example, the CEO of a California-based moving business recognized a need to more fully use the firm's delivery trucks. After all, it's frustrating to see the firm's major assets too often sitting idle in the parking lot collecting dust while the firm's loan payments, insurance payments, and tax payments continue to come due.

Management devised an Efficiency Diversification strategy whereby they would compete with U-Haul and Ryder Rental, but with a larger truck and trailer than those competitors provide. The firm began leasing their large tractor-trailer moving vans to area businesses during slack periods. They began leasing idle trucks at $50 per hour plus $40 a day for insurance. Leasing was a flexible business, since trucks were only leased if the regular moving business didn't need them *(2)*.

Another manager of a small business explained that she lowered her building overhead expense by leasing part of her firm's warehouse to another business. It would be years before her small firm grew large enough to use the entire warehouse. In the mean time, leasing a part of the warehouse gave the small firm a new revenue stream and made the remaining warehouse very economical.

In another small scale diversification, the CEO of Arkansas Woodworks Manufacturing Company studied the firm's Income Statement and decided that the firm's delivery expenses were too high. To offset the expense, the CEO approached a local craft producer with the idea of distributing its craft items to furniture retailers. The deal was struck, and profits from the distribution of the craft items offset a sizeable portion of the manufacturer's delivery expenses. Because craft items were small, they could be shipped inside the furniture; thus they easily fit within the already full delivery trucks without displacing any of the manufacturer's furniture.

Efficiency Diversification is common among small businesses, as these examples demonstrate:

- One small firm occasionally rents its forklift to a neighboring business.
- Another subcontracts time on some of its equipment.
- Another runs its own temp service by contracting out the services of some expensive employees on a part-time basis to area businesses.
- Another that has a repair service sought to become the regional repair facility for a large manufacturer to fully use its facility.
- Still another farms out an employee to a vocational college to conduct a training session.
- Yet another arranges backhauls for its delivery trucks that had been returning empty from a distant city.

All of these Efficiency Diversification examples have a common purpose, to offset the cost of an idle resource in order to boost profits.

Finding Your Growth Opportunities

Finding all your opportunities to use efficiency diversification involves two steps. First, identify your firm's idle resources. Second, find your firm's opportunities to use each idle resource.

Identifying Idle Resources. Begin with a management-by-walking-around technique. As you walk through each part of your business, look for idle resources such as idle computers, idle delivery trucks, empty warehouse space, an inside salesperson playing solitaire on the computer, a couple of empty offices being used to store junk, idle production equipment, and so on. Then, estimate the portion of the workweek the resource sits idle. Estimate how much profits might increase if your firm didn't have to absorb the overhead or direct expense of each idle resource. Make a list of idle resources that concern you, and prioritize the list by cost.

Next, analyze your Income Statement and Balance Sheet. Examine your expenses and assets line by line. Figure 14.1 shows how to analyze each type of expense.

Express each type of expense as a portion or percentage of one sales dollar. Then compare each expense percentage to those of other businesses like your own, and compare each expense percentage to your performance in previous months, quarters, and years. For example, consider Figure 14.1, if you discover that delivery expenses average 4 percent for other businesses similar to yours, you'll have an opportunity to increase profits by $2,500 (i.e., $250,000 times 1 percent if you lower costs to 4 percent) if you can duplicate their delivery systems.

FIGURE 14.1: Expense Analysis Example

Delivery expense ÷ total sales = portion of each sales dollar that goes to delivery.

If your income statement shows:

Annual Delivery Expense = $12,500

&

Annual Total Sales = $250,000

Then: $12,500 ÷ $250,000 = $.05 delivery expense for every one dollar of sales.

Also: ($12,500 ÷ $250,000) X 100% = 5% meaning that delivery expense is 5% of sales.

You may discover your delivery expense is slowly increasing over time. Such knowledge will motivate you to make your business perform as efficiently as other managers have made their businesses perform or to reverse your escalating cost trend.

As shown in Figure 14.2, assets are analyzed differently. For major assets, divide annual sales by the dollar amount of the asset shown on your balance sheet to get sales per asset dollar.

This will allow you to compare your business's performance with other, similar businesses. Suppose you discover that the average "Sales per equipment dollar" is $8.00 in your industry for firms of your size while your "Sales per equipment dollar" is $5.00. This could mean one of three things: 1) other business managers are making better equipment choices, 2) other businesses are using their equipment more effectively and efficiently than your business, or 3) you've overpurchased equipment in anticipation of rapid growth. Asset analysis is a way to recognize poor management, and if your numbers are poor, you'll be motivated to improve your management competencies. You'll be motivated to find out how other businesses your size manage to generate more sales for each dollar they invest in a given asset.

Idle resources always show up as assets with unusually low sales ratios — meaning low sales per dollar invested in the asset. Not every low number represents an idle resource, but every idle resource shows up as a low sales-to-asset ratio.

FIGURE 14.2: Asset Productivity Analysis Example

Total sales ÷ asset = the dollars of sales generated by each dollar invested in that asset.

If:

Annual Total Sales = $250,000

&

Equipment Assets = $50,000 (from the Balance Sheet)

Then:

$250,000 ÷ $50,000 = $5.00 in sales for every one dollar invested in equipment.

Examine the categories of expenses that are too high and determine which are too high because of idle resources. For example, building expenses can be too high because you've leased a very expensive location, or because the building is too big for your business. Keep in mind that a fast-growing business will occasionally incur expenses that are too high in some categories, but a fast-growing business will quickly grow out of its problems. The troublesome expenses are those that hold the business back, eat up too much cash flow, and keep the business from growing.

If you're unsure what good ratio numbers look like, contact a trade association in your industry to get the average figures for businesses of your size. Ask your CPA to compare your firm's figures with similar firms. You can occasionally, with the help of your suppliers or your trade association, contact businesses like yours in other geographic areas and swap figures.

Your Assignment. Now that you've identified your business's idle resources by walking around and by ratio analysis, your assignment is to find growth opportunities to use those idle resources. The best growth opportunity is to first identify new products and services you could add that would use the idle resources. Second, if this approach isn't possible, search for opportunities to rent, lease, or subcontract each idle resource to offset its costs to the business. These two types of searches require you, as the CEO, to use your industry, business, and community contacts to find opportunities to use the firm's idle resources. Also, review the emerging trends in your market for additional opportunities that will be developing in the near future.

Compatible Diversification: A Type of Related Diversification

Compatible diversification is known as *focused growth*. Focused growth refers to increasing sales by adding new products or new services that require the same or compatible skills, assets, and competencies as those the firm already possesses. The CEO achieves focused growth by listing the firm's existing skill strengths, asset strengths, and competencies (special abilities of employees and managers) and comparing these to the strengths that will be needed to pursue each diversification opportunity. If compatibility is high between the existing business and the new growth opportunity, the business expansion will be less disruptive to the organization, increasing the likelihood of success.

A CEO uses Compatible Diversification for two reasons: to grow sales and to lower costs. Compatible Diversification is the first alternative for a business in a sluggish market where sales growth has slowed or stopped. If there are no growth opportunities left within your market, look for compatible growth opportunities where your business's talents can easily be transferred to increase sales.

Sharon Lee-Tucci used Compatible Diversification because her business had run out of room to grow. Sharon founded a talent agency, Talent Plus in St. Louis, which grew to represent 700 clients to some 2,400 talent buyers. Her firm was successful and profitable, but additional growth in St. Louis wasn't possible. She searched for a Compatible Diversification opportunity, one that would let her use the skills and competencies she had already developed and that involved working with similar customers and similar clients.

Sharon found a Compatible Diversification opportunity. She formed a speaker's bureau. She had long observed the convention business in St. Louis, and convention planners were always searching for keynote speakers. Sharon decided to book celebrities to give headline speeches at conventions and corporate events.

The new service would require her to receive requests just as she did now from talent buyers, to find the talent just as she did now with her 700 clients, to handle similar contracts, and to schedule appearances in a similar fashion. The new growth opportunity required highly compatible skills and competencies to those she had already mastered, so it was a "focused" growth opportunity *(3)*.

Bill Engler used Compatible Diversification to increase sales and profits and to cut costs. In 1984 Kaytee Products Inc. of Chilton, Wisconsin, was a producer of pet foods for hamsters, gerbils, rabbits, and similar small animals. The moderately sized company had about 60 employees and sales of $10.6 million, but CEO Bill Engler wanted more. He considered the purchase of a compatible business in Southern California that produced wild bird foods and small pet foods.

Buying the business would increase Kaytee's sales and profits. Buying the business would also greatly improve Kaytee's economy of scale in several major ways. First, since both firms' products were sold to the same pet stores, a Kaytee salesperson could make a larger sale on each sales call, so the selling cost per sales dollar would decline. Second, instead of both companies running advertisements to target retail pet stores, only one set of advertisements would be required that showed all the products. Therefore, advertising cost per sales dollar would decline. Third, existing warehouses on opposite coasts could stock both sets of products, so warehousing overhead per sales dollar would decline. Fourth, material-handling equipment would be more fully utilized. Fifth, deliveries to pet stores would be more efficient. Sixth, billing could be consolidated. Seventh, management overhead could be consolidated. Seven economy of scale reasons why operating the combined company would lower the firm's per product costs.

Finally, Kaytee would strengthen its sales triggers. Small pet food retailers could meet minimum order volumes with the wider product line, which would trigger more orders. West coast products would now be stocked in the East and vice versa, speeding up delivery times to customers. With faster deliveries, many retailers would be able to operate with less inventory *(4)*.

Compatible Diversification doesn't require that you buy another business, like Kaytee did. However, like Kaytee, you should consider each Compatible Diversification's potential to create economy of scale cost savings and to strengthen your KSFs.

Finding Your Growth Opportunities

Searching for opportunities to use Compatible Diversification is much the same as searching for Marketing Diversification opportunities (See Chapter 12), but a CEO's search is much broader and his or her motivation for the search is different. A CEO turns to Compatible Diversification when growth opportunities in the firm's existing markets are poor. A CEO turns to Compatible Diversification in order to reduce costs through economy of scale. A highly aggressive CEO turns to Compatible Diversification to achieve extremely fast, low risk sales growth.

Your search for opportunities to use Compatible Diversification begins by listing your business's strengths — particularly KSF strengths — and weaknesses. When you find new diversification opportunities, analyze each opportunity's compatibility with your existing business to identify focused growth opportunities.

Make a list of your business's compatible growth opportunities. Analyze their compatibility. Analyze each opportunity's economy of scale advantages, ability to strengthen existing KSFs, sales growth potential, and profit growth potential. Prioritize your list.

Opportunistic Diversification Sales Growth Strategy

Opportunistic Diversification is an aggressive plan to seize any realistic opportunity to expand sales and add profits without any self-imposed restrictions that the new growth be related to the existing business in any manner or that the new growth be focused. Whether focused or unfocused, compatible or incompatible, any growth opportunity that will produce a good profit is added to the list of opportunities. New products don't have to be related to current products. New markets don't have to be related to current markets. New opportunities aren't required to use similar resources, competitive strategies, skills, assets, and competencies or to produce additional economy of scale cost reductions. In fact, some business owners love the challenge of tackling a completely new business venture.

Using this strategy, Ralph McCormick bought the stock of a local bookstore that closed down and added a book corner to his furniture store. After he gained sufficient experience, he leased space in the local mall and opened Bach's Books. Ralph's wife, Sudie, runs the furniture store, and Ralph runs the bookstore. What do the two businesses have in common? Each makes a profit, and Ralph can tell the book buyer where to get a good reading chair and lamp.

Ralph's chance to use Opportunistic Diversification was sudden; the opportunity popped up when an area bookstore closed, leaving local consumers without a place to buy books. Many opportunistic opportunities are sudden. For example, a bank with a pressing problem unexpectedly contacted one small business owner in Alabama. The bank was holding loans on a business whose owner had just died in a plane crash. The bank and the deceased owner's spouse, a member of the bank's board of directors, were offering to finance the purchase of the business. The only requirements were finding a buyer with business experience and a buyer willing to quickly seize the opportunity.

Another opportunity arose quickly in a Mid-Western community when an area businessman declared both personal and business bankruptcy. The bank auctioned off his business. The bankruptcy was due to personal problems — a romantic peccadillo and a divorce — that sank a good business. This was an opportunistic event for some lucky entrepreneur to grab a business on the cheap.

Opportunistic Diversification is often used to take advantage of growth trends outside your present market. For instance, if your business was located in Southern Florida, you'd be tempted to diversify to pursue some type of growth opportunity to profit from the ever-increasing number of retirees moving into that area. The increasing number of elderly in Southern Florida is a demographic trend that has created many growth opportunities for businesses serving the elderly.

Your business can gain a competitive advantage with Opportunistic Diversification if you are the first manager to recognize the changing remote trends in your market. A manager should monitor demographic, technology, economic, political, ecological, and attitude trends.

That's what Joe Alvarez did. Joe changed the nature of his commercial construction business, DCC Constructors Inc., because of a demographic change. In the mid-1980s, Joe realized that the central Florida apartment rental market was going to boom. However, building apartments is a wood frame construction business. Joe had been building shopping plazas, parking garages, and churches. His strengths were in steel and concrete construction techniques, not wood. The two types of construction were not compatible.

The new opportunity required new employee skills as well as new marketing and management competencies. Joe believed he could hire employees that had some of the needed skills and competencies, and he believed he could develop the rest. Today, thanks to Opportunistic Diversification, DCC's apartment construction business accounts for 40 percent of DCC's revenue *(5)*.

Dave Longaberger built a solid business using Opportunistic Diversification, but he didn't do it overnight. Dave opened a restaurant in 1963 in Dresden, Ohio; then he opened a grocery store. In 1972 he began The Longaberger Company to produce and sell woven baskets. Over the next 30 years, Dave added the Longaberger Family Restaurant, Longaberger Construction, eight Longaberger Shops, and even the Longaberger Museum, which houses a complete collection of Longaberger products.

Most of Dave's businesses are so unrelated that each requires its own management skills and competencies, not a task most managers of small businesses would like to tackle. Perhaps some of Dave's success was due to the length of his career, and the fact that he took his time to learn one type of business before embarking on another *(6)*. Dave has since passed away, but in keeping with Dave's long tradition of Opportunistic Diversification, Dave's family is constructing the Longaberger Golf Course, theme park, and convention center.

Remote Trends Generate Many New Opportunities

Remote trends are the single most important source of new opportunities, and the entrepreneur who first identifies a new remote trend in his or her community is in the best position to profit from it. You should monitor all six types of remote trends: demographic, technological, economic, political, attitudinal, and ecological, and try to imagine what type of business diversification would profit from the changing trends. Keep in mind, Opportunistic Diversification involves all types of products and services outside your current market, so you'll need to study trends that affect all types of businesses, not just trends that affect your current business. You need to develop a wide-ranging interest in how society is changing.

Demographic changes often create the most new opportunities. Demographics, as previously discussed, are the categories, characteristics, and variables used to describe people. Think of a demographic characteristic as a description about people in your area that you can get by counting the number of people with that characteristic. For example, the U.S. Government has counted and reported the number of people aged 45 to 54 in their 1960, 1970, 1980, and 1990 census reports. Those reports show a dramatic increase in the number of 50-year old people and project even more growth in their numbers in the future. This increase creates a growing market for skin creams, suntan lotions, hair coloring, cosmetics, vitamins, nutritional supplements, new cars, new trucks, and many other products and services purchased by that age group *(7)*.

Imagine the new demand for products and services in your community if the number of families with incomes over $75,000 began increasing rapidly. Such families spend large sums on entertainment, restaurants, vacations, housing, home furnishings, clothes, and so on. Imagine if the number of college graduates began increasing; the sale of books, magazines, and VCRs in your community would increase. College graduates also purchase different types of cars, clothes, food, and beverages than those purchased by high school graduates. Almost every demographic change in your area will result in changes in purchasing patterns. For instance, if the average age that couples marry increases, then young people will remain single longer, which will affect both apartment rentals and home purchases, as well as the sale of some types of clothes, entertainment, and cars, just to name a few. New purchasing patterns create new sales growth opportunities. (See Appendix A for a list of demographic characteristics you could choose to track in your community.)

Technological advances allow new products and services with improved benefits to be created and even whole new industries to develop. For example, Sony invented the VCR, and soon thereafter consumers in every community wanted to rent movie videos. Small video rental stores were quickly established.

In 1977 Apple Computer and Tandy Corporation launched the personal computer industry; four years before IBM entered the market. As the new technology evolved, small firms sprang up in every community to sell and fix computers, to customize computer programs, and to offer training programs. Computer Temp Agencies sprang up to provide businesses with part-time workers with guaranteed computer skills. Even small cabinet shops with fewer than five employees began using a computer to develop cutting and assembly instructions for each custom job, to receive orders by fax, and to do their bookkeeping. The effects of computer advances have spilled over to industries as diverse as airplane navigation and grocery store checkout systems. All of these changes were brought about by a technological trend.

Political trends — legislative, bureaucratic, judicial, and Presidential jawboning — create many opportunities. In fact, political trends make and break whole industries. For example, financial judgments awarded by the judicial system and political inaction drove manufacturing companies like Cessna out of the single engine airplane business in the mid-1980s. With Cessna's departure, the kit plane industry quickly emerged. Small businesses were formed to supply partially built airplane kits from which owners could build their own planes. Since the planes were classified as experimental, the kit plane firms were able to avoid the legal problems that plagued the large corporations. The kit plane industry has become vibrant. Kit planes are plush, sleek, and attractive, as well as fast and safe. One firm even offers a general aviation jet in kit form.

Opportunities for kit plane businesses developed because of judicial actions against the conventional small plane industry. However, the judiciary is only one part of government. Other political trends should also be watched. Presidential pressures can affect markets and opportunities, as can congressional and bureaucratic actions.

It's important to recognize that a relationship exists between attitudes and purchases that can generate many new opportunities. Consumer attitudes often change, and the change creates opportunities for new products, new services, and new businesses. For example, according to one attitude study, the number of Americans who believe crime has become a serious problem has risen to 90 percent. Changes in consumer attitudes about personal safety stimulated opportunities to make and sell security products. As a result, according to a 1993 Gallup poll, 43 percent of Americans have purchased and installed special locks on their doors, 18 percent of Americans have installed burglar alarms, 50 percent of American households have purchased a gun, and personal security devices that consumers carry have sold briskly *(8)*.

Sadly, most managers of small businesses respond only to changes in consumer purchase patterns, not to the changes in attitudes that caused the altered buying patterns. You can gain a significant competitive advantage if you respond to shifts in consumer attitudes and if you're the first business in the community to offer the new products or services in response to that shift in attitudes. Anytime you can spot changing consumer attitudes, you can expect inevitable changes in purchase patterns in your community or in the geographic area your business serves.

Economic trends affect how much money consumers have and how much money they expect to have. Even very small firms can track local economic trends by reading their regional Federal Reserve Bank's newsletter. Call your bank and get the name and address of the Federal Reserve Bank serving your area. One businessperson reported that the first two times they contacted their Federal Reserve, they were told no such publication existed. The third try was successful, and now they routinely get economic forecasts for their parts of their state. The forecasts should affect the timing of your business expansions. The best time to expand is when your community's economy is growing, which allows you to recover your investment faster.

Ecological trends have created many new opportunities such as recycling businesses, businesses that collect and spray hog manure on fields, organic gardening magazines, and biodegradable packaging, just to name a few.

Finding Your Growth Opportunities

Opportunities to use this strategy can arise from changes that are the result of either opportunistic events or remote trends, but the most changes are created by remote trends. To find your opportunities to use this strategy, first identify the remote trends that are changing in your area, and then try to estimate the magnitude of change. Study each type of remote trend, one type at a time. Talk to your chamber of commerce officials about emerging community trends. Call your Secretary of State's office and track down the people who monitor trend changes in your state. Contact your congressman or congresswoman, your local library, or your nearby college to get copies of the last several census track studies in your area, and study them to identify changes. Ask your Small Business Administration office, your local chamber of commerce, or your nearby college to sponsor a presentation about changing trends.

Most remote trend changes will create new consumer purchasing trends. It's up to you to determine what new demands customers will develop and identify new opportunities to provide those customers with the products and services they need.

Your assignment is to study the six types of remote trends and speculate about the opportunities each changing trend is creating. These are your opportunities to grow with Opportunistic Diversification. Prioritize the list by profit potential, investment cost, and likelihood of success.

Opportunistic Diversification also involves taking advantage of opportunistic events such as when a profitable business in your community suddenly goes up for sale. Most opportunistic events will take you by surprise. However, you can maintain an investment reserve or credit reserve to allow you to move quickly if an opportunity to your liking arises. You can also build a network of business owners, friends, and acquaintances through meetings at your Chamber of Commerce, Rotary Club, Country Club, and various associations, so you can hear about opportunistic events. Let your network of friends and associates know you're interested in growing through diversification.

If you're interested in pursuing opportunistic events, list the topic on your list of growth opportunities. Then, decide how much investment money or credit to hold in reserve for an opportunistic event of your liking to develop.

Forward Integration Sales Growth Strategy

Forward integration increases sales and increases the business's knowledge of customers by moving the firm's services closer to the customer. This strategy involves both expensive leaps and inexpensive little steps forward on the distribution chain that provide the customer with additional convenience and the business with a wonderful opportunity to learn more about its target customers.

Distribution Chain Moves

Every small business is part of a chain of distribution that begins when suppliers ship raw materials to manufacturers, who send finished goods to distributors, who supply them to retailers, who sell them to customers. Chains of distribution vary greatly from industry to industry. Some manufacturers, like Gateway 2,000, sell computers directly to customers. Others, like Amway, sell to individuals acting as jobbers who stock Amway products and sell directly to the final consumers. While a manufacturer-to-distributor-to-retailer-to-final-consumer distribution chain is common, many distribution chain variations are formed with the addition of manufacturer's representatives, wholesalers, and rack jobbers (firms that stock racks with consignment merchandise in retail stores).

Any business in a distribution chain can forward integrate by purchasing a chain member (business) who's located nearer the final consumer in the distribution chain — hence the name, "Forward" Integration. This type of Forward Integration increases sales in two ways. First, each chain member purchases products and services from suppliers, performs work and incurs additional costs, adds a margin of profit, and charges higher prices than its suppliers. Therefore, the prices of products and services charged by a retail business are always higher than the prices charged by a distributor, and the prices charged by a distributor are always higher than prices charged by the manufacturer. The result is that a Forward Integration strategy whereby a manufacturer buys the distributor or the distributor buys a chain of retail stores would always increase the sales figure on your Income Statement even if manufacturer, distributor, and retailer sold exactly the same products and services.

Second, a manufacturer sells a few products. A distributor represents several manufacturers and sells many products. A retailer represents several distributors and sells even more products. Therefore, Forward Integration always increases sales because it increases the number of products and services a firm sells. As you move forward on the chain, the opportunity exists to sell more and more products and services.

In addition to increasing sales, Forward Integration improves a firm's access to its final consumers. Sometimes a manufacturer uses Forward Integration and builds a system of retail stores because existing retailers are blocking the manufacturer's access to customers. The manufacturer can't sell his or her product unless they are readily available to customers.

Arkansas Woodworks Manufacturing Company used Forward Integration when it built a 2,600 sq. foot building adjacent to its small factory and opened a factory outlet store. The store, located 80 miles from the firm's nearest retail account, sold a wide variety of the firm's products, all its blemished items, some special orders, and a variety of products purchased from other manufacturers for resale.

A less expensive way to use Forward Integration is to build a second, direct distribution chain to customers located outside your normal sales area. Continue to use your existing distribution chain to serve present customers, and set up a new catalog or direct mail distribution chain for customers in a new area. To establish such a catalog, advertise with mail-in coupons or use a contest with a mail-in entry form to build up a customer mailing list. In addition to those names, you'll find thousands of good mailing lists that can be purchased economically. Business reference books at most large public libraries can supply you with a list of companies that sell mailing lists — call the reference desk and ask first before traveling to the library. These are lists of consumers who have recently purchased your type of products from a catalog or a direct mail promotion. Just look up your type products or services — farm products, swimming pool products, cosmetics, vitamins, sporting goods, etc. — and you'll discover a current list of customers who have a track record of direct mail purchases.

Mailing lists are also sold by customer type. For example, you can purchase mailing lists of newlyweds, people who just had their first child, first divorce, or, sad to say, first death in their family. The choices are endless.

Most lists are sold on a state-to-state basis, so you can purchase only the Utah list or the Alaska list. Lists can be purchased by zip code, by age, by gender, by income level, etc. Costs are usually $50 to $75 per thousand names. Stick-on mailing labels are extra.

Another, less expensive way, to use Forward Integration is to build a second distribution chain to target a different type of customer either inside or outside your normal sales area. You can sell to individual customers through retailers, and use a direct sales chain for contractors and high volume buyers.

Some businesses establish two brand names: one they use for retailers and one for contractors. Thus, you might sell lighting fixtures through retail stores under one brand name, and sell the same lighting fixtures direct to apartment builders and contractors under a second brand name.

Moving Closer to Customers

Forward Integration also includes adding services that move a business nearer to its customers by improving customer access to the business or bringing the business's products and services physically nearer to where customers live or work. Small, added services take your business to your customers and increase sales. Getting closer to customers allows you to collect valuable information about them that will be useful when 1) profiling target customers, 2) designing your next promotions, and 3) identifying more opportunities to grow with marketing sales growth strategies during your next growth planning session. Of course, you have to be prepared to collect the information, it doesn't just happen.

If you're prepared, traveling to customers' homes lets you build a descriptive profile containing customers' area of residence, whether they own or rent, type of neighborhoods where they reside, size of family, ages, lifestyle, occupation, apparent income, hobbies, preferred magazines, and newspapers. The more you know about your customers, the better promotions you can design and the more you'll know about how to reach target customers.

Some carpet and home decorator businesses have forward integrated by adding outside sales people who set up appointments and travel to the customer's home with samples. Many customers prefer to coordinate their selection of carpet colors, textures, and wallpapers in their home. They prefer to see each item's color in their home's lighting system, which can differ significantly from the color produced by a store's fluorescent lighting. Plus, many customers like to coordinate color and texture combinations with their furniture, pictures, and decorations in their home or office. Of course, many customers simply like the convenience of in-home shopping.

One small manufacturer reported an interesting twist to Forward Integration. It added a delivery truck and began direct shipments to its retail customers, eliminating common carriers. The sales manager occasionally drove the delivery truck, so he could gain access to customers' warehouses while the merchandise was being unloaded. The firm was able to boost sales by boosting its knowledge of competitive activities while it cut delivery costs.

Most small businesses can use some form of Forward Integration. For instance, a retail store might add an outside salesperson to provide an in-home or off-site shopping service. A bookstore might send a sales person to area retirement homes, nursing homes, and hospitals to directly serve shut-in customers. Adding either a telephone order service or a home delivery service moves the business closer to existing customers and adds additional customers such as those with inadequate transportation, disabled customers, and customers with too little time to shop. Remember, the latest study said 43 million Americans complained that they didn't have time for shopping, which suggests that many small Forward Integration opportunities exist to boost sales.

Finding Your Growth Opportunities

First, consider the amount of effort customers must expend to purchase your products and services. Next, search for small opportunities to decrease that effort by adding services that move your business closer to customers. Small opportunities are less expensive and may include simple expansions like adding a part-time or full-time salesperson to travel to customer homes and provide in-home product demonstrations, adding home deliveries, adding a telephone ordering system, and putting up a demonstration and sales booth at community events. Your objective is to find opportunities to take your business to customers instead of customers having to come to your business.

Make a list of small Forward Integration opportunities. Prioritize them by potential profits and costs plus their potential for collection of customer information to guide the development of future promotional programs and product and service improvement programs.

Forward Integration also encompasses opportunities to move closer to customers by moving forward on the distribution chain. Opportunities include buying a downstream business or adding a downstream business. Opportunities also include adding a second chain of distribution with catalogs or direct mail programs.

Make a list of the large Forward Integration opportunities to increase sales. Evaluate each opportunity's profit potential, costs, and risks. Prioritize your list.

Horizontal Growth Strategy

A Horizontal Growth Strategy is a plan 1) to expand by forming joint alliances and strategic alliances with other small businesses and 2) to expand rapidly by purchasing a competitor's business. Horizontal growth can be useful in quickly overcoming a major business weakness. For instance, if your business has a weak Key Success Factor, forming an alliance with a competitor whose strengths can offset your weakness may immediately improve your firm's ability to trigger many more sales.

Small Business Alliances

Small business alliances take two basic forms: joint ventures and strategic alliances.

Joint Ventures. Small businesses sometimes combine to form a strong joint venture, a type of alliance, that can provide more benefits for customers. For example, one joint venture occurred when an engineering and surveying firm, a homebuilder, and a real estate firm combined to develop a new subdivision. Another occurred when an automotive repair shop and a car body repair shop combined to provide a wide range of one-stop services for customers.

Joint ventures can be beneficial anytime several small businesses sell or provide complementary products or services. Complementary products and services are those that customers use or consume together, so customers would prefer purchasing them at one business instead of having to shop at several different businesses. Joint ventures can be developed in several ways. First, small firms that are geographically separated so to pose no threat in stealing one another's customers can expand by supplying the other with their products and training each others' employees.

Second, small firms can combine to form a new, joint business in another location. For instance, rural firms can join together and establish a co-owned store or facility in a nearby city. Joint ventures lower each individual business's investment and financial risk, plus joint ventures allow each firm to share the managerial burdens.

Strategic Alliances. A strategic alliance is used to license or contract with a business in another community to sell, make, or distribute your products and services. If you've developed a unique business system, you may want to license someone in a distant community to duplicate your successful system and pay you a royalty on their sales. If you make a unique product, you can license another small business in a distant community to make your products and even use your brand name, product name, or business name. Retailers who develop a "formula for success" often license their entire operation by selling franchises and collecting royalties. A franchise is simply a strategic alliance between businesses and business owners.

Another form of strategic alliance used by retailers is to enter into a formal inventory agreement with a smaller business in a distant community. The larger, more profitable retailer provides its most popular or most profitable merchandise to the smaller retailer and recoups its cost plus a share of the product's markup as the merchandise is sold. The smaller retailer gains access to items it couldn't otherwise afford and makes additional profits. Until the required level of trust is built, the smaller retailer is furnished with demo products and catalogs and timely deliveries are made when the sales are made. After some experience, larger inventories are shipped to the smaller firm on consignment.

Strategic alliances not only provide additional sales and profits; they can increase your orders to suppliers which will qualify your business for larger price discounts. However, be sure to formalize your relationship with a written contract or licensing agreement, otherwise, you'll just be training a future competitor.

Buying Competitors

Another Horizontal Growth Strategy includes purchasing your competitor's business. Purchasing a competitor provides three major advantages. First, if the competitor is located too close to your business, if the competitor uses the same competitive strategy, and if the competitor aggressively competes with the same sales triggers to attract your customers, a buyout can eliminate a troublesome competitor.

Second, if you have developed a winning success formula, you may want to purchase an ailing competitor in another area at a cheap price and install your winning success formula for rapid sales growth.

Third, your business may be too small to generate the economy of scale cost reductions necessary to be successful. Buying a competitor and combining both volumes may qualify the new business for steep supplier discounts, better freight rates, and lower advertisement costs while improving many of the business's operating efficiencies. It can lower management overhead costs because you can manage both locations. Many such purchases can be made with contractual agreements to pay the other firm's owners over time from the new profit stream.

The Unpainted Furniture Company in Little Rock, Arkansas, had three small retail stores, a modest central warehouse, a small custom finishing shop, and a good management system. It bought a smaller competitor in Conway, Arkansas, just 30 miles from its central warehouse. Buying the competitor increased sales, and it also created several economy of scale cost reductions. Conway residents watched Little Rock's television stations, since they had none of their own, so The Unpainted Furniture Company could simply add the Conway location to its advertisements, lowering the advertising cost per sales dollar. The Conway store's inventory could be reduced when it joined the central warehouse system — liquidating part of the inventory would generate much of the cash needed for the purchase. The finishing shop could also serve the Conway store. Finally, buying merchandise for more stores gave The Unpainted Furniture Company more purchasing muscle and greater supplier discounts.

Buying competitors is a fast way to increase sales and instantly capture additional economy of scale advantages. Two firms with decent sales and poor profits can be combined into one firm with good sales and good profits when enough economy of scale savings can be captured. Just keep in mind that the business you're acquiring must be able to pay a manager, retire its debt, and yield a respectable return on investment. Some small firms show a profit on the books only because the firm's owner is an unpaid, part-time manager and full-time laborer who works overtime for free. Be cautious when purchasing an owner-operated small business.

The safest business to purchase is one with full time salaried management and excessive inventories that can be sold off to allow you to recoup some portion of your initial investment. Then you can use the economy of scale cost advantages of the combined businesses to drive down your operating costs. Finally, with more purchasing clout, you can push suppliers to alter their delivery routes to make more frequent deliveries. With frequent small deliveries, you can operate a larger, combined business on less inventory than either one of the separate businesses previously required.

Finding Your Growth Opportunities

Business alliances, joint ventures, strategic alliances, and purchasing competitors are not opportunities that are highly visible. You have to dig them out. You have to develop an alliance idea and hunt for partners. You have to first envision the joint venture opportunity before you start searching for business partners. Competitors don't hang signs in their windows advertising their business for sale — if they did, they would scare off customers, employees, and suppliers. Even when competitors are for sale through commercial real estate brokers, you'll have to sign a non-disclosure agreement before the broker will give you the details. Don't wait to hear about someone wanting to sell his or her business, go ahead and initiate the first contact. Ask. A business owner who hasn't thought about selling may have to consider the idea for a time before warming to the idea. Call back later and ask again.

There are some great opportunities waiting to be uncovered. Particularly vulnerable to your offer is a business that suffers from a lack of economy of scale advantages that's managed by an owner who doesn't understand how to use economy of scale to drive down costs. They typically feel helpless and panicky. Then, if they think you might expand to their area if they don't accept your offer, you may be able to purchase the firm on your own terms.

Business alliances are easier to form. Firms with weaknesses are very receptive to offers that will erase their shortcomings.

Make a list of the types of opportunities you're interested in pursuing — joint ventures, strategic alliances, and purchases. Search for growth opportunities by visiting competitors and businesses with complementary products and services. Identify the opportunities. Analyze each opportunity's sales and profit potential, plus the risk associated with each. Prioritize your list of growth opportunities.

Management Profit Growth Strategies

GROWING SALES IS GREAT, BUT EVERY business owner will agree that growing profits is better. As owner, boss, President, or Chief Executive Officer of any size small business, the responsibility to produce profits and profit growth sits on your shoulders. If you're a big enough business to have a Director of Marketing or a Vice-President of Marketing, let them fixate on sales. You are solely responsible for profits, so you should fixate on growing profits. If you do both jobs, as is the case in many small businesses, you can't discover all your opportunities to grow unless you can stop thinking about sales growth and take a look at your business from a different perspective, a strictly management perspective. As your business's top manager, your main job is to plan, organize, and control the business's competitive and growth strategies in order to create healthy, growing profits even if you have to cut sales and layoff employees to do it.

Not even top managers of not-for-profit organizations escape the responsibility of continuously improving their firm's financial health by controlling costs. All top managers of any type business need to use profit growth strategies. If you're unwilling to exert control over costs and make tough financial decisions, then you should step down, step aside, sell out, get out, or turn your business over to someone with more fortitude before you either run the business into bankruptcy, or perhaps worse, cause it to become stagnant with little or no real growth, providing little or no opportunity for your employees. For the sake of your employees, you have a duty to provide good financial leadership.

Don't blame your financial problems on misfortunes; every business experiences misfortunes. Suppliers unexpectedly raise their prices, and your business can't immediately pass the higher costs on to customers. Formerly contented customers develop new needs and new desires and become increasingly critical of your products and services. A previously weak competitor introduces wonderful new products with benefits your business can't match immediately. A new competitor enters your market and slashes prices to buy their way in. Purchasing mistakes and operating problems occasionally plague even well run businesses. The price drops on a product that customers can substitute for yours, and customers suddenly start switching. Bad as these misfortunes may be, most can be handily offset with good profit growth strategies.

Profit growth strategies cut costs, and cutting costs will increase your profits faster than expanding sales. **One dollar saved in costs is a one-dollar increase in profits, while one more dollar of sales will only increase profits by a few pennies.** Assume for a moment that the profit shown on the bottom line of your Income Statement is 10 percent of sales — an extremely high percentage (your real profit percentage is probably closer to 5 percent). Now, which would you rather have: a $20 per week reduction in costs or a $7,500 increase in annual sales? A $20 cut in costs per week for 52 weeks yields a profit increase of $1,040 in a year's time. At a 10 percent profit margin, you'd need a sales increase of $10,400 to produce that much additional profit. Don't think of controlling small costs as penny pinching. Controlling small costs produces big profits.

The profit growth strategies you will choose to pursue depend on how your business is performing today. Strategies differ for businesses that are healthy versus those that are losing money or those that are terminally ill.

Profit Strategies for Healthy Businesses

The next three Management Profit Growth Strategies should be included in every year's growth plan. Every year you should try to trim your business's costs, and these are three strategies you can depend upon to do the job. They are used in combination with sales growth strategies. In fact, these strategies may generate the extra cash needed to fund sales growth strategies. The three are:

1. Backward Integration
2. Process Re-Invention
3. Divestment/Reinvestment

Profit Strategies for Troubled Businesses

Perhaps your business isn't healthy, it's losing money, or its profits are lackluster and disappointing. Unlike common ups and downs experienced by growing businesses, serious financial problems are of two types. One type of financial malaise involves a small business that was once profitable, but now the business almost seems to have outgrown its profits. Even though it seems abnormal and anti-capitalistic, the owner yearns to reverse course and return to simpler times. Under the right circumstances, a reversal is wise. The other more serious type of financial malaise involves a small business that's taking a severe financial beating at the hands of aggressive competitors, unfavorable remote trends, or management misadventures. Bankruptcy could be in the business's future. Strong actions must be taken to address serious problems.

These two strategies are medicines for sick businesses.

1. Retrenchment
2. Revitalization

Retrenchment is a strategy for the small firm that has actually outgrown profitability. Revitalization is a strategy for the small firm whose losses are threatening its very existence. Both are powerful strategies that require major changes in your business.

A Revenue Maximization Strategy

Some financial troubles are terminal; not every business can be turned around with a Retrenchment or Revitalization Strategy. You'll learn when it's time to voluntarily close your doors. Surprisingly, the vast majority of unsuccessful small businesses that shut down aren't forced by bankruptcy to do so, the vast majority close their doors and liquidate their businesses voluntarily. Some profit handsomely through liquidation. Unfortunately for many small firms in financial trouble, they don't liquidate soon enough. This final management strategy, Liquidation, helps you choose your timing and develop a plan to maximize the revenue you can recoup from a dying business.

Compatibility of All Types of Growth Strategies

Five of these six Management Profit Growth Strategies are compatible with all of the previous Marketing and Management Sales Growth Strategies. Only Liquidation must be used by itself.

The Backward Integration Growth Strategy

Backward Integration is a strategy used to reduce costs by performing tasks or work in your own business that suppliers have previously done for you.

Forward Integration, a sales growth strategy discussed in Chapter 14, moves the business closer to its customers; in contrast, Backward Integration moves the business closer to its suppliers. Backward Integration can involve small changes like purchasing components and assembling a final product instead of purchasing an already assembled product. Backward Integration can also involve larger changes like doing a job or task previously done by a supplier, distributor, transportation firm, accounting firm, cleaning firm, etc. Finally, Backward Integration can involve huge changes like buying out your supplier or adding the capability to become your own supplier.

For example, Spacesaver, a small business in Fort Atkinson, Wisconsin, used a Backward Integration strategy when it built a plant to make steel shelving for its custom bookcase systems. In addition to reducing costs, Spacesaver was able to eliminate some supplier restrictions and supplier delays, which had forced them to maintain large and costly inventories of shelving. The strategy cut costs, and, at the same time, improved Spacesaver's ability to serve its customers *(1)*.

On a much smaller scale, one small manufacturer used a Backward Integration strategy to make a series of small changes over several years to slash its costs significantly. Arkansas Woodworks Manufacturing Company, like many small woodworking businesses, initially purchased doors for its furniture from a door manufacturer. The small company's first Backward Integration move was to add two inexpensive machines to make flat panel doors. This allowed the firm to use scrap wood it had previously thrown away and to cut the costs on its most popular style doors by 80 percent. Over the next few years, the firm added more equipment to make its own raised panel doors. One year it added a machine to make its own drawers, and the next year it added a molding machine to make decorative trim. Each year the small firm depended on Backward Integration to cut costs and to cut its dependence on the delivery schedule of its suppliers.

Backward Integration can be used by many different types of businesses to perform some activity or service previously done by suppliers. For example, a men's clothing store used Backward Integration to add a monogram machine to lower its costs and increase its service speed. Another small business added a box machine to cut boxing costs, cut breakage, and eliminate its costly box inventory. A small restaurant owner began growing tomatoes to serve on hamburgers to cut costs and to improve the burger's taste.

Backward Integration both cuts cost and allows a business to better serve its customer by freeing the business from supplier restrictions. Even though cost cuts may be small, they add up to big profits. For example, cut your costs by $1.93 per week for 52 weeks, and you'll increase annual profits by $100. Cut costs by $193 per week, and you'll boost annual profits by $10,000. Since your business won't have to wait on suppliers, customers get faster service, which is a competitive advantage for businesses using a Speed Enhancement Competitive Strategy. And, since you're no longer restricted by the type of product your supplier wants to provide, you may have the ability to customize some products, which is a competitive advantage for businesses using a Flexibility Enhancement Competitive Strategy (see Chapter 6).

However, Backward Integration does have a negative side; it can tie the firm to one type of technology. For example, suppose your firm purchases a used injection-molding machine and begins making its own plastic parts. Then, suppliers introduce a new, superior material — maybe a lightweight composite metal with special benefits. Your firm will be reluctant to lose its investment in plastics equipment and return to purchasing from a supplier, so you continue to use the less desirable plastic parts because you're tied to one type of technology by your investment. When technologies are changing rapidly, your firm might be better off to maintain its flexibility by purchasing from a variety of suppliers. Therefore, always analyze the limitations caused by any proposed Backward Integration project. Most Backward Integration opportunities are beneficial, but not all.

Finding Your Growth Opportunities

Examine each of your business's suppliers, distributors, and service providers to find opportunities for your business to assume part or all of the work done by them. Remember, as a customer you're buying four things from each supplier: product, service, personnel, and image. Become a Prudent Shopper and try to trade portions of these four factors for a lower price. Can you make your own product? For example, the Illinois Association of School Boards added a print shop, so it could cut costs by printing some of its own publications. Are there any supplier products you can make? These are your opportunities to cut costs.

Can you perform some of the services presently provided by suppliers and marketing intermediaries such as advertising firms, researchers, or manufacturers' representatives? Packaging is often a merchandising service. Ask suppliers to sell items in bulk at a reduced price and then provide your own attractive display. Deliveries are a service. If you're paying a high freight rate for deliveries, search for a local manufacturer who would like to have a backhaul from your supplier's location. Assume the responsibility for coordinating your orders with the local manufacturer's backhaul opportunities to cut costs.

It's expensive for suppliers to deliver small amounts to several stores. If you have more than one store, ask for a distributor's discount or a functional discount in return for letting the supplier drop all merchandise at one store, then you distribute the merchandise to your other stores. You're probably running a truck from store to store anyway.

Suppliers have personnel costs. It costs suppliers plenty to send a sales person to your business every week or two. Offer to reduce a supplier's selling expense by simplifying your procurement process. Offer to give a blanket purchase order or contract for six months or a year in return for a discounted price. To keep the salesperson up to date, suggest the two of you talk once a week by phone, and promise never to switch suppliers without giving the current supplier time to respond.

Suppliers provide your business with four things: products, services, their personnel, and their image. Backward Integration trades a reduction in one or more of those four factors for a lower price. Make a list of your opportunities to cut costs with Backward Integration by 1) making all or part of a supplier's product, 2) performing services that you've directly or indirect paid suppliers to perform in the past, 3) trading reduced supplier personnel costs for a lower price, and 4) trading reduced supplier image building expenses for a lower price.

Analyze each opportunity's potential cost savings. Identify any risks associated with becoming your own supplier, such as tying your business to one type of technology. Prioritize your list.

Process Re-Invention

Everything your business does costs money. Making products, marketing products, performing a service, running a credit check, handling customer complaints, developing new products or services, hiring an employee, planning growth strategies — each of these things is accomplished through a sequence of routine work tasks that can be called a work process. Each work process costs money, raises your expenses, and lowers your profits.

The natural evolution of a work process is for it to get bigger and more costly. Each time an employee makes a mistake or a problem is encountered, a new work step is added to make the process error free. Eventually a work process can become bloated, slow, and unduly expensive.

Process Re-Invention is a plan to reduce the number of steps in a work sequence to make it more efficient and to increase productivity. The goal is to make work faster by cutting out unnecessary steps, combining steps, and incorporating new technology to speed up steps. Costs go down, work speed goes up, profits go up.

The word "process" refers to the sequence of routine work steps or actions taken to complete a job. Think about the number of routine steps or tasks performed when someone in your business makes a routine purchase from a supplier. The purchasing process begins by determining inventory on hand, projecting usage, writing up the order, talking to the supplier about possible delivery dates, submitting the order, tracking the order, receiving the order, rectifying invoices and delivery paperwork, and paying the supplier's bill. There's a sequence of people involved in the purchasing process. There's a sequence of information gathered during the purchasing process. There's a sequence of decisions made during the purchasing process. You could easily draw a map that would show each step in your purchasing process. And, with the help of a Revitalization Strategy, you could streamline that sequence to cut your costs.

As you just saw, the purchasing process involves three major components: the physical flow of material, the information flow, and the sequence of decisions. The purchasing process could be streamlined by improving all or any one of the three components. Or, the purchasing process could be drastically shortened for inexpensive items, and maintained as it is for expensive items. As you will see, Process Re-Invention has many cost-saving options.

Each of the many processes in your business is made up of the same three components: material flow, information flow, and a sequence of decisions. The critical point is that all internal and external work performed by your business and by its employees is the product of a process — a sequence of work steps — that can be improved, shortened, made more productive, and made less expensive.

To use Process Re-Invention, you must first stop thinking of your business as a collection of functional parts — receiving, operations, marketing, personnel, purchasing, etc. — and start thinking of your business as a collection of work processes. Try mentally dividing your business into its processes and assigning costs to each. Yes, this is difficult, maybe impossible, because of the way the IRS has forced accountants to set up "the books," but mentally picture it anyway because it will help you to understand how work is performed and how costs are really incurred.

Since everything that gets done in your business is the result of a process, all costs can be split up and re-assigned to each work process. Your most costly processes are the external processes that serve customers, the ones that are directly connected to providing products and services to customers, such as the customer order-filling process (starts with the customer order, includes production or retail procurement, and ends when the customer takes possession of the merchandise and pays the bill), the new product development process, the credit approval process, the complaint resolution process, and so forth. A business also has a great many vital internal processes that support the customer processes: the inventory control process, the employee training process, the payroll process, the equipment maintenance process, etc. These too can be costly to operate.

You might consider abolishing functional areas (i.e., marketing, operations, purchasing, personnel, etc.) and replacing them with processes. Then, instead of employees working in engineering, production, and marketing, they might work in one of the processes like maybe the "New Product Development Process." Maybe then they would quit trying to protect and build their own departments and start helping each other speed up new product development. By shifting from departments to processes, you could get reports by process, see the costs of performing each type of work, and manage the effectiveness and efficiency of each entire work sequence. Your management job would become the planning, organizing, and controlling of work processes.

You should occasionally reinvent your business's work processes to increase efficiency and decrease costs. In the last 30 years, three major methods of Process Re-Invention have been developed to help you accomplish this feat:

- Benchmarking
- Total Quality Management
- Process Re-Engineering

Benchmarking Profit Growth Strategy

Benchmarking is a Process Re-Invention technique that transfers an efficient work process from another business to your business. For example, if another business has a superior inventory control process or sales force training process, your business could copy it with Benchmarking. Benchmarking requires the permission and cooperation of the other business to allow you to draw a map of the physical, information, and decision-making components of its process.

Benchmarking is versatile and is used in both product or service businesses. It is used for all types of external customer processes and internal support processes. Here's how one manufacturing firm used benchmarking to cut its costs.

The firm assembled and shipped a wide variety of small and medium sized copiers, accessories, inks and toners, and repair parts. Its distribution center was slow, costly, and inefficient. The facility needed a faster process to receive, fill, and ship customer orders — it called this process the Order Fulfillment Process. This process included many major steps, such as receiving the customer's order, checking credit, preparing the shipping authorization, sending paperwork to the warehouse, retrieving stored items from bins in the warehouse, backordering out-of-stock items, preparing the packages for shipment, routing, shipping, and billing. The Order Fulfillment Process had to be reinvented. But where should the firm begin?

The firm looked around for a model that could be copied. Competitors weren't going to help. So, the manufacturer searched elsewhere. They turned away from their industry and sought to find the most efficient business in any industry that handled a high volume of small orders. They found L. L. Bean, the Maine-based outdoor apparel company that sells coast-to-coast and internationally by catalog. A company whose distribution center was renowned for speed, accuracy, efficiency, and low costs.

L. L. Bean agreed to help; and why not, the copier company would never pose a competitive threat to the apparel company. The copier company sent a team of people to study L. L. Bean's Order Fulfillment Process. The Re-Invention team had to identify and measure Bean's paperwork (information) flow, merchandise storage and retrieval methods, the material handling equipment, the computer system, each employee's job design, employee work habits, company policies — every part of the system that made L. L. Bean so productive and efficient. Each factor that contributed to Bean's efficiency was documented and measured, and those measurements became known as "benchmarks" that the copier company would try to duplicate. The copier company's use of benchmarks to guide its Process Re-Invention was very successful — productivity, efficiency, and accuracy were drastically improved. Costs dropped. Customer satisfaction increased. Profits increased.

Okay, you don't have a team of people to send to Maine for months, but Benchmarking can work for you, here's how.

Determine what work system or work process in your business needs to be more efficient, more productive, and less costly. Find another business — it can be in another market, industry, or field — with a similar but highly productive work process. Ask them to help you. Most small business owners are proud of their achievements and willing to share their knowledge. Then, to the best of your ability, study these three process components: the Physical Work Flow, the Information Flow, and the Sequence of Decisions.

One component or a combination of all three components may be responsible for the other business's process efficiency. They may have faster equipment, or they may have the same equipment as your firm but they've delegated the decision-making authority to the equipment operator to speed up decision making. Perhaps they move information around more efficiently. You have to discover their secrets. How much time you spend examining their process depends on their cooperativeness and your available time. Fortunately, small businesses employ simple systems, so don't be scared off because the following suggestions sound like they will require too much time and effort, they won't.

Enormous amounts of time are required to Benchmark a complex system in a big corporation; small amounts of time are required to Benchmark a simple system. Still, you'll need to examine each of the following three process components when you're trying to copy another business's superior system:

1. **The Physical Work Flow:** first, make a map of the other firm's physical layout, which includes machines, desks, technology, and materials. Draw a sketch of the physical workflow, step by step, showing how work proceeds through the work process from each job's origin to its completion. Describe the technology used at each step. Second, make a map of each worker's job — a job design. Job designs are the STANDARD sequence of steps used to perform each job. Job designs are how the job is standardized. Describe how the job is MECHANIZED — what machines or technical systems are used. Record each person's work cycle times (the time it takes to complete each job). Record how fast each employee completes each of their work tasks. Record all work methods. Draw a sketch of the way each employee organizes his or her personal work area.
2. **The Information Flow:** make a map of the paperwork and electronic information flow connected to each job; of course, the paperwork may be the job. Make a map of how the paperwork travels from person to person and from folder to drawer to desk to computer file through the modem to another location, back, over to the boss, until the job is completed and terminated. Describe in detail what is done with the information at each step, what information is added or deleted at each step, and how long each step takes.
3. **The Decision-Making Flow:** make a map of the sequence of decisions made for each job — when, where, why, and by whom each decision is made.

Study how the three components interact to deliver the other business's process speed. And don't forget to ask about their reward and punishment policies and motivational techniques.

Every important fact or significant measurement becomes a benchmark that you will use to reinvent your work process. The other business's work process is your model, and the benchmarks are the pieces of the model that you will copy as you transfer their process to your business.

Finding Your Growth Opportunities

Benchmarking is one way to fix a broken or poorly performing work process, but you first have to recognize that a process needs fixing. If you're like most owners and managers of small businesses, it's difficult to admit that a process you developed doesn't work properly. Don't let pride stifle your opportunity to increase profits.

Make a list of processes in your business that need to be more efficient and more productive. Next, search for similar-sized businesses in any industry that have similar but superior processes. Ask the suppliers of your equipment, computer system, material handling system, etc. for information about any other types of businesses that use the supplier's system and use it with remarkable efficiency. These suppliers sell to various markets and often use well run businesses as examples of how well their equipment or systems work. Ask the supplier to introduce you. Or, pick up the phone and ask the other owner for help. They'll likely be flattered when you tell them about their reputation and be willing to let you observe their process to get improvement ideas. Then, get organized. Map each of the three components for your process so that you can spot the differences at the other business.

When you've finished, analyze the investment required to transfer the process to your firm. Calculate the cost. Analyze the potential boost in profits. If you have more than one opportunity, you should prioritize your list.

Of course, you may not know that a process is inefficient. So, be observant. Watch how other firms do things. Compare your process efficiency to that of other businesses. Discuss processes with suppliers. Seek to discover if other types of businesses have developed more efficient and cost-effective ways to get similar work done.

Total Quality Management (TQM) Profit Growth Strategy

Here's a Process Re-Invention technique that works well, but takes a long time to implement.

Total Quality Management, its many variations, and many similar programs are used to inspire employees to reinvent their own work processes. TQM motivates employees to voluntarily eliminate their own wasted steps, wasted motions, and wasted efforts. At the heart of TQM is the fact that an employee knows more about his or her personal job process, the way they actually do their work, than anyone else in the business. Managers are often in the dark about the exact sequence of steps that each employee uses to perform his or her job. Remember that there are formal and informal ways to do things. While you may know the way a job is supposed to be done (the formal), you may not know the real sequence of steps an employee actually uses to get a job done (the informal).

Therefore, the first tenant of TQM is for you to admit that each of your employees owns the work process they use to complete each work task or assignment. Employees are the only ones who know exactly what formally proscribed steps in the physical work environment, information flow, and sequence of decisions they use and don't use. Individual inefficiencies will only be eliminated if employees voluntarily choose to eliminate the wasted steps. TQM programs are designed to slowly mold employee attitudes so they will voluntarily eliminate waste as they choose to improve their individual productivity.

People don't change their personal values quickly. TQM programs are understandably slow, but they do create a work atmosphere that encourages each employee to use personal learning curves and experience curves to continuously develop ways to improve their productivity and eliminate their wasted motions. Employees with a "just-tell-me-what-to-do" attitude are challenged by a TQM manager to help redesign their own jobs. This means management must make sure each employee is given and accepts the power to change (or at least propose changes to) his or her job. Employees must know that management expects them to help make their jobs more efficient. Management must also understand that not every employee's attitude will change at the same time; employees whose attitudes change quickly will subtly put pressure on the others to change.

TQM isn't magic. TQM is a tool, a system, and a lot of work that combines to motivate employees, educate employees, and empower employees to make changes, changes that only employees would know how to make. Many books have been written explaining various tools used in TQM programs. For the latest, see "Books in Print: Subject Guide" at your local library. But, here are a few of the common tools.

Quality Circles

Quality circles are one of the TQM tools often used by managers to encourage employees to help the business make productive changes and to alter the employees attitudes towards change. A manager creates a quality circle by assigning 2 to 10 employees to a group and giving them one of the firm's problems to solve. This may require group training to give them the ability to create a working solution. Usually the group is asked to define the problem, identify alternative solutions, choose the best solution, justify it to management, and help implement the solution.

Over the long haul, quality circles encourage employees to accept change and encourage each employee to propose process changes to improve efficiencies. However, in the beginning, management starts out by assigning easy waste reducing problems to build employees' confidence and mold their attitudes. The group slowly builds toward solving more difficult problems that management assigns and eventually to proposing problems to management that the quality circle might solve.

Quality circles were borrowed from Japan, where employees voluntarily participate after hours, without pay, to help the business. American employees haven't shown any eagerness to donate their after work time to building a stronger business. Most quality circles in America have operated during regular business hours; therefore, managers tend to push the groups for quick results. Unfortunately, like most TQM techniques, quality circles don't produce quick solutions. This fact has caused some dissatisfaction with them in our "fast-paced" society.

TQM and Quality circles work, but TQM sometimes requires employee training, reading assignments, or even coursework involving statistical quality control techniques. TQM requires a participatory management style where managers give employees lots of previously confidential information about the business and encourage employees to find new solutions to persistent problems.

Focusing on Customers

Another TQM tool is to focus every employee on customers, making each employee more customer oriented. Then, each employee is challenged to look at each step in their personal work processes and ask themselves if the step adds value for the customer or is a wasted effort. Waste is to be eliminated through personal Process Re-Invention.

Installing a TQM program and achieving a workforce focus on customers is a long, slow process because it requires that the entire work force change their work attitudes and beliefs. TQM programs strive to achieve these permanent changes:

- Employees should be able to define their personal processes and individual efforts in terms of customer satisfaction.
- Employees willingly strive for zero defects, zero mistakes, and the total elimination of waste. Over time they adopt the belief that it takes the same amount of time, materials, and costs to make a defective product or service as it does to make a good product or service, and they strive for perfection.
- Employees learn to measure and track the quality of their individual work. Employees begin to track their defects, mistakes, personal productivity, and group productivity.
- Employees learn to measure all process cycle times. When a lot of quality work is produced in a short amount of time, that cycle is studied to find

out how to repeat that set of conditions. When a lot of mistakes occur or when very little work is produced during another work cycle, that cycle is studied to find out how to avoid repeating that set of conditions. Understanding exactly why a work process is sometimes highly efficient and other times woefully inefficient provides the employees with valuable Process Re-Invention ideas.

- Employees learn to set targets for improving their productivity and keep striving to reinvent their work process to achieve their targets.
- Each time a target is achieved, the employee sets a new, higher target.

The 5-M Error Elimination Program

The 5-Ms is another TQM tool. Employees learn the 5-Ms method of identifying and tracking all process problems and mistakes. They learn to keep a permanent 5-Ms record for each work process that lists every mistake or problem under one of five categories: Manpower, Machines, Materials, Measurements, and Methods. All errors can be classified as one of these five types of error.

For example, an employee experiences a computer problem; it's recorded under the "Machine" category of problems. If an error in procedures causes a problem, it's recorded under the "Methods" category of problems. If the sloppy work of a co-worker causes a problem, it's recorded under the "Manpower" heading. From time to time, each employee tallies his or her problems. Suppose that tally shows that 89 percent of the employee's problems are in the "Machine" area, it becomes clear what part of the work process must be reinvented to increase productivity and cut costs. The 5-Ms technique draws attention to the part of a process that most needs to be reinvented.

Keeping a personal 5-Ms logbook can be very beneficial. For example, an employee operating a machine in the plant might document ten problems with "Material" from one supplier, two "Machine" problems, one "Measurement" problem that caused a part dimension to be mis-measured, three "Methods" problems that caused the equipment to be set up incorrectly, and one "Manpower" problem caused by a fellow worker. By keeping a 5-Ms log, the employee could make valuable Process Re-Invention recommendations that would increase output, cut waste, and cut costs.

Workplace Organization

Another TQM tool is to teach workplace organization. Employees are taught to clear and simplify their work areas. They are taught to establish a storage place for everything and that the only visible items in their work area should be those they are using to accomplish the current job. They are taught that storage places should be orderly and logical so time isn't lost looking for things. They are taught that their work process should use the same exact sequence of work steps every time to promote speed. Employees are encouraged to post their personal work schedule each day as a way to keep focused on personal goals. Employees are encouraged to display a chart of personal mistakes and a log of personal productivity; these are not public displays, they are private displays meant to inspire each employee to constantly reinvent their work process to eliminate waste and become more productive.

These are just a few of the many, many tools and techniques of TQM. By studying TQM, you could pick and choose the techniques that would be most beneficial for your type of business. Your business's TQM program would teach your employees only the appropriate techniques you approved.

Installing TQM Takes Years

How long does it take to install TQM at your business? TQM is similar to putting a person through college. It takes four or five years for a college to educate a person and change his or her thought process, objectivity, and attitudes. And every person who completes college gets something different out of it. Unfortunately, it takes four or five years to install TQM in your business, and every person will get something different out of it also. Lots of TQM books, consultants, and associations exist to help you design a TQM program for your type of business and your type of employees. TQM programs must be tailored to your needs and your employees' abilities, which vary according to their aptitude, personality, experience, training, education, and intelligence.

Small businesses sometimes shy away from TQM because of employee turnover. A firm with higher turnover fears they will be investing in a soon-to-be someone else's employee. However, TQM programs will raise the performance of the entire work force, and the improved work attitudes and methods of your experienced employees will quickly influence new employees. Also, TQM can spur sales and profit growth, creating more opportunities for the employees you most want to retain.

Finding Your Growth Opportunities

TQM is not meant to rescue a troubled firm from the jaws of bankruptcy, it's meant to make a good business better. Good businesses have time to make improvements and time to develop employees. You're in business for the long haul, and TQM is a long haul process improvement technique.

Which TQM techniques you use depend on three factors: the weaknesses of your employees, your knowledge of TQM, and your consultant's knowledge of TQM if you choose to hire a consultant.

Make a list of overall employee weaknesses you'd like to change, such as poor work habits, inattention, personal inefficiencies, or poor problem-solving ability. You'll add to this list as you study TQM and are better able to recognize categories of weaknesses.

Next, read current TQM books, join TQM associations (find them through your local library's *Directory of Associations*), take TQM classes, and talk to business professors at nearby universities and colleges. Then, teach various TQM techniques to your employees; set time aside for everyone to view TQM videotapes; and invite an occasional TQM speaker to address your work force. You'll discover that most local community colleges are happy to conduct a TQM short course at your business.

TQM isn't a technique you hurriedly adopt. Instead, target a few aspects of overall employee performance for improvement every year. Use TQM to encourage employees to continuously improve their work methods and increase their personal productivity.

Process Re-Engineering Profit Growth Strategy

Process Re-Engineering is the fastest and cheapest of the three Process Re-Invention techniques. You should include one or more projects using this technique in every year's growth plan. Process Re-Engineering is an effective method to correct minor problems that always crop up in any work process. It's a wonderful mechanism for introducing new technology like computers into a work process. It's also an effective and quick way to reinvent a work process completely. However, it requires creative thinking to imagine new ways to get things accomplished. You don't need help from outside your business. You, the manager, with the help of your employees, can do Process Re-Engineering.

One of the big successes of Process Re-Engineering has been to make managers realize that when it comes to work processes, one process shouldn't fit all size jobs. Big, complex jobs and small, simple jobs shouldn't travel through the same work sequence. Tasks or jobs should be classified quickly into simple and quick jobs and into complex and long jobs. A shortened process should be designed for simple and quick jobs. The normal process should be used only for the complex and long jobs.

For example, in his highly popular book, *Re-Engineering the Corporation*, Michael Hammer tells of a credit-approval process at a subsidiary of an equipment manufacturer. The average credit approval was taking seven days, and sales were being lost because the customers continued to shop around while their credit was being approved. Seven days is a long time to keep a customer hanging in suspense.

Then one frustrated manager devised a test. He grabbed a new credit approval request and carried it from desk to desk. He told each person to stop what he or she was doing and complete their portion of the credit application immediately. The whole credit-approval process took one and one-half hours — not seven days. The manager declared the process broken and set out to Re-Engineer it.

After thoroughly mapping the existing seven-day process's three components — physical work flow, information flow, and decision sequence — the manager decided the process was bottlenecked because every credit application, no matter how simple or how complex, went through the same sequence of steps. Here's the main point: if an employee had ten applications on her desk, the new application became number eleven, and work on it was delayed until the other ten were completed, even if number eleven was simple and quick to handle. Each application followed the same sequence of steps as it went from employee to employee and desk to desk in the order it was received. Therefore, a quick job was as slow as the most complex job in front of it. The speed of every job was determined by the speed of the slowest job.

Does this sound familiar? Is this mistake made anywhere in your business? If so, it's time for you to use Process Re-Engineering.

The Re-Engineered credit-approval process established categories of credit applications. The simple applications stayed on the first desk and were handled quickly with the use of a checklist established by the experts in the organization. The employee at the first desk wasn't an expert, but the employee applied the expert's guidelines. Only if the application failed one of the guidelines would it be sent to the next person. All applications were no longer handled by everyone, which meant far fewer applications flowing from desk to desk. This freed up the specialists to work exclusively on complex applications.

The result of the Process Re-Invention was that the average credit-approval time dropped to a third of its former time. The number of employees in the credit-approval process dropped by two-thirds. Costs dropped sharply. Happily, sales increased as the firm lost fewer orders *(2)*.

The First Major Process Re-Engineering Concept

The credit-approval example establishes a key concept of Process Re-Engineering:

A process can be made more efficient, faster, and less costly by developing a shorter process for simple and easy work. Getting the easy jobs out of the way leaves more time to do the complex jobs.

Creating work categories can work at your business. Perhaps you can write a set of guidelines, so an employee can handle the simple work. Then you'll have more time to handle the complex work.

A similar Re-Engineering took place at State Farm Insurance. State Farm reinvented their claims payout process. Instead of sending every claim to their adjusters for settlement, insurance agents in the sales offices are now allowed to pay claims with the guidance of checklists prepared by the adjusters. The agent instantly pays the simple and easy claims when the customer brings in the damage and loss estimates or the receipts from repairing the damage. A claim is considered simple and easy if the claim is under $2,500, if the customer has been with State Farm for several years without a claim, and if the claim fits into a normal profile of costs established by the adjusters. Most claims are simple and easy, and most customers are now paid by the agent instead of waiting for an adjuster.

The concept behind State Farm's use of Process Re-Engineering is one you can use: State Farm agents do occasionally overpay a claim by a few dollars or even a hundred dollars, but this is cheap compared to adding more adjusters. And besides, overpaying customers keeps them highly satisfied, and highly satisfied customers who tell their friends and co-workers about their wonderful insurance company are walking advertisements for State Farm.

The Second Major Process Re-Engineering Concept

The State Farm example establishes another basic concept of Process Re-Engineering that you should use when reinventing your processes.

Shortening a work process may result in a few errors. These errors are acceptable under two conditions. The errors must not hurt customer satisfaction (i.e., State Farm customers are happier with faster service and a few extra bucks), **and the cost of the errors must be small compared to the overall savings.**

In practical terms, creating a perfect process may be too expensive and too time consuming. A perfect process may require more employees and may actually lower customer satisfaction. Customers enjoy fast service, managers want cheap processes, and Re-Engineering can produce both.

During another Re-Engineering analysis, the manager of one small company reinvented his firm's purchasing process to avoid having to add another purchasing agent to buy office supplies. The departments and groups were issued a credit card with a monthly limit and a list of approved suppliers. They were told to order their own office supplies and charge them. Even if occasional purchasing errors did occur, the slight increase in costs would be much less than the cost of adding another purchasing agent.

Re-Engineering also works on a personal level. After all, each employee and manager has various individual work sequences they use to perform their own work, and these sequences can be improved. For example, an employee in a small association Re-Engineered her handling of customer requests. She decided to immediately and personally handle any customer request that took less than 10 minutes. So, if her work was interrupted by a customer who called with a request that would take less than 10 minutes, the job was completed immediately because it would consume too much time to make notes, later review the notes, and then complete the task, or explain the task to a secretary. Customer requests that would take 10 to 30 minutes were also handled on the same day, but she performed these requests when she wanted to take a break from the day's complex work. This system increased her productivity to two and a half times above departmental expectations, and customers loudly praised the fast service.

The Third Major Process Re-Engineering Concept

This example of handling customer requests establishes another important Re-Engineering concept.

Individual works process should be re-engineered.

Individual work processes are made up of the same three components: physical work flow, information flow, and the sequence of decisions. Individual work processes should be mapped and creatively reinvented to increase personal productivity.

How to Perform Your Own Re-Engineering Project

Re-Engineering has much in common with Benchmarking. Benchmarking requires that you map another business's work process; Re-Engineering requires that you map your own business's work process. You can't Re-Engineer a process until you completely understand it. Such an understanding comes from carefully studying and mapping the same three process components used in Benchmarking. Your analysis should include:

1. **The Physical Work Flow:** first, make a map of your firm's physical layout, which includes machines, desks, technology, and materials. Draw a sketch of the physical workflow, step by step, showing how work proceeds through the work process from each job's origin to its completion. Describe the technology used at each step. Second, make a map of each worker's job — a job design. Job designs are the STANDARD sequence of steps used to perform each job. Job designs are how the job is standardized. Describe how the job is MECHANIZED — what machines or technical systems are used. Record each person's work cycle times (the time it takes to complete each job). Record how fast each employee completes each of their work tasks. Record all work methods. Draw a sketch of the way each employee organizes his or her personal work area.
2. **The Information Flow:** make a map of the paperwork and electronic information flow connected to each job; of course, the paperwork may be the job. Make a map of how the paperwork travels from person to person and from folder to drawer to desk to computer file through the modem to another location, back, over to the boss, until the job is completed and terminated. Describe in detail what is done with the information at each step, what information is added or deleted at each step, and how long each step takes.
3. **The Decision-Making Flow:** make a map of the sequence of decisions made for each job — when, where, why, and by whom each decision is made.

Next, study the three component maps to discover Re-Engineering opportunities. Play a "What if" game. "What if" Bob had a computer terminal, so he got the information immediately? "What if" Joyce made that decision with a few guidelines instead of waiting on her supervisor? "What if" those two tasks or jobs were combined? At each step on your three process component maps, stop and ask, "What if we changed the process at this point. What could we do to improve the process's efficiency?" Re-Engineering requires a bunch of creative "what ifs" to create a new process.

Every step on each map of the existing process must be questioned and challenged. Your objective is to:

1. **Shorten the process.** All work should not be treated the same: quick tasks should be done quickly, easy tasks should not be made difficult, and experts should work only on complex tasks. So, change your process. Combine jobs, combine tasks, redesign the work area, shift decision-making authority, add new technology, speed up the flow of information, and analyze the effect of process tiers for easy, moderate, and complex work.

2. **Use fewer employees.** Reduce the number of people involved in a process to speed it up. Can three employees' jobs be redesigned to be done by two employees?
3. **Accept some errors.** Errors that benefit the customer and lower costs are okay. Perfection may be too expensive.
4. **Apply Re-Engineering to personal work processes.** Have every employee draw process maps for each type of work they do. Have all employees play their own "What if" games and then present their process maps to their manager or supervisor with proposals for personal improvements.

Re-Engineering produces some creative and surprising results. One small firm changed its ordering system for routine items. It turned receiving, ordering, and payment authorization for routine inventory items over to one person in the receiving department. Since that person was already tracking inventory and reporting daily amounts, it was decided the same person should monitor inventory, order material, receive material, document shortages, and authorize accounting to make payments. Accounting could send checks to suppliers. Purchasing could concentrate on negotiating prices and handling complex orders.

Finding Your Growth Opportunities

It's difficult to estimate the potential savings that a Re-Engineering project will generate. Since you don't know ahead of time how successful Process Re-Invention will be, you've no way to accurately estimate its savings. However, it's important to Re-Engineer one or more of your work processes every year in order to continuously improve efficiency, increase productivity, increase customer satisfaction, and cut costs. Don't let your business become one of those sadly mismanaged organizations that must resort to massively reinventing itself and laying off (downsizing) lots of employees. Re-Engineering should be used continuously to improve the way your business works.

Here's a recommended sequence for using Re-Engineering. First, Re-Engineer any poorly working, inefficient process. These may be processes that serve your customers or processes that perform internal work.

Second, use Re-Engineering to speed up any process that provides a customer service or benefit. This will both cut costs and increase customer satisfaction. Examine every process that serves customers. Identify those that could be speeded up by designing different processes for different categories of customer work. Also, identify those where you might trade-off occasional errors that benefit customers in return for lowering your costs.

Third, use Re-Engineering to improve good processes. Good processes can be improved, often by adding the latest computer technology to consolidate steps or speed up steps. Remember that the natural evolution for any process is to grow in size over time. Combat that tendency by occasionally Re-Engineering every process, or, at least, by occasionally studying every process.

Fourth, ask every employee to map their personal processes, develop some ideas for improvements, and present their ideas to their supervisor. Remember, the learning curve (see Chapter 3) proves that when employees perform the same manual tasks over and over, they can do the work faster. Likewise, the experience curve (see Chapter 3) proves that when white-collar workers do the same tasks over and over, they can also do their work faster. However, the learning and experience curves only prove that employees can speed up, not that they will speed up. By implementing a Process Re-Engineering strategy, you will encourage employees to use their acquired knowledge to become more productive.

Don't be surprised if some of your employees' wasted steps disappear before they ever show their personal process maps to supervisors.

Divestment/Reinvestment Profit Growth Strategy

Divest your losers. Reinvest the cash. A common strategy used yearly by all small and large businesses. A product, group of products, or whole product line that isn't performing well is liquidated and the cash reinvested in other products. Likewise, services that aren't generating good sales are discontinued, equipment used for the services liquidated, and new services are added.

Good managers are constantly monitoring products and services and making Divestment/Reinvestment decisions. Managers have a variety of tests to determine if a product should stay or go. The simplest is to measure each item's sales. Or, measure each item's sales or profits per square foot of floor space or shelf space; such measures are useful if you have a large choice of items to stock and a limited amount of space. Try to make each item earn its spot. Of course, some items earn their spot not as moneymakers but because they generate traffic. Some stores attract shoppers because of their wide variety of merchandise even though 20 percent of their items account for 80 percent of sales. In this case, the slow-selling items are the *traffic builders* that earn their spots by attracting the customers.

One furniture store manager said that she had to keep cheap items in several categories for phone-in shoppers. Shoppers would call and ask about the store's lowest price for a nightstand or bookcase, etc. Unless they heard a cheap price, they wouldn't travel to the store. Once in the store, 90 percent of the phone-in customers bought a more expensive item.

Segment your current products and services into two categories: moneymakers and traffic builders. The Divestment/Reinvestment decision is different for each category. Use a strict return on sales or return on investment analysis of moneymakers to determine which to keep and which to replace. Measure or estimate the traffic-building effectiveness of the traffic builders to determine which to keep and which to replace.

The decision to divest isn't strictly a monetary decision. Some products waste too many of the firm's resources. They may require too much training, too much after-the-sale support, or too much effort to close the sale. Therefore, you may decide to divest a product or service because it's too much trouble, particularly when you have better options.

Divestment decisions should involve more than which products aren't producing a reasonable profit return; it should also involve the profits your business could make if you invested your time and energy in other products or other services.

The first stage of a Divestment/Reinvestment strategy is to critically examine all your current product lines or types of services and see if any of them aren't living up to your expectations. The second stage is to look for better opportunities to reinvest your money and effort. This is exactly what Ed Rawlings, President of General Mills, did when he decided to divest his company's animal feed division in the 1960s and reinvest the funds in other areas of the remaining business. In the year following his Divestment/Reinvestment decision, sales dropped 6.5 percent, but profits rose 49 percent *(3)*. That's the type of effect you're seeking, higher profits because of smart decisions.

Small business owners use the Divestment/Reinvestment strategy exactly as big business managers use it, just on a smaller scale. Take the case of James Baum who operated his family's 114-year-old department store in Morris, Illinois. The store's fabric department had lost its competitive advantage, so sales and profits were unsatisfactory. There were two reasons for this turn of events. One, new competitors had a much wider variety of merchandise. And two, his competitors' prices were lower.

Even though the fabric department had been a historical mainstay of the family business, James decided to divest that product line. He then successfully reinvested the cash from liquidating the fabric department into a women's sportswear department and a department for the larger woman. Profits were further improved by hiring more part-time employees who received fewer benefits *(4)*.

Your decision-making process doesn't have to follow a Divestment/Reinvestment sequence of thoughts; it can look more like a Reinvestment/Divestment sequence. For example, Paper Cutters of Greenville, S.C., found a new growth opportunity first and then searched for a way to find some investment money. They devised a plan to divest the business of its fleet of company-owned cars and trucks. This move not only generated the cash necessary for the new growth opportunity, it cut their cost of vehicle purchases and repairs, and simplified preparing tax reports. By divesting themselves of their fleet and leasing the vehicles they needed, they lowered their costs, rid themselves of many problems, and raised the funds they needed for reinvestment *(5)*.

Of course, you could just divest yourself of your headaches like Mike Weaver. Mike divested himself of the things that were robbing him of the time to be creative. He reinvested his time in himself. You see, Mike knows his strengths and weaknesses. He considers himself an inventor and an entrepreneur. He doesn't consider himself an administrator. So when Mike's Hand Held Products Inc. business had grown to employ 50 people with sales of $15 million, he knew it was time to divest himself of his managerial responsibilities and turn his company over to someone with the right competencies to plan, organize, lead, and control his growing business.

In 1992, Mike turned the company over to a professional, proven manager. The new manager did all the things Mike didn't want to be bothered with. Things like reducing costs in an orderly fashion, cutting inventory, and cutting personnel. All this let Mike reinvest his time in Mike. He went back to being an inventor and having fun *(6)*.

Pet Supplies Plus in Livonia, Michigan, wanted to expand by adding more stores, and they needed the cash to invest. Management decided the cash was sitting on their shelves in the form of large inventories. So, they constructed a novel Divestment/Reinvestment plan. They searched for new wholesalers with a wide product line who could make frequent, small deliveries. They found a willing wholesaler. This allowed them to divest their current inventory to fund growth. As a bonus, the new supplier provided them with a wider variety of retail products. They were able to display a wider variety of products with less on-hand inventory. Less on-hand inventory reduced insurance, taxes, and even reduced the utility bills. Best of all, since 1988, Pet Supplies Plus has expanded to 35 locations *(7)*.

Finding All Your Growth Opportunities

Divestment/Reinvestment is a routine strategy for all businesses. It's like the normal pruning and fertilizing of fruit trees to make them more productive. As you have seen, the strategy is used in two ways. First, you may decide that there are unproductive parts of your business that need to be divested, then you can look for more lucrative growth opportunities to reinvest your money. At this point in the book, you probably have a promising list of new growth opportunities to consider. Second, you might have already identified a lucrative growth opportunity, and now you're trying to find ways to raise the investment money you need. Some type of divestment might raise the cash. Either way, take these steps to develop your divestment list:

1. Examine your existing products and services, your product and service lines, and the markets you serve. Are any of the items you consider profit makers losing money or performing poorly? Are any traffic builders not doing their job? Is there any reason not to divest of the bad performers?
2. Examine your assets. How could you liquidate some of your assets to fund a new investment? Can you sell and then lease back some of your assets? Can you find ways to operate with less inventory? Can you liquidate part of your operation and rely instead on suppliers and subcontractors?

These are your opportunities to grow.

Retrenchment: A Profit Growth Strategy for Financially Troubled Businesses

Small businesses have a "best" size that generates the greatest profits, just as any machine has a "best" operating speed or any building has a maximum capacity. Operating above or below the "best" size will decrease profits. Lots of small business owners know this is true, they just can't explain why it's true. The owner of a car repair shop, himself a working mechanic, said that he figured out he could make more money hiring three mechanics than he could hiring six mechanics — he didn't know why, but experience had taught him that this was true. Several custom homebuilders have reported similar experiences. These firms grew too much, and then shrunk or retrenched back to the "good old days" — back to a smaller size with fewer sales but better profits.

Your Costs Look Like the Letter "U"

Retrenchment is a strategy to shrink a business that's grown too big back to its "best" size, the size that generates maximum profits. Retrenchment works because every business and every work process in the business has a "U" shaped cost curve like Figure 15.1.

Imagine a new business that sets up and operates at a low sales level, a very inefficient sales level where every employee, every piece of equipment, and every work process is often idle. If you added up the new firm's total costs and divided total costs by the small number of units sold, the per unit cost would be high; that's point 1 on the U-Curve. Point 1 is a typical situation for new firms and new processes. As the business becomes successful, sales increase. Now if total costs are added up and divided by the relatively large number of units sold, per unit cost is much lower; that's point 2 on the U-Curve.

The U-Curve graph shows unit costs (average per product or per service costs) steadily declining from point 1 as the business's volume increases. This relationship is true for all retail, service, and manufacturing businesses, and it's true for all individual work processes because they have individual U-Curves.

Per unit costs decline from point 1 to point 2 for many reasons. Going from point 1 to point 2, the business buys increasingly larger quantities from all its suppliers and gets increasingly larger price discounts. Raw materials, components, office supplies, repair parts, advertising, etc. all get cheaper per unit when the business purchases larger quantities. Bigger shipments from suppliers will lower freight rates. If outbound shipments to customers are involved, those freight rates also decline. Employees who were drawing full wages even though they were idle part of the time at point 1 are drawing slightly larger wages and are never idle at point 2. They are more productive. Therefore, labor cost per unit declines steadily from point 1 to point 2.

The U-Curve graph shows that eventually a business's per unit cost reaches its lowest level. From that point on, additional sales are subject to diminishing returns. Meaning that, at some sales level, profits are maximized, and

FIGURE 15.1: The U-Curve

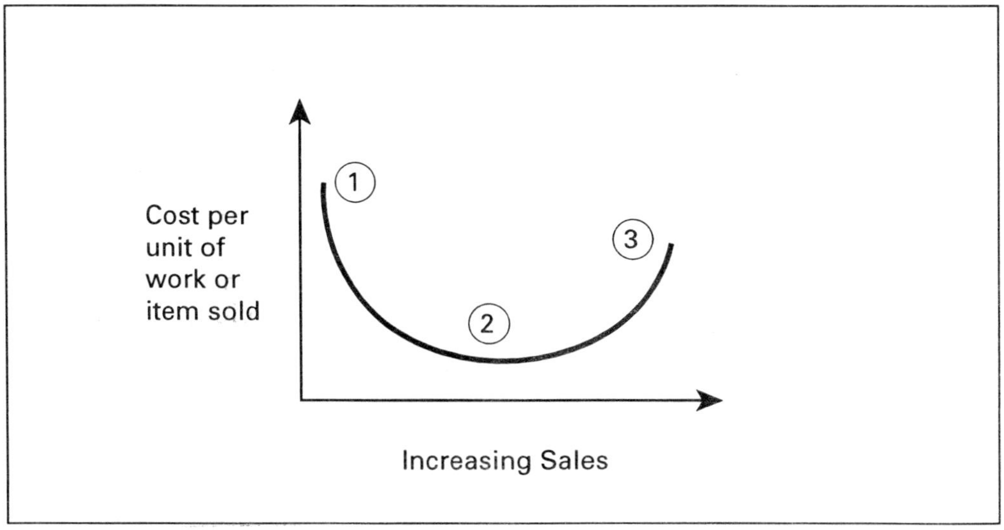

beyond that optimum level total costs rise faster than sales, and the business heads toward point 3 on the U-Curve. From point 2 to point 3, increasing sales cause the business to experience overtime labor expenses and an increasing number of worker mistakes, scheduling errors, product breakage, and damage. As the business approaches point 3, the facility becomes excessively crowded, and both employee injuries and equipment failures increase due to pushing people and equipment beyond their capacities.

Also, as the business approaches point 3, a part-time manager must often switch to full-time to cope with the business's growing pains. In many cases, small businesses are managed by part-time managers who spend most of their time working as the firm's best craftsman, or as the small firm's star salesperson. On the way to point 3 this part-time manager switches to full-time, hires a worker or salesperson to replace him or her, and attempts to solve the range of growth problems. Often losing the firm's star worker in this way pushes the firm closer to point 3.

When per unit costs start increasing and keep on increasing as more and more sales are added, *the business has passed its best operating point.*

The classic U-Curve explains the normal "unit-cost" phenomenon that's an unexpected event for many managers of small businesses. They thought bigger sales always meant bigger profits. The problem is that the business isn't designed to be efficient at the higher volumes: *the business has to change.* Change means expanding. Change means taking actions like ridding the business of a bottleneck by replacing a slow machine with a new, high volume machine; moving to a larger location; getting a larger warehouse; and reinventing critical work processes. At point 3, the business either has to reinvent and redesign itself to create a new U-Curve or it has to retrench back down its existing U-Curve.

Creating a New "U-Curve"

When a small manufacturer encounters rising unit costs, they usually upgrade their equipment. So, a machine that requires three workers to produce 10 units per hour is replaced with a new machine that requires only one worker to produce 25 units per hour. Perhaps a manual information system is replaced with a computerized information system. Such changes create a new U-Curve that's located to the right and below the old U-Curve. Retail and service firms make similar moves to increase their productivity and create a new U-Curve (Figure 15.2).

The newly created U-Curve presents the firm with a new problem. If sales decline past the intersection of the new and old U-Curves, the per unit costs will

FIGURE 15.2: Creating New U-Curves

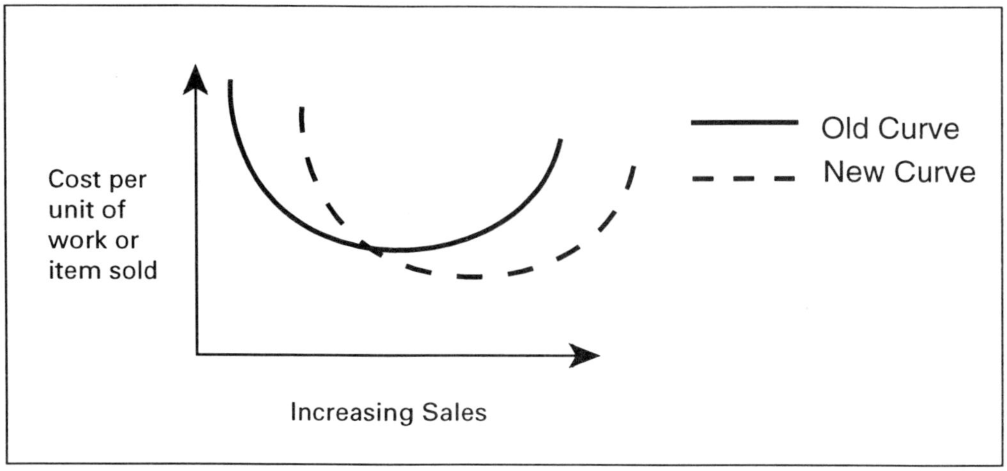

be higher as the firm tries to produce less volume with its new, high-volume facility. In other words, the bigger business is more costly to operate at a lower sales level than was the smaller business.

Every business, whether retail, service, or manufacturing, has a U-Curve. Every business, small, medium, or large, can expand beyond its "best" operating level. Every business either copes with too much growth by creating a new U-Curve, by making significant changes in the way work is performed, or the business must retrench.

All U-Curves are Not Alike

Small businesses have different shaped U-Curves. Some businesses, like custom homebuilders, have sharp curves like the Sharp U Cost Curve shown in Figure 15.3, and their costs quickly increase when they past their optimum sales volume. Sharp U firms often become unprofitable with too much growth and need to use a Retrenchment Strategy to return to profitability. Other businesses, like retail stores, have lazy-sided curves like the Soup-Bowl U shown below, and as they past their optimum sales volume and continue to grow, costs per unit slowly rise and profits slowly decrease. Soup-Bowl firms more often need a Re-Invention Strategy to cut costs rather than a Retrenchment Strategy to shrink sales.

In fact, both type firms can use either a Re-Invention Strategy to cut costs or various growth strategies to increase profits. Unfortunately, some owners with Sharp U Cost Curves get trapped in a situation where they can't make the

FIGURE 15.3: Different Types of U-Curves

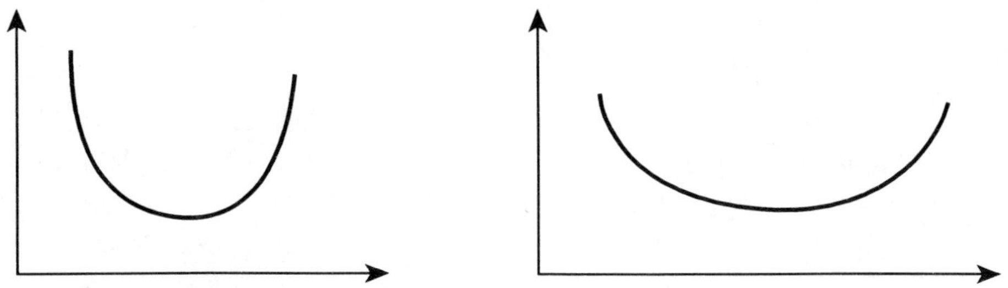

significant business changes required to reinvent or redesign their firms in order to create a new U-Curve.

The Owner-Manager-Worker Trap

Here's a common trap, already alluded to, that requires a Retrenchment Strategy. A person starts up a business as an owner who makes an investment, acts as the firm's sole manager, and performs as the small firm's most productive worker or star salesperson. The business never pays dividends to the owner on the money invested, the business pays nothing or very little to the owner for managing the business, but the business pays the owner a good wage for work performed. As sales increase, the business goes down the U-Curve, around the bottom of the U where profits are good, and starts up the over-capacity, over-worked side of the U-Curve. It's time to expand, but expanding would require the owner to quit the worker role and become a full-time manager — a double whammy. First, hiring an additional employee would increase costs. Second, losing the firm's most productive worker or star salesperson would hurt sales and cut profits. A price increase would offset the extra expense, but the market won't support a price increase, because there are a lot of similar owner-manager businesses that have established the market's low prices. Therefore, the owner is trapped in a position he or she can't easily change. This is the Owner-Manager-Worker Trap also known to some as "buying a job."

Since expanding is unwise and remaining in an over-capacity position is unbearable, the solution is to Retrench back to the firm's most profitable size. If possible, do this with a slight price increase to trim volumes. The next step is to start working with this book's marketing and management sales growth strategies to find opportunities to grow out of the trap. Usually this involves Opportunistic Diversification, Market Diversification, and Market Development.

The Cheap-Overhead Trap

A similar trap involves setting up a business on-the-cheap. This is accomplished by purchasing used equipment at an auction, getting a sweetheart deal on rent from a relative, or some other one-time deal that provides low overhead costs. Then, the business establishes its prices based on its cheap overhead. Finally, sales volume steadily increases, the business travels down its U-Curve, across the bottom, and arrives at the over-capacity position. Then the owner discovers he or she can't afford to expand. Expanding into a more expensive new facility or adding expensive new equipment would cause costs to rise too high. Higher costs would require higher prices, and the market won't support higher prices. Facing this alternative, the business has to Retrench back down its U-Curve to return to profitability. Then turn to the sales growth strategies in this book to find new growth opportunities.

The Large-Incremental Expansion Trap

Sometimes a small expansion isn't possible. Expansion might require too large an increase in capacity — too large for the limited number of customers in your local market or your customer segment. In other words, an expansion would create a new U-Curve for your business, but you'd be on the inefficient (left side, point 1) side of the new U-Curve with too small a market to ever increase sales enough to move you down the curve and into a new "best" range — a fact some small businesses discover only after they expand. Retrenchment is much easier before an expansion. It's still possible after an expansion, but it takes more work and some luck.

A business owner in Memphis over-expanded then used a Retrenchment Strategy in a gutsy and illegal way. He broke some contracts and reneged on a retail store lease. No one bothered to sue him because of his bad financial condition. After all, "You can't get blood from a turnip." He was able to retrench and eventually regain his old profitability.

The Owner-Manager-Worker trap, the Cheap-Overhead trap, and Large-Incremental Expansion trap aren't the only traps a small business owner can create; they are just the most common ones.

Finding Your Profit Growth Opportunities

Before you decide to use a Retrenchment Strategy, you must be convinced of four facts.

1. The U-Curve properly describes the relationship between your business's per unit costs and your business's sales volume.
2. Your business's per unit cost is traveling up the right side of your U-Curve, toward point 3. In other words, your costs are increasing faster than your sales.
3. You know how to reverse your situation. Your Retrenchment plan must cut sales in such a way as to cut the costs of overtime, breakage, mistakes, and the errors caused by being overworked.
4. Finally, you know you're trapped. Trapped for reasons you can clearly identify. Trapped in a way that keeps you from significantly reinventing and redesigning the way your business works to create a new U-Curve and boost efficiency and productivity. Trapped usually means you can't afford to add more productive equipment, can't afford to change processes to make them more efficient, can't afford to move to a more effective location, and can't afford the expense of shifting your U-Curve. In short, you can't find a way out through growth.

The best Retrenchment plan is usually to lower overall sales volume by slightly increasing overall prices. It's also common to drop certain types of customers when you determine that they cause most of your growth problems. Retrenchment can be used selectively on a part or piece of your business. If only one area of your business is in trouble, just shrink that area.

Make a list of your opportunities to increase profits with Retrenchment.

Revitalization: A Profit Growth Strategy for Financially Troubled Businesses

Revitalization is surgery that cuts away the cancerous parts of a financially troubled business, so the remaining organization can be returned to good health. It's an extreme measure to treat a very sick business. A revitalization strategy requires an owner or top manager to make deep cost cuts, to sell off assets, and to eliminate the losing parts of the business. These moves are designed to shrink the business back to a smaller, profitable core. These moves can range from a delicate pruning and trimming exercise that takes place over many months to an emergency plan that's quickly deployed to rescue the business. However, cutbacks cause lingering employee morale and productivity problems that must be dealt with to avoid losing the key employees that are most needed to operate the remaining business.

Revitalization is used to avoid bankruptcy or liquidation. Normally, it's a strategy used in an older business that was once profitable, but it can also be used on a newer business that has some good and some bad parts. For the older firm, revitalization usually means turning back the clock and returning to a core business that was profitable before adventurous attempts to grow turned sour. If the business's older core has gone sour, Revitalization can be used to jettison it.

Foremost, revitalization involves finding a vital and viable business core that is profitable or can be made profitable once it's freed from having its profits and cash flow sucked away by the losing parts of the business. Eliminating the losing parts of the business will boost profits, and liquidating the assets of the losing part will help replenish cash flow. The next hurdle is to operate the remaining business core at a profitable level, and this often depends on deep cost cuts and on quickly rebuilding employee trust and support. Rebuilding morale depends largely on whether employees believe the firm's financial troubles were primarily created by external market forces or internal management blunders.

One Firm's Experience

The Missouri School Boards Association (MSBA) became one of the largest such state organizations in the United States under very creative and competent leadership. By 1995, the nonprofit organization had grown to 49 employees and provided numerous services for school board members. But the firm found itself losing money, falling far behind on its payments to suppliers, and even having trouble paying employee insurance premiums and reimbursing employees' expense accounts. Faced with threats of foreclosure by its suppliers, it turned to a Revitalization Strategy.

An internal analysis showed that several core services generated positive revenue. MSBA operated a state mandated new school board training program, paid for by the State of Missouri, that was highly profitable. A profitable policy services department kept school board members up-to-date on the latest legal requirements. The association's lobbying efforts, while not revenue producing, were highly valued by members and a major reason why members were willing to pay their yearly dues to belong to the association.

However, the association had several big losers. It operated a large technology department designed to provide school districts with computer hardware, software, and networking capabilities, as well as provide training for teachers, administrators, and support staff — it was bleeding red ink profusely and causing massive cash-flow problems. The association operated a money losing educational satellite network for school districts and a video production facility. Closely related, the firm also operated a satellite up-link truck to broadcast remote events into Missouri classrooms. All were wonderful services, but they were costly, and were not highly valued by the membership.

Management's Revitalization Strategy eliminated or downsized those parts of the business that were losing money. It included laying off 17 out of 49 employees, most from the technology and video production areas. Assets were liquidated to generate cash, including selling the association's interest in a twin engine plane flown by the executive director. The up-link truck and its driver/operator were contracted out to various TV networks, thus covering all expenses. The firm even attempted to sell and lease back its office building to generate additional cash.

Asset liquidations, quick elimination of the losing parts of the business, and employee layoffs shrunk the association back to a profitable core. Unfortunately, management misjudged its need to rebuild employee morale. The remaining employees blamed management for the firm's problems. Morale continued to sink. At the time the association desperately needed revenues that could only be generated by the remaining highly productive workers, productivity declined, slowing the firm's recovery. In fact, almost half of the remaining employees left the association in the next six months. The firm did recover, but, with some serious morale-building efforts, it could have recovered faster.

The MSBA example demonstrates the five key elements of a revitalization strategy.

1. Identify a profitable vital core.
2. Cut costs by eliminating the losing portions of the business.
3. Rebuild cash flow by liquidating assets.
4. Eliminate costly perks — including yours.
5. Rebuild employee morale.

The Vital Core: Revitalization works only if you can find a part of your business, called a vital core, that's generating profits or can be reorganized to generate profits. The vital core is often the firm's original business area that generated the investment money used to expand into ill-fated ventures. However, the vital core can also be one or more of the new business ventures or some combination of old and new parts of the business.

Finding a vital core may not be easy. This search often requires segmenting customers into separate groups and analyzing the profitability of each group. If your pricing has been held down to appeal to the widest range of customers, search for smaller segments of customers willing to pay a higher price for your products and services.

Next, look for ways to reduce the expenses of the vital core to make it profitable. Examine each of the vital core's expenses, starting with the largest, and determine how much it would have to be reduced for the new core to be profitable; then devise a wide range of options for reducing expenses to targeted levels. Also, don't ignore the small expenses, sometimes you can cut enough small expenses to be significant. Next comes the chore of cost cutting.

Severe Cost Cutting: Your biggest savings normally come from closing down the losing parts of your business; those parts outside the vital core. The shutdown includes eliminating product lines, service systems, retail stores, and warehouses plus laying off employees connected with those parts. These cuts should produce a drastic cut in variable costs.

Cost reduction always involves eliminating people because wages are a major expense for every small business. Some full-time employees can be replaced with part-time or temp-service employees. Eliminating people will force you into reinventing many of the remaining jobs. Use the Process Re-Invention techniques previously discussed to reorganize the new workforce.

Cost reduction also includes delaying the replacement of existing equipment, buying used equipment instead of new, and leasing rather than buying.

Asset Liquidation: Troubled firms are almost always short on cash. Cash flow is rebuilt by selling off the non-core portions of your business, those being eliminated, as well as non-essential land, buildings, equipment, and inventories. Obviously the inventories connected to portions of the business being closed can be liquidated, but perhaps other inventories can be trimmed to generate extra cash flow. Try to replace current suppliers with new ones that can make small deliveries more frequently to reduce inventory levels.

Some vital fixed assets like land, buildings, and trucks can be sold and leased back to generate cash without losing their benefits. Leasing produces another cost-cutting benefit. Leasing lets you shift upkeep and maintenance to the new owner, allowing your business to operate with even fewer people.

Sell your personal perks like company cars, airplanes, boats, etc. to generate cash and to signal your remaining employees that you're affected too.

Timing: The timing of cost-cutting measures such as laying off employees, eliminating portions of the business, and liquidating assets to improve cash depends on the urgency of your situation. If your problems are serious, but you still have good cash flow and some financial reserves, you can devise a plan to minimize the impact on employees. You can encourage some employees to seek other jobs and not replace those employees who leave.

On the other hand, if bankruptcy is imminent, your cost cutting and asset liquidation plans must be implemented swiftly, having a devastating impact on the morale of remaining employees.

Rebuilding Employee Morale: As soon as employees suspect a cut is coming, and continuing well after laid-off employees have departed, morale drops into the toilet and so does productivity. Just when the business needs remaining employees to be highly productive, employees turn in their worst performances. Instead of working, employees console one another, exchange current rumors, and bad mouth management. Understandably, employees are upset and bitter. The business has broken its promise to employees. There is an unspoken but understood and valid covenant between employees and the business: employees will help build the business, and the business will take care of its employees. If employees believe they have lived up to their half of this tacit agreement, they are going to be upset, bitter, and vocally resentful when management fails to live up to its half.

A manager can greatly influence morale even when laying off people. The first step is to anticipate employee morale problems and then to take actions to boost morale. Failure to deal with lingering morale problems will result in high turnover levels. The standing joke among businesses using a Revitalization Strategy is, "How can you tell who the best and brightest employees are? They're the ones who are leaving." And without a plan to counteract morale problems, the good employees will find new jobs and leave you with a business full of mediocre, depressed, unmotivated, confused, unproductive workers.

Your first job is to persuade key employees to stay. Your second job is to minimize morale problems. Your success will be influenced by the state of the economy and the job market. The better the job market, the bigger your problem.

First, develop a one- to two-year special bonus system for key employees guaranteeing them a specific reward for specific personal achievements; achievements that support your revitalization goals. Don't make the goals impossible for employees to attain. Try offering multiple levels of goals and rewards. Tiered goals reward employees in direct proportion to their achievements — small rewards for small achievements up to large rewards for big achievements. Because trust between employees and management is at extremely low levels, goals must be clearly achievable. Furthermore, to build trust, employees should participate in collecting the data used to measure their achievements.

Second, try to influence where employees place the blame for the business's troubles. Morale is easier to rebuild when employees feel the firm's problems were caused by competition in the market place or external forces and events largely beyond the control of top management. Morale is hardest to rebuild when employees feel management's internal blunders are mainly responsible for the firm's problems. Unless management mounts an offensive, employees will tend to blame management. Here's how to deflect employees' bitterness.

Employees Understand External Problems: Employees understand competition. Most are sports fans and most were raised in a culture of capitalism. So deflect blame by arguing that the business fought a good fight, a smart fight, but lost to a competitor or lost to unforeseeable outside forces that were beyond management's control.

Outside forces that cause understandable misfortunes include events like a competitor achieving an unexpected technological breakthrough, interest rates suddenly going up, a key supplier having unusual problems, lawsuits, and changing trends in the marketplace. Perhaps shifting customer attitudes or damaging political decisions caused your problems. Employees understand that every firm faces risks; the world isn't risk free. Life is a cycle of ups and downs. Few remaining employees will blame management for fighting and losing a battle in the marketplace. However, employees will not continue to work for managers who they believe are likely to lead them into similar problems in the future. You must argue that you have learned to avoid such problems in the future.

Employee morale is rebuilt more easily when management convinces employees that one or more external forces caused the business's misadventures, not poor management decisions. And, thank goodness, you have a plan to get the firm out of its quagmire. Then, present a sound Revitalization plan with rewards for their active participation.

Employees Don't Forgive Internal Blunders: Maybe it was your fault. Employees are understandably afraid of management incompetence. Scott Adams has made a lucrative career out of his Dilbert cartoon strip by appealing to the common fear that managers are really stupid. It should come as no surprise that the long lasting and most severe morale problems occur when employees believe that the need for severe cost cutting, asset liquidations, and layoffs was management's fault. Morale is difficult to rebuild when employees believe management tried to compete in areas where there was no reasonable likelihood of success. Morale is difficult to rebuild when employees blame management for not understanding the firm's weaknesses, for making unwise investments, for squandering the firm's resources, and ruining the employees' futures.

When management's poor leadership obviously caused the problem, morale can only be rebuilt after top management is replaced or most of the employees are replaced. New managers can inspire employees with new ideas, inspire employees by leading the firm in new directions, and inspire employees by making believable promises of better days to come. While replacement of top management is a common action taken by larger corporations when they use a Revitalization Strategy, the top manager of the small firm is usually the owner who isn't going to fire himself. If you're an entrenched manager whose employees blame you for their problems, be prepared for an extended period of depressed morale, spotty employee performances, and increased tardiness, absenteeism, and turnover. It will take time to revitalize the core of the business to its maximum profit potential.

A Final Checklist: Before pursuing Retrenchment, do a couple of things. First, read about remote trends in Chapter 16. If your business is positioned to take advantage of emerging new trends, a reversal of your fortunes may be in sight if you can hold on. Second, if you have a profitable core but too much debt and repaying the debt would take more time than suppliers and loan officers would allow, visit a bankruptcy attorney. It's their job to find a way to buy you some time.

Third, you can cash in part of your ownership. If there are attractive ways out of your hardships that require cash investments you don't have, draw up a growth plan proposal and sell it to investors. Sell part of your business to get the cash needed to survive and grow. If you want to maintain control, devise a plan like placing advertisements in all the surrounding area newspapers and find ten small investors instead of one large one. Try to maintain control by holding onto the largest share of the business.

Your Opportunity to Grow Profits with Revitalization

Use a Revitalization Strategy when you don't have any other choice. Use a Revitalization Strategy when you're losing money and when you can't afford to pursue any of the marketing or management sales growth opportunities that you've identified. Revitalization is chosen by eliminating all the other growth strategies because they are not feasible in your situation. Revitalization is your last growth choice.

To use this strategy, develop the following five-part plan for your situation:

1. **Find your vital core.** The vital core is a part of your existing business that would be profitable if it didn't have to carry the financial burden of the losing parts of the business. The vital core may be original business before the firm expanded, or it may be a new growth opportunity that's having to carry the old business to which you're emotionally attached.
2. **Aggressively cut costs.** Devise a plan to severely and aggressively cut costs. Shut down the losing portions of the business. Lay off employees. Cut expensive promotional programs. Eliminate the "perks."
3. **Liquidate assets.** Sell assets to raise cash. Sell the portions of the business you intend to shut down. Sell unneeded assets. Sell and lease back buildings, equipment, or vehicles. Liquidate the excess inventory. Sell the perks like company cars, planes, and boats.
4. **Plan to rebuild morale.** Rebuilding morale is critical. If possible develop a convincing explanation that blames the firm's problems on external forces, factors, and events. You must aggressively sell your explanation of the business's financial problems to the remaining employees. Devise a one or two year bonus system for key employees that will financially reward them for staying and rebuilding the business. If management blunders caused the problem, replace management. Unless of course, you're management.
5. **Timing.** How swiftly you implement your revitalization plan depends on the severity of your problem. Go slowly if you can afford it.

Liquidation: A Cash Flow Maximization Strategy

Liquidation is a plan to sell off your business in pieces or as a whole. Owners can be forced into liquidation by declining profits, or they can choose to liquidate voluntarily.

Voluntary Liquidations are Common

The authors formulated and implemented a voluntary liquidation plan to sell their small manufacturing business to someone who would move the equipment to another location, allowing them to split their plant site and buildings into three parcels for separate sales. This plan extracted the authors from their business, maximized their cash, and freed them from a seven-day a week work routine that had grown old.

Barbara Todd and Sandy Anderson jointly founded "Orchids Only!" and grew the business to an enjoyable size with good profits. After developing a list of growth opportunities, they realized that the next expansion step did not interest them. More growth would involve assuming a lot of risk, they would have to make a big investment in phone systems, employees, computers, and equipment. If they didn't make the investments, they would be inviting competition. They opted to voluntarily liquidate by selling the operation to a larger mail-order operator to maximize their cash flow from their successful venture *(8)*.

Such voluntary liquidations are common in the small business community. The motivation of many small business owners is to maximize personal control over their own lives, not, as the general public believes, to make themselves rich — although a combination of the two would be considered perfect by all owners. When an owner chooses to start up a business, it's often a quest for more personal freedom. When an owner chooses to voluntarily sell the business, it's often because the business has become a burden that severely restricts personal freedom. Voluntarily choosing to liquidate is done for a variety of personal reasons, and there are many fine books to help you develop strategies for selling your business.

Forced Liquidations

If you're forced to liquidate, hire an attorney. Your attorney should handle liquidations forced by bankruptcy proceedings. Always hire an attorney.

In between the two extremes of voluntarily liquidating a business and being forced to liquidate by creditors are small businesses in financial trouble whose owners are trying to determine if they should liquidate or not.

When You Should Choose Liquidation

Liquidation should be chosen if you were unable to devise a feasible Revitalization Strategy. When Revitalization isn't feasible, Liquidation is your only alternative. If your business is constantly losing money, delaying liquidation will only decrease the cash you'll get from your business when you finally do liquidate. The earlier you liquidate, the more money you'll take with you.

Take the advice of A. J. Cohen; liquidating sooner is better than liquidating later. He depleted much of his personal money by covering three years of losses in his Savannah business. All the time his accountant was advising him that padlocking the door would maximize his personal money. Cohen didn't want to let his employees down, but he finally faced an inevitable choice — let them go now, or let them go later because of forced bankruptcy. So, in September 1992, A.J. Cohen liquidated Lady Jane, Inc. of Savannah, Georgia *(9)*.

Even though Cohen didn't have a viable core, he was still reluctant to use a Liquidation Strategy. Cohen's reaction is common among owners facing deep financial trouble; they are reluctant to use Liquidation. However, if you wait until you are forced to liquidate, you may be ruined financially. Unfortunately, like Cohen, most small business owners delay the inevitable for years and lose a lot of personal money. Don't delay the inevitable, you'll only lose more money. If you couldn't find a viable core for a Revitalization Strategy, liquidate!

Your Opportunity to Maximize Your Cash

If you're out of options, face facts, visit your local library, look up some of the books on liquidating a business, and devise a plan.

CHAPTER 16

How to Choose the Best Growth Opportunities

"OPPORTUNITY LOST" OCCURS WHEN YOU INVEST in one growth opportunity then discover a better opportunity that you can no longer afford to pursue. You've gotten in too big a hurry and chased the wrong growth opportunity. Now you realize you should have analyzed all your growth opportunities before making your choice. This chapter is dedicated to helping you avoid that type of mistake. This chapter is dedicated to helping you find the "best" opportunity to pursue.

As an owner or manager of a small business, you need help. Yes, you need help making the right growth choice. Managers of big businesses have lots of help. Why shouldn't you get some? Every owner of a small business faces a serious lack of objectivity when they discover a new growth opportunity, and they analyze its potential — it's like asking new parents to judge their baby's looks. Like a proud new parent, an owner of a small business is too quick to see a new opportunity's potential to boost sales and profits and too slow to see its risks and problems. It's even more difficult to give each its proper weight. Is it a small, medium, or large risk? How serious are the problems? And so forth.

By contrast, in a large business, people who are not connected to the discovery of a new opportunity are called upon to analyze its potential objectively. Unfortunately, you don't have the same depth of people and can't assign competent and objective key employees to analyze your growth idea. So, you need help to become more impartial and objective. No one can transform you into a completely impartial and totally objective analyst, but this chapter offers you many factors and issues to consider before deciding which of your growth ideas to pursue. Reading this chapter will improve your objectivity, and the only thing you'll lose is 20 minutes of your time and maybe your chance to experience "Opportunity Lost."

This chapter presents a number of different factors and issues you should analyze before selecting which growth opportunities to pursue. They are not and can not be arranged in the order of importance because the order of importance varies for each business and each situation. Any single issue or factor might be the reason you decide to give one opportunity a higher priority than another. Some issues will tempt you to scratch off a growth idea as unworkable in your situation, don't do it. Instead, push it to the bottom of your priorities. You may want to reconsider it next year when you do this all over again.

Your goal is pick the best opportunities to pursue in the foreseeable future. How far is foreseeable? It varies, but don't be shortsighted. Don't choose only opportunities that can be implemented immediately. If you plan one year at a time, you might lose ground to a competitor who plans five years at a time and updates his or her five-year plan every year. Some plans take several years to implement. For instance, you may want to pursue a Process Re-Invention opportunity during the next year and invest the savings in a marketing growth opportunity during the second year. Most owners and managers will want to choose several growth opportunities and weave them together into a multiple-year plan which they will update and improve each year. With each passing year, you'll be a more experienced planner and have more knowledge about what does and doesn't work for your business and your target customers. Every year you'll be able to design a better growth plan.

One last suggestion. Develop three prioritized lists of opportunities: a marketing sales growth list, a management sales growth list, and a management profit growth list. This will keep you from burying a small Backward Integration or a small Process Re-Invention opportunity under a list of exciting marketing opportunities. It's wise to pursue a variety of growth strategies.

Now, here are some issues you should consider when analyzing each growth opportunity.

Project Sales, Costs, Profits, and Competitive Reactions

For each growth opportunity, project sales, costs, profits, and competitive reactions. Actually writing down your projections in detail helps you become more objective. Make month-by-month predictions for the next 12 months.

Before Arkansas Woodworks Mfg. Company pursued a Market Development opportunity to add a factory outlet retail store, it constructed a five-year financial projection. The plan required erecting a small building, investing money in inventories of furniture built in-house, investing money in inventories of other manufacturers' furniture, funding an advertising program, and incurring many new costs. The owners realized their emotions were clouding their judgment as they dreamed of huge new profits. They needed a dose of objectivity.

The owners decided to use a large customer's retail business in Little Rock, Arkansas, as a model. Since the manufacturer's rural trade area had 12 percent of the number of customers that were in the Little Rock trade area, they projected sales to reach 12 percent of Little Rock's within five years. They put together a five-year estimate of sales, costs, and profits that would take them in increments to the "12 percent size." They had one weak competitor and projected pushing them out of business within a year with the aid of an aggressive and costly advertising program. They predicted that their Little Rock retailer would complain that their supplier was getting into the retailing business, and they developed a plan to calm that customer.

Using this more objective projection, first year profits looked as though they would be much less than previous emotional guesses, but still attractive. The project would still pay for itself. Therefore the building was constructed and the outlet store opened. Their weak competitor closed down within three months, allowing them to cut their advertising budget to a more reasonable level. First year's sales and profits were better than projected, matching those projected for year two. Over the next few years, sales grew as projected. No gold mine, but solid profits.

Managers of small businesses easily become infatuated with their growth ideas and need to find a way to return to reality. Forecasting based on objective numbers, while boring, usually is a good reality check. For example, one potential owner of a small business envisioned opening a new liquor store in a small community that had three existing stores. Imaginary profits soared through the new owner's mind. Then came the consultant's recommendation. Go sit in front of each of the three stores for a week and estimate their sales. Then project annual community sales. To verify and improve the projections, seek out the area's liquor distributors and quiz them about total area sales. Assume you'll eventually capture your 25 percent of the community's spirit purchases. Further assume your new business's sales will be 10 percent the first year, 15 percent the second, 20 percent the third, and top out at 25 percent of total community sales the fourth year. Next project costs and profits. Finally, factor in competitive reactions and new firm advantages. As you can see, emotional infatuation is being replaced with some objectivity — not complete objectivity, but a definite improvement.

Objective numbers are numbers you can't easily manipulate. In the first example, the furniture manufacturer knew the Little Rock customer's total sales.

The size of both communities came from a U.S. Government census count. These were objective numbers that couldn't be manipulated. Likewise, the total current liquor store sales in the local community was an objective number.

To avoid being misled by your emotions, base your forecast of sales on as many objective numbers as possible. If your growth plan calls for targeting a new segment of customers in your market area, try to find a way to count that group. Ask a local marketing instructor at your community college for help. Ask the Chamber of Commerce for help. Ask newspaper, radio, and television advertising salespeople for help — you'll be surprised to learn that they've already built a demographic profile of the area. Then measure your penetration of existing target customers in your existing business. If your business has worked up to a 22 percent share of your target customers, maybe you should project new growth opportunity sales to your new customer segment to follow a similar trend — you'll work up to a 22 percent share over time. Call this Scenario Number 1. Scenario Number 2 might be a more favorable forecast because of factors you can identify. Try developing several scenarios that each deviate from your most conservative scenario if something favorable happens. By improving your objectivity, you'll avoid over estimating a favorite growth opportunity's expected sales and profits and making the wrong choice.

Risks

Evaluate two types of risks that are associated with each growth opportunity: Known Risks and Unknown Risks.

Known Risks

Known Risks are questions without answers that you have about the probability of success or failure of a new growth opportunity. Questions like, "What's the likelihood of my new product failing?" Because you know what question to ask, you can analyze it. If 60 percent of past new products have failed, the Known Risk of failure is 60 percent plus or minus unusually favorable or unfavorable factors for this proposed new product. A favorable factor that would lower the risk of failure could be a new product feature that has been frequently requested by your customers.

The purpose of analyzing Known Risks is to estimate the likelihood of your business actually receiving the projected profits from each of your growth opportunities. One growth opportunity may have a huge potential profit and an extremely high Known Risk of failure. Another may have a moderate, attractive potential profit with an extremely low Known Risk of failure. No one can tell you how much risk is too much, but such an analysis will help you understand the risks you are facing.

Two systems are valuable when assessing risks: the Internal Risk Evaluation System and the External Risk Evaluation System.

The *Internal Risk Evaluation System* involves comparing the skills, assets, and competencies (special abilities) required by each new opportunity to those the firm 1) now has, and 2) believes it can realistically develop or purchase in a timely manner. The less certain you are that you can develop or purchase a required skill, asset, or competency in the time required, the more Known Risk your firm is assuming. This comparison should be done function by function. The most common business functions are: Receiving, Operations, Marketing, Shipping, Service-After-the-Sale, Purchasing, Personnel, Technology Management, Credit, Cash flow, Finance, and General Management. (Some businesses have functions like housekeeping, millworking, player development, or entertaining, to name but a few.)

The *External Risk Evaluation System* involves five areas of risk that you should consider.

1. Each Growth Opportunity's Target Customers
   - Are the individual wants or needs of the new target customers consistent or do they vary greatly from customer to customer?
   - Can you accurately identify and measure the size of the target customer segment?
   - Can you reach those target customers with a promotional message?
   - What specific medium (TV, radio, newspaper, direct mail, Internet, etc.) will reach new target customers?
   - How can you influence target customers to respond to your business's promotions?
   - Do target customers have any existing brand loyalties?
   - What is your firm's competitive advantage (sales trigger KSFs) with target customers?
   - Are target customer numbers growing or declining?
   - Are you part of the right distribution chain to best serve the customers?
   - Are there any powerful customers, buying cooperatives, or emerging customer trends that can force prices down?

2. Each Growth Opportunity's Suppliers
   - Can the suppliers for the new opportunity ship the quantities and qualities of goods needed (low-cost businesses need low-cost suppliers and so forth)?

- If new raw materials or components are involved, are there few or many suppliers to choose from? Are their numbers increasing or decreasing?
- Will you be tied to one supplier? Will you be important to that supplier? Does being tied to one supplier pose a threat to future profits?

3. Each Growth Opportunity's Competitors
   - What is the Competitive Strategy of each competitor?
   - Which competitors are your "Real" competitors (actually target your customer segment)?
   - What are the *relative* sales trigger strengths and weaknesses of each competitor?
   - How are competitors likely to respond when you pursue this new opportunity?
   - Is market growth sufficient to keep competitors from trying to steal one another's customers? Is growth slowing down so that competition will likely increase?
   - If your business is entering a new market, what are all the business practices concerning samples, consignment, coop advertising, normal payment terms, special deals for big buyers, building loyalties, and so forth.
4. Each Growth Opportunity's Substitute Products and Services
   - What can customers substitute for your new product or service?
   - Are substitutes likely to get more expensive or less expensive over time *relative* to your products and services?
   - What improvements could producers of substitute products and services develop that would lure away your customers? How likely is this to happen?
5. Each Growth Opportunity's Potential New Competitors
   - What new competitors might emerge?
   - If your new opportunity generates a big sales or profit increase, what new competitors might enter this market? How might these affect sales?

If you can't answer all these questions or the additional questions you will undoubtedly add, your likelihood of failure increases because each incomplete answer means you're assuming more Known Risk. During your analysis, some growth opportunities may accumulate too many Known Risks to be attractive.

Unknown Risks

Unknown Risks are difficult to assess. For example, one business owner was pursuing a Market Development opportunity and lost a large initial order from one of the new market's largest customers. The order was lost when the big customer asked for consignment products for a showroom display, a practice unheard of in the small business's existing market. The request was turned down, and the account was lost. The business owner later discovered that showroom consignments were a common practice in the new market. Try as it may, the small firm was not able to get the order re-instated. Selling always involves good timing, and the owner of the small business had lost the timing.

Like that business owner, no one ever knows all the problems and all the risks that will be discovered when pursuing a new opportunity. Some of the risks a business will face will remain unknown until encountered. However, some growth opportunities obviously involve more Unknown Risks than others. For example, if your growth opportunity depended on the development of a new chemical process, you would immediately and emphatically admit that you faced a high level of Unknown Risks. In fact, you would readily admit that the whole project might be impossible for reasons no one could foresee at the beginning of the project. And yet, business managers often ignore the existence of Unknown Risks in other types of business ventures.

You can't really measure the amount of Unknown Risks associated with a new opportunity. You can't write down everything you don't know you don't know. Yet, it is possible to predict when to expect surprises that might jeopardize the success of a new opportunity. The rule of Unknown Risks is: the more dissimilar a new opportunity is from your existing business, the more Unknown Risks the venture contains. Therefore, if you operate a restaurant you'd expect many surprises, Unknown Risks, if you diversified by purchasing a small manufacturing plant that molded plastic parts. If you can estimate the degree of dissimilarity between your existing business and your growth opportunity, you can guess that this is a reasonable estimate of the number of surprises to expect.

The degree of dissimilarity between your growth opportunity and your existing business is controlled by four factors:

1. Customers: The greater the differences between your existing customers and your new customers, the more surprises you're likely to experience.
2. Products or Services: The greater the differences between your existing products and services and your new products and services, the more surprises you're likely to experience.
3. Markets: The greater the differences between your existing market and your new market, the more surprises you're likely to experience.
4. Technology: The greater the differences between your existing technology and your new technology, the more surprises you're likely to experience.

You should rate the degree of dissimilarity of each of your growth opportunities as a way of estimating each opportunity's Unknown Risks. Any growth opportunity that's rated highly dissimilar on all four factors might be suicidal. You'll never uncover every Unknown Risk, but you can make better growth opportunity choices by estimating your likelihood of encountering Unknown Risks.

Every growth opportunity will involve risk; no act in life is risk free. Your objective is to estimate the Known and Unknown Risks associated with each opportunity, so you can guess how likely you are to succeed. Successful business people aren't afraid to take risks, but they do try to avoid doing something stupid. However, don't study every opportunity until it disappears. Good timing is the key to turning many opportunities into success stories, so don't delay pursuing an opportunity until you have all the answers. You might miss your window of opportunity.

Competitors

Most opportunities either involve competitors or will involve competitors if you are successful. New competitors always spring up to chase new profits. Your short- and long-term success depends on you having the right strengths and on your competitors having the right weaknesses. For each growth opportunity, identify the Key Success Factors that trigger sales and control costs. Then compare each competitor's KSFs. You're most likely to succeed if your KSF strengths are superior to your competitors' KSF strengths. The ideal growth opportunity pits your KSF strengths against your competitors' KSF weaknesses.

Market Growth Rates

Each growth opportunity exists in a market. You should estimate each market's growth rate for the next several years. Wars between competitors are less likely to occur in fast-growing markets. Fast growth lets all competitors expand their sales and profits without having to steal customers from each other. Conversely, if a market has stopped growing, a business can only increase its sales by stealing customers from competitors, so competitive rivalry heats up. Therefore, the best growth opportunities are usually in growing markets.

However, an opportunity in a declining market (total sales for all the competitors combined is declining) can be attractive if enough competitors are pulling out of the market. Sometimes big competitors are particularly quick to pull out of a declining market, leaving a great opportunity for a small firm.

Concentrated Business versus Diversified Business

At startup, most small businesses are narrowly concentrated in one product or service area. Eventually, the owner feels threatened by the possibility of market ups and downs that are beyond his or her control — an all-my-eggs-are-in-one-basket fear. This causes the owner to pursue diversification strategies.

Should you give extra consideration to the diversification opportunities on your list? Not if 1) target customers are highly satisfied, 2) your business's sales are growing, 3) your market's sales are growing, and 4) your business has a clear KSF competitive advantage over your competitors.

Diversification should be given extra consideration if your market's sales are unstable, your business's sales are seasonal, or industry technology is changing rapidly and in unpredictable ways. Technology changes outside your industry must also be considered in your decision to favor diversification. For example, technology devastated the carbon paper industry when copy machines were invented in a different industry. Likewise the typewriter industry was severely harmed by the computer industry. Rapid technological changes inside or outside your industry favor your pursuit of diversification opportunities.

Competitive and Growth Strategy Compatibility

A companion issue to diversification is the degree of compatibility between your growth opportunity and your competitive strategy. You could restrict your choice of growth opportunities to only those that are compatible with your competitive strategy, this is called Focused Growth. Or, you could pursue Opportunistic Growth whereby you seek the highest potential profit regardless of compatibility. The choice that's best for you depends on your business goals and on your growth opportunities.

Focused Growth has its advantages. By choosing growth opportunities that require your business to develop skills, assets, and competencies that are very similar to existing skills, assets, and competencies, your business develops in a consistent manner. Employees and managers can more easily master the required new skills and competencies because they are similar to the ones they already possess. Highly similar skills have a synergistic affect. In other words, mastering new skills improves a workers ability to perform existing skills, and existing skills speed up the acquisition of new skills. This happens when old and new skills share similar learning curves. Likewise, the same is true of existing competencies (special abilities of management and key employees) and new competencies. The result of Focused Growth is that both existing and new KSFs will be increased, boosting the business's competitive advantages in both its existing business and new growth area.

For most firms, Focused Growth will be easier to manage and will produce higher long-term sales and profits.

On the other hand, Opportunistic Growth can generate exceptional profits. You may be presented with an opportunistic event that's a chance of a lifetime. Should you pass it up? Any businessperson who gets the opportunity to make a low-risk investment and get rich should take it. However, such opportunities are rare.

On balance, Focused Growth exposes the business to less risk and exposes you to fewer management problems. Unless the expected profits from Opportunistic Growth are too high to pass up, you'd be wise to favor compatible growth opportunities. Measuring compatibility is easy. Just list your KSF strengths and your other strengths in each functional area and compare them to the strengths your growth opportunity requires. Some growth opportunities will be highly compatible, others highly incompatible.

Ultimately, you must decide what type of business you want to build over time. Keep in mind that small businesses like Wal-Mart, Southwest Airlines, and the Bic Corporation grew large with focused growth. It's doubtful they would have achieved greatness through haphazard, Opportunistic Growth.

Remote Trends

The best growth opportunities are the ones supported by the strongest remote trends. Favorable remote trends not only support new opportunities, they actually create them. Positive trends will cause your sales to increase; negative trends will cause your sales to decrease. For example, technological trends in the computer industry created opportunities for many small, software support firms all across the United States. Similarly, demographic changes in California have created many opportunities to prosper by targeting Hispanic-Americans. And, the enactment of the General Aviation Revitalization Act of 1995 is creating new opportunities for fixed-based operators at small airports all across the U.S.

Growth opportunities created by and supported by strong remote trends will generate the most long-term sales growth. The remote trends influencing and affecting each of your growth opportunities should be studied carefully. Here's what you're looking for:

1. What are the **Demographic Trends** among the target customers for your new growth opportunity? If the growth opportunity will target professional men in your community, are their numbers increasing or decreasing?

If you're targeting a certain age group, income group, religious group, educational group, gender group, family size, married people, gays, lesbians, and so on, are their numbers increasing or decreasing in your market area? If you're targeting people who like to backpack, garden, attend musical events, fly airplanes, etc., are their numbers expected to increase or decrease in your market area? Try to determine the demographic profile of each growth opportunity's target customers and find out how the number of people with that profile is expected to change. Ask your local community college marketing instructor for help, call your Chamber of Commerce, get census track information from your local reference librarian, ask your congressman for assistance. Get the numbers.

2. Are **Society and Community Attitudes** changing in favorable or unfavorable ways? New spending patterns by consumers are preceded by changes in consumer attitudes. For example, consumer attitudes about saving the environment must develop before a market emerges for recycled products, biodegradable plastics, etc. Likewise, the attitudes of older consumers first shifted towards a more healthy and active lifestyle, and then a market emerged for healthy foods for older consumers and exercise equipment made for older consumers. Also, societal attitudes have to change before you can promote your products or service in certain ways or target certain customers. For example, before your travel agency can target gays and lesbians in your market area, community attitudes must first become more accepting of alternative lifestyles — an attitude shift that can be measured. Identify what attitudes would favor each of your new growth opportunities and find out if those attitudes are shifting in your favor.

3. What **Technological** trends might affect each growth opportunity? You need to consider technological trends inside and outside your industry. Often the biggest threats come from outside an industry. For example, FAX machines ruined the courier business in New York City, but the relationship between bicycle couriers and fax machines wasn't immediately obvious. Study the technological trends inside and outside your industry that might affect the success of each of your growth opportunities.

4. What **Political** trends might affect each growth opportunity? There are four types of political trends you should consider: legislative, bureaucratic, judicial, and jawboning.

   - New laws and programs enacted by the federal and state legislatures affect opportunities. For example, the federal gasohol program made corn growing more profitable for farmers while deregulation of the trucking and airline industries created many new opportunities for small transportation businesses. Are any new laws or programs being considered by legislative bodies that might affect one of your growth opportunities?

- Changes by governmental bureaucracies often affect the success of a growth opportunity. OHSA rulings have created new opportunities for small firms making safety equipment. NIST created a nationwide system of Manufacturing Technology Centers and Manufacturing Extension Centers to help small firms improve their technologies which has made it easier for many small firms to pursue their growth opportunities. Are any federal or state bureaucracies expected to make rule changes or spending changes that will affect one of your growth opportunities?
- The judicial system often changes the economics in an industry. Court rulings made insurance costs so expensive for airplane manufacturers in the 1980s that single engine airplane production dropped by 95 percent. With the demise of single engine aircraft production, great opportunities opened up for small manufacturers of kitplanes. Are any judicial decisions likely to affect one of your growth opportunities?
- Jawboning by the President or your state's governor can create a climate favorable or unfavorable for your opportunities. President Bill Clinton's criticism, early in his first term in office, of the pharmaceutical industry made it very difficult for small startup firms to attract investors. Likewise, Illinois Governor Edgar and Chicago Mayor Daley's squabble over control of Meges Field hurt many small businesses expecting to profit from that piece of real estate. Are top level politicians speaking out in favor or against any of your growth opportunities? The press is likely to magnify the comments of top elected officials, which can affect growth opportunities.

5. What **Ecological** trends are influencing your opportunity? Almost every product has a substitute. Steel 2 x 4s are a substitute for wooden 2 x 4s, plastic bottles can be substituted for glass bottles, and farm raised salmon can be substituted for ocean salmon. Every ecological problem hurts one market and helps a substitute market. Are any ecological trends such as natural resource shortages or environmental problems likely to affect one of your growth opportunities?

6. **Economic** trends affect growth opportunities in two ways. First, the best time to make large investments to pursue new opportunities is when the

economy is expanding because you'll recoup your investment and rebuild your cash flow faster. Second, a sluggish economy favors focused growth because you want to reduce the number of unknown risks your business has to face. The effects of unknown risks are easier to overcome during good economic times when the firm's overall profits are higher. What are the economic growth predictions for your market area for the coming years?

These six remote trends are called remote because they exist outside the influence of your business, yet they greatly influence the success or failure of your business. You're powerless to change or alter remote trends, but you can take advantage of them by choosing to pursue growth opportunities with strong supporting trends.

Growth Phase Balance

It is wise to have a mix of products and services in various growth phases to protect your future. Consider a typical product, the 8-track tape. Yes, it's dead and gone and that's the point. A product like the 8-track tape is Introduced; it enters a Growth Phase where sales for the industry increase for months or years. For most products and services, sales growth will eventually slow and then peak as the product enters its Mature Phase. In the Mature Phase sales remain at a high level, growth stops, and profits are at their maximum.

Then a new replacement product is introduced, becomes popular, and begins to steal sales from the older product. That's what happened as cassette tapes began to replace the older 8-track tapes. Sales of 8-track tapes finally entered the Declining Phase where sales continuously dropped month after month until 8-track tapes died. In the Declining Phase, the product usually dies and is withdrawn.

Most products and services move through the Introduction, Growth, Maturity, Declining, and Death Phases. However, they don't have to. A few products avoid the declining and death phases by entering a commodity phase. Common necessities like toilet paper, light bulbs, and gasoline go through the Introduction, Growth, Maturity, and into a Commodity phase. The sales of commodities continue to increase forever at the same rate the population increases. Nevertheless, most products and services go through these phases, don't become commodities, and die — yours probably will. Therefore, you should be concerned that unless you have some products in each phase, you may end up with all your products entering the Declining Phase at the same time, causing your entire business to die as your old products and services die.

So, even if current sales and profits are good, to ensure a good future, new growth opportunities should be pursued. You should strive for a balance of new products and services just being Introduced, some products and services in the Growth Phase, some in the Maturity Phase paying the bills and funding the others, and some in the Declining Phase, but still generating profits.

Products and services in the Introductory and Early Growth Phases require more cash than they generate. Products in the Late Growth Stage generate good profits. Products in the Mature Phase generate lots of profits. Products in the Declining Phase generate good profits if their costs are carefully controlled. Therefore, some of the profits created by Mature and Declining Products should be used to develop, refine, and promote new products. You should attempt to maintain a mix of products in most growth phases.

Industries can also go through growth cycles: Introduction, Growth, Maturity, and Decline, and even Death. For example, the blacksmith industry died, for all practical purposes, when the automobile industry entered its Growth Phase. The vacuum tube industry died when the transistor industry entered its growth phase. The coffee industry is in Decline due to a combination of weather-related setbacks which have increased prices and concerns about the negative effects of caffeine. Surely the cigarette industry will be dealt a deathblow by a combination of the actions by the attorneys' general and judicial judgments. If your industry is in a Declining Phase, you should pursue growth opportunities outside your industry. That's why cigarette companies are diversifying by buying beer, cheese, and snack food businesses; they fear the cigarette industry is entering its Declining and Death phases. Cigarette firms are diversifying to related consumer goods industries where their KSF strengths can easily be used.

The Final Words

MANY OF YOU HAVE JUST COMPLETED your first growth strategy session using this book's fourteen growth strategies. Congratulations. Now, make a note on your calendar to do it again next year. By next year, new growth opportunities will be waiting to be discovered. And to help you prepare for next year, start a system to collect growth ideas and customer information to make it easier. Make a list of the information you want for next year's growth session, and set up a system to collect it all year long. Don't let calls from other industries and other markets be turned away by a salesperson, the receptionist, or a secretary. Encourage everyone to keep a log of odd requests with the names, industries, and phone numbers of the people who called. Encourage everyone to pay close attention to calls and visits from non-target customers because they represent opportunities to grow with Segment Development and Segment Diversification. Keep logs of customer complaints and suggestions to guide your search for new products and services. Publicly reward and praise the employees who do the best job collecting the information you need.

Next year's growth planning session will be easier and more productive than this year's because you'll be smarter and better prepared.

Dear Readers,

We truly care about your future and would love to hear your success stories, comments, and book criticisms. The publisher will forward your letters to us or you can reach us by e-mail at wlovern@aol.com or annalovern@aol.com.

We wish you increasing sales and profits.

Wayne and Anna Lovern

APPENDIX A

Segmenting

SEGMENTING SIMPLY REFERS TO THE PROCESS of finding useful ways to describe the characteristics of different groups of customers. The most important descriptive characteristics about customers are those that help you, the manager

- Separate customers into segments;
- Determine the wants, needs, or behaviors of each segment;
- Target selected segments; and
- Reach the targeted segments with the right promotional messages.

For example, suppose you determine that the few characteristics that best describe your target customers are

- Men,
- Over the age of 55,
- In professional occupations, and
- Earning over $75,000 per year.

Then you could

- Study the exact product, service, personnel, and image desires of that segment;
- Build a competitive advantage with that segment by supplying the perfect mix of those four factors;
- Discover how to appeal to and reach that segment with targeted promotions;
- Measure or estimate the size of that segment; and
- Forecast the expected sales growth of that segment.

One of the keys to business success is knowing more about your segments of target customers than your competitors know.

The first value of segmenting is that it helps you, as manager, identify, describe, study, and fully satisfy target customers who then reward your business with a high level of customer loyalty. To survive and grow, every small business needs a core of loyal target customers. Every small business needs the majority of its sales to come from this core of loyal target customers.

Most businesses have a broad mixture of target customers as well as various groups of non-targeted customers shopping at their businesses. Customers from all these segments make purchases, offer suggestions, and lodge complaints. However, if a business attempts to either: please customers from all the segments with compromise products, services, personnel skills, and image, or be all things to all customers by offering a wide variety of different products and services, providing different personnel skills for each type of customer, and presenting a different image for each type of customer, the business risks not fully satisfying any segment of customers. And if your business doesn't develop a core of loyal customers, competitors can easily target and steal your customers.

The second value of segmenting is that it offers a small business opportunities to grow. In the process of identifying and describing target customers, you're able to more easily recognize new groups of customers that your business could pursue. Segmenting can boost sales anytime you recognize a new group of customers who

- want a different variation of a product, service, personnel skill, or image,
- respond to different types of promotions, and/or
- derive significantly different benefits from the same product or service.

Often, you can target one or more of these new groups of customers by making simple improvements to products, services, personnel skills, image, or promotions. Your sales grow as you are able to better satisfy additional groups of customers.

Without calling it segmentation, managers of small businesses already segment a market's customers by their choice of which products and services to sell, which personnel skills to develop and which image to portray. When you make those selections, you have decided to offer selective benefits to a segment of customers seeking those benefits. This selection process is called benefit segmentation, and it works fairly well. However, this simple segmenting technique can often be improved.

How to Divide Your Customers into Segments

Finding the best descriptive characteristics and dividing customers into useful segments is a trial-and-error exercise. There is no one-best-characteristic that will divide customers into various segments according to their different purchasing patterns. Some firms discover that customers with different levels of income purchase different products, and they choose to target a certain level of income. For example, Wal-Mart targets families with under $25,000 income with low-price products and in doing so is able to appeal to all types of price-sensitive customers.

For other firms, the level of income isn't the best descriptive characteristic for separating customers into segments. For instance, customers with different levels of education often buy different books, tires, and wines. The occupation of customers is often associated with many types of purchases. For products as simple as pencils, customers can be separated into segments with different needs according to their occupation because carpenters, teachers, artists, seamstresses, and doctors each buy different pencils. Still other firms separate customers into segments according to personalities, opinions, attitudes, and lifestyles.

When attempting to segment customers into groups with similar wants, needs, behaviors, and reactions to promotions, always search for the minimum number of characteristics that best divides customers into useful segments. You can accomplish this in three ways. First, you can observe the descriptive characteristics of various customers and then use those characteristics to describe various customer segments. Second, you can collect descriptive customer information from warranty cards, credit applications, pre-approved check writing applications, games, and contests then use those characteristics to describe various customer segments. Third, you can collect descriptive information from face-to-face interviews, telephone interviews, questionnaires, and chat (focus) groups and then use those characteristics to describe various customer segments.

Descriptive characteristics questions used with any information-collecting technique should use the following easy-to-answer, multiple choice form:

Your family status is:

_____ Single
_____ Bonded with a Companion
_____ Married
_____ Married with Children under 6 years old
_____ Married with Children, Youngest over Six
_____ Married with Empty Nest
_____ Widowed

Your combined household income is:

_____ Under $10,000
_____ $10,000–19,999

_____ $20,000–29,999
_____ $30,000–39,999
_____ $40,000–49,999
_____ $50,000–74,999
_____ Over $75,000

Of course, there's more than one way to ask any question, for example, it might be better for your business if you structured the household income question this way.

Your combined household income is: _____ Under $25,000
_____ Between $25,000 and $50,000
_____ Over $50,000

What type of descriptive information you should collect depends on the type of business and type of products and services you sell. However, there are five types of descriptive characteristics that you can collect.

Geographic Descriptive Characteristics

For a variety of reasons, where customers live can greatly influence many of the products and services they purchase — particularly those seen by their neighbors. Most people try to fit into their neighborhoods by purchasing products and services that make them compatible with their neighbors. Also, customers' purchases are somewhat forced by where they live. For instance, living in suburbia forces most people to buy lawn tools, just as living on a golf course, in a high rise apartment, or in a very wealthy subdivision forces customers to make other types of purchases. As a result, where people live will often divide them into segments that tend to purchase certain types and qualities of products and services. Knowing this, you may want to collect descriptive information about where customers live and determine if this information is a good indicator of what your customers will likely purchase. If geographic segmentation is discovered to be useful, it will guide future promotion efforts and help you to develop products and services for customers who reside in different subdivisions or geographic areas. You should collect customer information about whose customers live like, but not limited to:

- Geographic region: states, counties, zip codes, etc.
- Community or suburb: especially useful around cities.
- Actual addresses: search for clusters of customers and determine how to find other such clusters.

After collecting this information, you should analyze the purchases of customers in each area to determine if geographic characteristics predict what customers will buy. If they do, you've found some useful geographic or geodemographic segments.

Demographic Descriptive Characteristics

Demographic characteristics are things you can easily count. For example, age can be divided into ranges; each age range becomes a segment. You can count the number of customers in each age range, and study the wants, needs, and purchasing behaviors of each age segment. Often, customers in different age ranges purchase different types of products and services, use different media, and are motivated to make purchase by different promotional messages.

You may want to study the purchasing patterns and needs of segments formed with the following few demographic characteristics:

- Age: divide customers into age ranges
- Religion: divide customers by their religion
- Race: divide customers by race or ethnicity
- Income level: divide customers into income ranges
- Nationality: divide customers by their country of origin
- Gender: divide customers into male and female
- Sexual orientation: divide customers into heterosexual, gay, and lesbian
- Family type: divide customers by their family type such as single, married, children, divorced, etc.
- Family size: divide customers by the number of children in each household
- Occupation: divide customers into blue collar, white collar, professional classifications, or even place of employment
- Education: divide customers by their educational level
- Social class: divide customers by lower, middle, or upper class
- Languages spoken: divide customers by language spoken at home, preferred language to read, or languages spoken
- Military experience: divide customers by military experience

After collecting this information, you should analyze the purchases of customers for each demographic segment to determine if that descriptive characteristic predicts what customers will buy. If it does, you've found a useful demographic segment.

Lifestyle Descriptive Characteristics

Lifestyle characteristics are those that separate customers into segments according to differences in their attitudes, interests, and opinions. For example, customers in many markets can be separated into segments that are strongly-in-favor-of, in-favor-of, slightly-against, and strongly-against recycling. Each segment would respond differently to higher prices for recycled products, products made from recycled materials, and promotions with recycling themes.

Customers' opinions can be used to segment them into different groups with different purchase behaviors. For example, opinions about how to live a healthy life often affect customers' choices of which foods to purchase and what exercise equipment to buy.

The success of some businesses is determined by their ability to tailor their products, services, personnel skills, and images to be compatible with the attitudes, interests, and opinions of target customer segments.

You may want to study the following few lifestyle characteristics:

- Work: divide customer by type of work they perform
- Hobbies: divide customers by their hobbies and the degree of interest in the hobby
- Social events: divide customers by the social events they attend
- Vacations: divide customers by the type vacations they take
- Entertainment: divide customers by their choice of entertainment
- Club membership: divide customers by the clubs they belong to
- Sports: divide customers by the sports they play or watch
- Outdoor activities: divide customers by their outdoor activities
- Family: divide customers by their family interests
- Home: divide customers by their different home interests
- Fashion: divide customers by their different fashion interests
- Food: divide customers by their different food interests
- Media: divide customer by their different interests in TV, radio, Internet, newspapers, magazines, and direct mail
- Social issues: divide customers by the opinions they hold on social issues
- Politics: divide customers by their political opinions
- Products: divide customers by the opinions they hold about products and businesses

After collecting this information, you should analyze the purchases of customers for each lifestyle segment to determine if that descriptive characteristic predicts what customers will buy. If it does, you've found a useful lifestyle segment.

Behavioral Descriptive Characteristics

Behavioral characteristics are those that describe customers' shopping habits and purchasing patterns. This is a relatively easy way to segment customers into groups who behave differently.

Therefore, you may want to study the purchasing patterns and needs of customers with the following few behavioral characteristics:

- Product or service use rate: divide customers into heavy, moderate, light, occasional, former, and non-users
- Brand loyalty: divide customers into national brand, private brand, and no brand loyalty
- Payment method: cash, credit card, debit card, or other type of financing
- Price sensitivity: divide into various cheap, low-price, high-price groups
- Store cluster preference: central business district, big shopping malls, strip malls, neighborhood shopping centers, stand alone stores
- Occasion use: divide customers by their purchase patterns on special occasions
- Use situation: home, work, parties, vacation, etc.
- Risk status: degree of risk aversion (high, moderate, low)
- Innovativeness: first buyer, early buyer, late buyer

After collecting this information, you should analyze the purchases of customers for each behavioral segment to determine if that descriptive characteristic predicts what customers will buy. If it does, you've found a useful behavioral segment.

Psychographic Descriptive Characteristics

Psychographic characteristics are those that describe a customer's psychological motivations and attitudes. This is a difficult, often expensive, but useful way to segment customers when the other methods fail.

Psychographic research is subtle. For example, imagine a travel agency trying to build a prospective customer list for a direct mail promotional campaign. The travel agency sets up a table in a local mall, offers a prize, and requires people to fill out a short questionnaire which includes the following psychographic questions that can be answered with a simple yes or no:

1. I would rather go to a party than spend a quiet evening at home.
2. I like to belong to groups.
3. I enjoy shopping.
4. I am sometimes accused of being a big spender.

Any person answering Yes to all four questions would then be placed into a cruise ship vacation segment and targeted with appropriate promotions. In fact, the travel agency could devise a wide variety of questions that would separate potential customers into psychographic segments that were likely to prefer different types of vacation experiences.

Psychographic segmenting divides customers into groups according to both their lifestyles and their personalities. So, in addition to collecting information about customers' attitudes, interests, and opinions, you might collect personality information such as (but not limited to) customers':

- Degree of masculinity or femininity
- Degree of sophistication
- Desire to be active or sedentary
- Tendency to be reserved
- Tendency to be outgoing
- Tendency to be materialistic
- Tendency to be spiritual
- Tendency to be liberal vs. conservative
- Tendency to be adventuresome

Then, you would study the purchasing patterns and needs of segments formed with the various psychographic characteristics to determine if what characteristic predicts what customers will buy. If it does, you've found a useful psychographic segment.

Another cheap and simple way to collect psychographic information about customers is to collect information about the magazines, TV channels, TV shows, movies, and activities preferred by different customer segments. Then, you can make educated guesses about the psychographic differences of each customer segment, improving your ability to target selected segments.

Controlling Costs

EXPERIENCE, ALWAYS THE BEST TEACHER, has repeatedly proven that great sales alone don't produce great profits. Only when great sales are combined with the right cost controls will a small business enjoy big profits.

Lots of money can be misspent generating sales. As established in Chapter 2, the first step toward controlling the cost of making-the-sale is for a manager to separate the firm's business factors into

1. a few Key Success Factors (KSFs) that are used to trigger sales to target customers, and
2. the many Support Success Factors (SSFs) that must be maintained at an adequate level so as not to hurt sales.

For example, establishing adequate support levels for factors like advertising, location, inventory, and personnel training when these are your business's SSFs will help you, as a manager, avoid wasted expenditures. Recall that SSFs must be maintained at sufficient levels, and KSFs must be improved continuously. Money saved by not overspending on SSFs can be used to boost profits or used to fund further KSF improvements which will generate even more sales. So, as a business manager, your first task is to control the cost of making the sale.

The next task is to control the operating costs of your organization. Also established in Chapter 2 was that a small business's primary cost-controlling systems are Key Success Factors. Like the factors that trigger sales, these KSFs must also be continuously used and improved. Cost-controlling systems are chosen by you, the manager, then deliberately implemented and constantly monitored. Several such systems that you might use are briefly presented in this appendix. Each of the following systems can be researched in depth at any public library. If your local library is small, ask for the *Books in Print — Subject Guide*, search by topic, and if the library doesn't have the books you want, ask your librarian to borrow the books through their Inter-Library Loan Program.

Rigid Budgets Are Often KSFs in Small Businesses

Budgets are simple estimates of all costs a manager thinks the business will encounter in a specified period of time. Once prepared, budgets become guidelines that managers and employees are expected to follow, and these guidelines are often expressed as percentages rather than absolute numbers. For example, Total-Cost-of-Goods-Sold must increase as Sales increase because the business will have to put more money into raw materials, processing, inventories, or all three. So, when preparing a budget, many of the costs and expenses that are part of your firm's Total-Cost-of-Goods-Sold should be expressed both as projected numbers and as a percentage of projected sales.

Preparing a budget for a small firm begins by preparing a projected Income Statement for the next year. Accountants call this projected budget a Pro-Forma Income Statement. Using previous years' Income Statements as guides and making adjustments for anticipated changes, a manager projects the next year's expected sales, costs, and expenses. Next, a manager uses his or her judgment and past sales and costs experiences to divide the Pro-Forma Income Statement into seasons, quarters, or months. This takes into account that sales may be higher in the fourth quarter, but promotional expenses may be higher in the third quarter, and so forth. These budgets become the guidelines that are used to control costs in each time period.

No doubt each season, quarter, or month's sales will vary from the estimated Pro-Forma numbers. Some expenses can be expected to rise and fall with sales while others should stay constant regardless of sales. Despite sales variations, a manager periodically compares the budgeted costs, expenses, and guidelines to the actual costs and expenses. The manager then attempts to make adjustments to force costs and expenses to stay within the budget guidelines.

Rigid budgets differ from normal budgets only in the way they are used. Costs and expenses shown in budgets are often treated as amounts that should not be exceeded without good reason. With rigid budgets, the costs and expenses become amounts that will not be exceeded without top management's prior approval. Rigid budgets allow a manager to exercise stronger control over costs, expenses, and the decisions of employees.

Go/No-Go Evaluation Points Control the Costs of Projects

Budgets and rigid budgets are used to control everyday operating costs as well as the costs of special projects. Go/No-Go Evaluation Points are used to control the costs of special projects like — but not restricted to — technology upgrades, market development, marketing diversification, developing new products or services, basic product research, and process improvement research. Go/No-Go Evaluation Points are scheduled project review dates that are established at the beginning of a project. For example, if a business was funding a project that was supposed to take 18 months to complete, a manager might, at the beginning of the project, establish a 6-month and a 12-month Go/No-Go review. On those dates all project progress, costs, expenses, and expectations will be reviewed to determine whether or not to continue the project or kill it.

Several benefits are gained from establishing scheduled Go/No-Go points at the beginning of a project. First, the employees will know that costs are being tracked and analyzed and that project progress will be measured at specified points to determine if the project should proceed or be terminated. Second, with this system, employees are more likely to both control their expenses and strive for significant progress in each time frame. Third, if a project is terminated, employees are less likely to feel it was terminated for personal reasons. Without pre-established evaluation points, employees on a project will often feel that a manager's decision to suddenly evaluate then terminate a project was due to some personal disapproval of the employees assigned to the project. The result is that the employees involved become unhappy and seek employment elsewhere. But, when Go/No-Go Evaluation Points are established before the project begins, the aspect of personal disapproval is removed. Managers are perceived as more objective.

Project Go/No-Go Evaluation Points should also be used for personal projects. Set up review dates at the beginning of the project and conduct a thorough review of your own progress, costs, and expectations on those dates. This keeps you from continuing to waste money on a pet project that should have been scrapped.

Management by Objectives is a Common KSF

Peter Drucker eloquently explained in *Practice of Management* (Harper & Row, 1954) and later in *Management* (Harper & Row, 1973) that managers and employees have a natural tendency to have disjointed objectives. This tendency raises the small business's costs and hurts its sales. After all, a business is a collection of individuals with their own motives, interests, and communication problems. As a result, each employee interprets the objectives of top management differently. Each group of employees, each department, or each functional area in the business tends to develop and define its own purpose and its own objectives. Those differences cause

- Inevitable internal friction;
- Unnecessary duplication of effort; and
- Loss of performance.

To combat these common organizational problems, an owner or top manager must clearly establish the objectives of the business and constantly take steps to ensure that all employees, groups, and functional areas perform as a team. Management by Objectives includes identifying, explaining, and motivating employees to fully support your firm's objectives and strategies. Management by Objectives requires you, as a manager, to be a leader. And part of your leadership job is to repeatedly focus employees' efforts on the firm's

- Plan to satisfy target customers;
- Competitive strategy;
- Key Success Factors that employees must use and help to improve continuously; and
- Growth strategies.

Each employee should then be challenged to define his or her job in terms of helping to achieve the business's objectives. Furthermore, each employee's contribution to the firm's objectives should be measured and rewarded.

The goal of Management by Objectives is to increase the organization's effectiveness, efficiency, and productivity by getting all the employees to work together as a coordinated team. So whatever your firm's mix of goals and objectives, employees must understand how their personal work efforts can best support the firm's goals.

Just-in-Time Philosophy is Sometimes a KSF

Much has been written about the Just-in-Time (JIT) Inventory system whereby major suppliers (not every supplier) frequently deliver small quantities of raw materials and components just as they are needed. This type of JIT keeps inventory low, cash flow high, and boosts profits.

There is also a Just-in-Time Philosophy that can substantially lower the costs of some types of businesses. It is an operating system used to eliminate all forms of waste in a business and to find permanent solutions to problems that hurt efficiency and productivity. The philosophy consists of six parts.

1. **Workplace Organization.** All work areas are cleared of everything not needed for the immediate job or task. Cleaning up work areas helps to avoid distractions that cause mistakes and work delays while instilling a sense of employee discipline in the workplace. JIT requires employees and managers alike to clean up and organize their workplaces to improve efficiency.
2. **Visibility.** Visual communications between all employees are improved. Work schedules are posted. Where several employees work in a process, the work is made to flow from one person to the next in a uniform pattern, and no work is allowed to accumulate at any person's workstation. The work area is redesigned to promote visibility, so all employees can see work flowing through the organization, make quick adjustments when the pace is changed, and identify potential problems.
3. **Work Control System.** JIT works best for businesses whose work flows from workstation to workstation in an assembly line manner. Inventories of work-in-progress at each workstation are reduced to a bare minimum because large inventories are viewed as a way to hide problems. When an employee has a large amount of work-in-progress, problems can be set aside to be redone and reworked while other work is completed and forwarded to the next employee. When work-in-progress at each workstation is reduced to a bare minimum, problems become immediately evident because they will stop the flow of work through the entire process. When the entire work process stops, everyone — workers, managers, and technicians — will search for a permanent solution to the problem so it will never again shut down the entire work process. While obviously very disruptive, over time the JIT Philosophy greatly improves productivity by permanently eliminating problems that were once hidden under a mound of work-in-progress.
4. **Total Quality Management** (see Chapter 14). The JIT Philosophy also incorporates the use of TQM. Employees are trained in various aspects of TQM to improve their ability to recognize productivity problems and to give them the tools to solve those problems. All employees learn to define their work in terms of satisfying customers. All employees strive to perform defect-free work, track their problems, set goals to eliminate

personal errors, and continue to make improvement in all facets of their work.

5. **Timing.** Employees learn to time everything they do. They become cycle oriented and strive to produce work in regular time intervals. Steady work rates are believed to eliminate confusion and mistakes.

6. **Timing and Flexibility.** Most employees perform several different types of work, so to improve their productivity, they must learn how to switch from one type of work to the next with a minimum of in-between time. This is called reducing the set-up time.

The Just-in-Time Philosophy is not for every business, but it can boost productivity for any business with a high volume of routine work that can be arranged like an assembly line. Whether the work is product assembly or the routine handling of paperwork makes no difference as long as the work process can be organized like an assembly line.

Works Cited

Chapter 2

1. Mitchell, A. A. & J. C. Olson. "Are Product Attributes the Only Mediators of Advertising Effects on Brand Attitude?" *Journal of Marketing Research*, Aug. 1981, pp. 318–32.

Chapter 3

1. *Discount Store News*, Dec. 18, 1989, p. 168.
2. Barrier, M. "Hawaii Calling." *Nation's Business*, June 1993, p. 16.
3. Peters, T.J. & R. H. Waterman, Jr., *In Search of Excellence*. New York: Harper & Row, 1982, pp. 73–78, 280-286. T. J. Peters & N. Austin, *A Passion for Excellence*, New York: Random House, 1985, pp. 279–286. A. A. Thompson, Jr. & A.J. Strickland, III, *Strategic Management, 8th Ed.*, Chicago: Irwin, 1995, pp. 280–285.

Chapter 4

1. Hodgson, B. "Buffalo: Back Home on the Range." *National Geographic*, Vol. 186, No. 5, p. 80.
2. H. G. Gough, T.J., M. Fioravanti, and R. Lazzari. "Some Implications of Self Versus Ideal-Self Congruence on the Revised Adjective Check List." *Journal of Personality and Social Psychology*, Vol. 44, Issue 6, 1983, pp. 1214–20.

3. Mitchell. A. A. & J. C. Olson. "Are Product Attributes the Only Mediators of Advertising Effects on Brand Attitude?" *Journal of Marketing Research,* Aug. 1981, pp. 318–32.

4. Barrier, M. "Are They Still Making It?" *Nation's Business,* Sept. 1992, p. 14.

5. Dunn, W. "The Move Toward Ethnic Marketing." *Nation's Business,* July 1992, p. 39.

6. *Ibid.*

7. *Ibid.*

8. *Ibid.*

9. Nelton, S. "Rustic and Wonderful." *Nation's Business,* Dec. 1993, p. 18.

10. G. Tom et al. "Cueing the Consumer." *Journal of Consumer Marketing,* Spring 1987, pp. 23–27.

11. Whittemore, M. "Survival Tactics For Retailers." *Nation's Business,* June 1993, p. 22.

12. Kaufman, S. B. "Freshness By The Bottle." *Nation's Business,* Feb. 1994, p. 14.

13. Barrier, M. "Doing Well What Comes Naturally." *Nation's Business,* Sept. 1992, p. 25.

14. King, B. *Better Designs in Half the Time: Implementing Quality Function Deployment (QFD) in America.* Methuen, MA: G.O.A.L., Inc., 1987.

Chapter 5

1. Conway, A. Sr. "When The Customer Needs It Yesterday." *Nation's Business,* April 1994, p. 6.

2. *Kansas City Star,* Oct. 1, 1995, Sec. F, p. 2.

3. Barrier, M. "Re-engineering Your Company." *Nation's Business,* Feb. 1994, p. 20

Chapter 6

1. "Tailoring Products For A Niche Of One." *Nation's Business,* Nov. 1993, p. 42.

2. Barrier, M. "Re-engineering Your Company." *Nation's Business,* Feb. 1994, p. 22.

3. Barrier, M. "One On The (Movable) Aisle." *Nation's Business,* Oct. 1992, p. 13.

4. Barrier, M. "The Customer Is The Answer." *Nation's Business*, Oct. 1993, p. 16.

Chapter 7

1. Denalli, J. "An Airline Of Her Own." *Nation's Business*, Aug. 1993, p. 15.

2. *Ibid.*

3. Altman, H. "How A High-School Coach Became The "Farmer" In The Discount Dell." *Nation's Business*, July 1991, p. 12.

Chapter 9

1. King, B. *Better Designs in Half the Time: Implementing Quality Function Deployment (QFD) in America*. Methuen, MA: G.O.A.L., Inc., 1987.

Chapter 11

1. Bellizzi, J, A. Crawley, and R. Hasty. "The Effects of Color in Store Design." *Journal of Retailing*, Spring 1983, pp. 21–45.

Chapter 12

1. Booz, Allen, and Hamilton. *New Product Management of the 1980's* (New York: Booz, Allen, and Hamilton, 1982). & M.G. Duerr, *The Commercial Development of New Products* (New York: Conference Board, 1986).

2. Thompson, R. "The Handicap That Wasn't." *Nation's Business*, May 1992, p. 18.

3. Kotler, P., & G. Armstrong, *Principles of Marketing, 5th Ed.* (New Jersey: Prentice Hall, 1992).

4. Maynard, R. "What Do Customers Think of Your Firm?" *Nation's Business*, April 1993, p. 62.

5. Kotler, P., & G. Armstrong, *Principles of Marketing, 7th Ed.* (New Jersey: Prentice Hall, 1996) p. 3.

6. Barrier, M. "A New Sense of Service." *Nation's Business*, June 1991, p. 19.

7. Macnow, G. "Small Firms' Senior Links." *Nation's Business*, Sept. 1992, p. 40.

8. Whittemore, M. "PR On a Shoestring." *Nation's Business*, Jan. 1991, p. 30.

9. Barrier, M. "Permanently Temporary." *Nation's Business*, Sept. 1993, p. 18.

10. Barrier, M. "How An Oregon Shopkeeper Spreads His Light Across The Country." *Nation's Business*, Jan. 1992, p. 13.

11. Jaravis, C. "Prescribing Good Manners." *Nation's Business*, May 1994, p. 18.

12. Resnick, R. "Front Porch On the World." *Nation's Business*, Sept. 1993, p. 17.

13. Hawkins, D.I., R.J. Best, & K.A. Coney. *Consumer Behavior: Implications for Marketing Strategy, 5th Ed.* Irwin, 1992, p. 78.

14. Miller, C. "Gays are Affluent but Often Overlooked Market." *Marketing News*, Dec. 24, 1990.

15. Barrier, M. "On a Washington Island, Two Entrepreneurs Grew Red Currants — And a Business." *Nation's Business*, Feb. 1992, p. 14.

16. Marklein, M. B. "Selling To Uncle Sam." *Nation's Business*, March 1991, pp. 29–30.

17. Mora, J. M. "A Gooey Inspiration." *Nation's Business*, April, 1993, p. 16.

18. Webster, F. E. Jr. *Industrial Marketing Strategy*, Wiley and Sons, 1991, p. 9.

19. Marklein, M. B. "Selling To Uncle Sam." *Nation's Business*, March 1991, pp. 29-30.

20. Kaufman, S. B. "Building Blocks of Success." *Nation's Business*, May 1994, p. 16.

21. Willen, J. L. "Marketers to the World." *Nation's Business*, Feb. 1994, p. 11.

Chapter 13

1. Booz, Allen, and Hamilton. *New Product Management of the 1980's* (New York: Booz, Allen, and Hamilton, 1982) and M.G. Duerr, *The Commercial Development of New Products* (New York: Conference Board, 1986).

2. Lawton, L. and A. Parasuraman, "So You Want Your New Product Planning to Be Productive." *Business Horizons*, Dec. 1980, pp. 29–34.

3. Nelton, S. "Gourmet Food for Thought." *Nation's Business*, May 1994, p. 20.

4. Dalrymple, D. J. & L. J. Parsons. *Marketing Management, 6th Ed.* Wiley & Sons, 1995, p. 177

5. Holly, S. "A Country Twist at Every Turn." *Nation's Business*, March 1993, p. 37.

6. *Prescription for New Product Success*, (New York: Association of National Advertisers, Inc., 1984.

7. Whitford, D. "The Snack Food That's Packing America." *Inc.* Magazine, Oct. 1996, pp. 51–5.

8. Barrier, M. "On a Washington Island, Two Entrepreneurs Grew Red Currants — And a Business." *Nation's Business*, Feb., 1992, p. 14.

9. Barrier, M. "Meeting The Challenges." *Nation's Business*, April 1992, p. 32.

10. Barrier, M. "The Portable Tycoon." *Nation's Business*, March 1993, p. 20.

Chapter 14

1. Pearce, J. A. II & R. B. Robinson, Jr. *Strategic Management: Formulation, Implementation, and Control, 5th Ed.* Irwin, 1994. p. 235.

2. Maynard, R. "Managing Your Small Business." *Nation's Business*, Oct. 1993, p. 10.

3. Jarvis, C. "A New Midwestern Crop." *Nation's Business*, Sept. 1992, p. 16.

4. Nelton, S. "Flying High On Bird Food." *Nation's Business*, Sept. 1993, p. 16.

5. Alvarezz, J.A. Jr. "When Status Quo Just Won't Do." *Nation's Business*, Oct. 1993, p. 6.

6. Nelton, S. "A Basket Maker with Vision." *Nation's Business*, July 1993, p. 14.

7. Russell, C. "The Baby Boom Turns 50." *American Demographics*, Dec. 1995, pp. 22–33.

8. Russell, C. "True Crime." *American Demographics*, Aug. 1995, pp. 23–4.

Chapter 15

1. Barrier, M. "One On the (Movable) Aisle." *Nation's Business*, Oct. 1992, p. 13.

2. Hammer, M. and James Champy. *Re-Engineering The Corporation: A Manifesto for Business Revolution*. HarperBusiness, 1993

3. Clamp, J. C., et al. "General Mills, Inc.: A Food Company or a Diversified Conglomerate?" In J. A. Pearce II & R. B. Robinson Jr. *Strategic Management: Formulation, Implementation, and Control, 5th Ed.* Irwin, 1994, p. 808.

4. Whittemore, M. "Survival Tactics for Retailers." *Nation's Business*, June 1993, p. 20.

5. Candler, J. "Leased Wheels." *Nation's Business*, May 1994, p. 33.

6. Weaver, M. "Step Aside to Stay Ahead." *Nation's Business,* March 1993, p. 8.

7. McKee, B. "Pick a Distributor that will Grow with You." *Nation's Business,* April 1993, p. 12.

8. Barrier, M. "A Successful Oregon Sister Act Gets Ready for Its Second Act." *Nation's Business,* Dec. 1991, p. 14.

9. Whittemore, M. "Survival Tactics for Retailers." *Nation's Business,* June 1993, p. 24.

Index

G

H

I

J

K

T

U

V

W

The Oasis Press® Order Form

NAVG09/98

Call, Mail, Email, or Fax Your Order to: PSI Research, P.O. Box 3727, Central Point, OR 97502
Email: sales@psi-research.com Website: http://www.psi-research.com
Order Phone USA & Canada: +1 800 228-2275 Inquiries & International Orders: +1 541 479-9464 Fax: +1 541 476-1479

TITLE	✔ BINDER	✔ PAPERBACK	QUANTITY	COST
Advertising Without An Agency		❑ $19.95		
Bottom Line Basics	❑ $39.95	❑ $19.95		
BusinessBasics: A Microbusiness Startup Guide		❑ $17.95		
The Business Environmental Handbook	❑ $39.95	❑ $19.95		
Business Owner's Guide to Accounting & Bookkeeping		❑ $19.95		
Buyer's Guide to Business Insurance	❑ $39.95	❑ $19.95		
California Corporation Formation Package	❑ $39.95	❑ $29.95		
Collection Techniques for a Small Business	❑ $39.95	❑ $19.95		
A Company Policy and Personnel Workbook	❑ $49.95	❑ $29.95		
Company Relocation Handbook	❑ $39.95	❑ $19.95		
CompControl: The Secrets of Reducing Worker's Compensation Costs	❑ $39.95	❑ $19.95		
Complete Book of Business Forms		❑ $19.95		
Connecting Online: Creating a Successful Image on the Internet		❑ $21.95		
Customer Engineering: Cutting Edge Selling Strategies	❑ $39.95	❑ $19.95		
Develop & Market Your Creative Ideas		❑ $15.95		
Developing International Markets		❑ $19.95		
Doing Business in Russia		❑ $19.95		
Draw The Line: A Sexual Harassment Free Workplace		❑ $17.95		
Entrepreneurial Decisionmaking		❑ $19.95		
The Essential Corporation Handbook		❑ $21.95		
the Essential Limited Liability Company Handbook	❑ $39.95	❑ $21.95		
Export Now: A Guide for Small Business	❑ $39.95	❑ $24.95		
Financial Decisionmaking: A Guide for the Non-Accountant		❑ $19.95		
Financial Management Techniques for Small Business	❑ $39.95	❑ $19.95		
Financing Your Small Business		❑ $19.95		
Franchise Bible: How to Buy a Franchise or Franchise Your Own Business	❑ $39.95	❑ $24.95		
Friendship Marketing: Growing Your Business by Cultivating Strategic Relationships		❑ $18.95		
Funding High-Tech Ventures		❑ $21.95		
Home Business Made Easy		❑ $19.95		
Information Breakthrough		❑ $22.95		
The Insider's Guide to Small Business Loans	❑ $29.95	❑ $19.95		
InstaCorp – Incorporate In Any State (Book & Software)		❑ $29.95		
Joysticks, Blinking Lights and Thrills		❑ $18.95		
Keeping Score: An Inside Look at Sports Marketing		❑ $18.95		
Know Your Market: How to Do Low-Cost Market Research	❑ $39.95	❑ $19.95		
The Leader's Guide		❑ $19.95		
Legal Expense Defense: How to Control Your Business' Legal Costs and Problems	❑ $39.95	❑ $19.95		
Location, Location, Location: How to Select the Best Site for Your Business		❑ $19.95		
Mail Order Legal Guide	❑ $45.00	❑ $29.95		
Managing People: A Practical Guide		❑ $21.95		
Marketing for the New Millennium: Applying New Techniques		❑ $19.95		
Marketing Mastery: Your Seven Step Guide to Success	❑ $39.95	❑ $19.95		
The Money Connection: Where and How to Apply for Business Loans and Venture Capital	❑ $39.95	❑ $24.95		
Moonlighting: Earn a Second Income at Home		❑ $15.95		
People Investment	❑ $39.95	❑ $19.95		
Power Marketing for Small Business	❑ $39.95	❑ $19.95		
Profit Power: 101 Pointers to Give Your Business a Competitive Edge		❑ $19.95		
Proposal Development: How to Respond and Win the Bid	❑ $39.95	❑ $21.95		
Raising Capital		❑ $19.95		
Renaissance 2000: Liberal Arts Essentials for Tomorrow's Leaders		❑ $22.95		
Retail in Detail: How to Start and Manage a Small Retail Business		❑ $15.95		
Secrets to High Ticket Selling		❑ $19.95		
Secrets to Buying and Selling a Business		❑ $24.95		
Secure Your Future: Financial Planning at Any Age	❑ $39.95	❑ $19.95		
The Small Business Insider's Guide to Bankers		❑ $18.95		
SmartStart Your (State) Business... series		❑ $19.95		
PLEASE SPECIFY WHICH STATE(S) YOU WANT:				
Smile Training Isn't Enough: The Three Secrets to Excellent Customer Service		❑ $19.95		
Start Your Business *(Available as a book and disk package)*		❑ $ 9.95 (without disk)		
BOOK SUB-TOTAL (Additional titles on other side)				

TITLE	✔ BINDER	✔ PAPERBACK	QUANTITY	COST
Successful Business Plan: Secrets & Strategies	❑ $49.95	❑ $27.95		
Successful Network Marketing for The 21st Century		❑ $15.95		
Surviving Success		❑ $19.95		
TargetSmart! Database Marketing for the Small Business		❑ $19.95		
Top Tax Saving Ideas for Today's Small Business		❑ $16.95		
Twenty-One Sales in a Sale: What Sales Are You Missing?		❑ $19.95		
Which Business? Help in Selecting Your New Venture		❑ $18.95		
Write Your Own Business Contracts	❑ $39.95	❑ $24.95		
BOOK SUB-TOTAL (Be sure to figure your amount from the previous side)				

OASIS SOFTWARE Please specify which computer operating system you use (DOS, MacOS, or Windows)

TITLE	✔ Windows	✔ MacOS	Price	QUANTITY	COST
California Corporation Formation Package ASCII Software	❑	❑	$ 39.95		
Company Policy & Personnel Software Text Files	❑	❑	$ 49.95		
Financial Management Techniques (Full Standalone)	❑		$ 99.95		
Financial Templates	❑	❑	$ 69.95		
The Insurance Assistant Software (Full Standalone)	❑		$ 29.95		
Start Your Business (Software for Windows™)	❑		$ 19.95		
Successful Business Plan (Software for Windows™)	❑		$ 99.95		
Successful Business Plan Templates	❑	❑	$ 69.95		
The Survey Genie - Customer Edition (Full Standalone)	❑ $199.95 (WIN)	❑ $149.95 (DOS)			
The Survey Genie - Employee Edition (Full Standalone)	❑ $199.95 (WIN)	❑ $149.95 (DOS)			
Winning Business Plans in Color (MS Office Addition)	❑		$ 39.95		
SOFTWARE SUB-TOTAL					

BOOK & DISK PACKAGES Please specify which computer operating system you use (DOS, MacOS, or Windows)

TITLE	✔ Windows	✔ MacOS	✔ Binder	✔ Paperback	QUANTITY	COST
The Buyer's Guide to Business Insurance w/ Insurance Assistant	❑		❑ $ 59.95	❑ $ 39.95		
California Corporation Formation Binder Book & ASCII Software	❑	❑	❑ $ 69.95	❑ $ 59.95		
Company Policy & Personnel Book & Software Text Files	❑	❑	❑ $ 89.95	❑ $ 69.95		
Financial Management Techniques Book & Software	❑		❑ $129.95	❑ $ 119.95		
Start Your Business Paperback & Software (Software for Windows™)	❑			❑ $ 24.95		
Successful Business Plan Book & Software for Windows™	❑		❑ $125.95	❑ $109.95		
Successful Business Plan Book & Software Templates	❑	❑	❑ $109.95	❑ $ 89.95		
BOOK & DISK PACKAGE SUB-TOTAL						

AUDIO CASSETTES

Power Marketing Tools For Small Business	❑ $ 49.95		
The Secrets To Buying & Selling A Business	❑ $ 49.95		
AUDIO CASSETTES SUB-TOTAL			

You can learn more about and buy our books directly online!
Visit our store at http://www.psi-research.com

Sold To: **Please give street address**

NAME:
Title:
Company:
Street Address:
City/State/Zip:
Daytime Phone: Email:

Ship To: **If different than above, please give alternate street address**

NAME:
Title:
Company:
Street Address:
City/State/Zip:
Daytime Phone:

Your Grand Total

SUB-TOTALS (from other side)	$
SUB-TOTALS (from this side)	$
SHIPPING (see chart below)	$
TOTAL ORDER	$

If your purchase is:	Shipping costs within the USA:
$0 - $25	$5.00
$25.01 - $50	$6.00
$50.01 - $100	$7.00
$100.01 - $175	$9.00
$175.01 - $250	$13.00
$250.01 - $500	$18.00
$500.01+	4% of total merchandise

09/98

Payment Information: **Rush service is available, call for details.**
International and Canadian Orders: Please call for quote on shipping.

❑ CHECK Enclosed payable to PSI Research — Charge: ❑ VISA ❑ MASTERCARD ❑ AMEX ❑ DISCOVER

Card Number: — Expires:

Signature: — Name On Card: